THE FALL OF
THE IVORY TOWER

THE FALL OF
THE IVORY TOWER

*Government Funding, Corruption,
and the Bankrupting of
American Higher Education*

GEORGE ROCHE

Foreword by Malcolm S. Forbes, Jr.

REGNERY PUBLISHING, INC.

Washington, D.C.

Library of Congress Cataloging-in-Publication Data

Roche, George Charles.
The fall of the ivory tower : government funding, corruption,
and the bankrupting of American higher education / George Roche.
        p.   cm.
Includes bibliographical references and index.
ISBN 0-89526-487-0
1. State aid to higher education—United States.   2. Federal aid to higher
education—United States.   3. Universities and colleges—United States—
Finance.   4. Universities and colleges—United States—Costs.   5. Education,
Higher—Political aspects—United States.   I. Title.
L82342.4.U6R63   1994   93-47561
                                              CIP

Published in the United States by
Regnery Publishing, Inc.
422 First Street, S.E.
Washington, DC 20003

Distributed to the trade by
National Book Network
4720-A Boston Way
Lanham, MD 20706

Printed on acid-free paper.

Manufactured in the United States of America.

10 9 8 7 6 5 4 3 2 1

CONTENTS

PREFACE

———— 🏛 ————

It must be stated unequivocally that this book is not an "original work"; it is merely a compilation of facts and ideas—fascinating, revealing, and often horrendous—about higher education that have been collected over the last several years. What struck me most when reviewing them was that most people know so little about what really has been happening in higher education. They deserve to be told, and that is how this book came about.

I owe a great deal to many members of the Hillsdale College staff for helping me to put it all together. Their dedicated efforts and research gave it shape and organization.

It is to them, as well as the late Charles Nixon, who underwrote the entire project and who, to my regret, did not live to see it completed, that *The Fall of the Ivory Tower* is dedicated.

George Roche
February 1994
Hillsdale College
Hillsdale, Michigan

FOREWORD

———— 🏛 ————

American higher education is the best in the world, which is why it attracts tens of thousands of foreign students. The breadth and diversity of our institutions make their foreign counterparts pale in comparison. But our system today is in deep crisis, financially, morally, and academically.

George Roche ably catalogues the signs of decay: the growing allergy to undergraduate education manifested by the shrinking hours professors actually spend in the classroom teaching; the decline and debasement of academic standards and the concomitant grade inflation; "political correctness"; the bloat of non-teaching staff; scandals concerning the handling of government funds. *The Fall of the Ivory Tower* joins Thomas Sowell's *Inside American Education*, Allan Bloom's *Closing of the American Mind*, Charles J. Sykes' *Profscam*, and Martin Anderson's *Impostors in the Temple* in describing campus problems today.

But what will make this book a sizzling sensation is the answer Roche gives to the question: What is the underlying reason for these disturbing trends? His response: government funding. The author argues that massive infusions of money from Washington and the states to higher education institutions and to student assistance are the root cause of today's troubles. This funding has encouraged overexpansion, overstaffing, and overspending. It has subsidized skyrocketing tuition and fiscal mismanagement. It has twisted the thrust of many colleges away from educating undergraduates to attracting more government funds. It has been, he says, a Faustian bargain, and the price will be a dear one.

As long as the amount of money was growing—as it did almost nonstop from the end of the Second World War through the 1980s—colleges and universities could expand higgly-piggly with no real sense of direction or focus. Now this government funding flood is ebbing, and the results are, and will be, devastating. Most institutions are faced with serious budget pressures. Many will be forced to close their doors.

The immediate response to these financial pressures has been the so-called "Washington Monument Syndrome"—cut what will generate an immediate public outcry so that the money will be restored. Undergraduates are initially bearing a disproportionate brunt of the cut-backs. Thousands of students are discovering that it may take them five or six years to graduate because required courses are quickly oversubscribed.

This book will fuel the rage of parents and students who are increasingly asking: Why aren't the still-vast sums colleges and universities receive being used to provide a timely and sound undergraduate program. Why do so many of these institutions seem to have their priorities backwards—protecting staff and grossly underutilizing tenured faculty?

Roche's thesis will be hotly controversial among academics. But wise educators will recognize that there is validity in what he says about the governance of higher education. They will realize that the financial pressures are not temporary, particularly as government-financed research is scaled back in the post-Cold War world. And they will conclude that the management of many colleges and universities will have to be fundamentally refocused and restructured.

MALCOLM S. FORBES, JR.
Editor-in-Chief
Forbes

THE FALL OF
THE IVORY TOWER

INTRODUCTION

Higher education in America has become a popular bull's-eye, and with good reason. In spite of a massive infusion of money, including federal aid, which has doubled over the last few years, tens of thousands of students do not know when Columbus sailed to the New World, who wrote the Declaration of Independence, or when the Civil War was fought. Businesses complain that they must reeducate college graduates in such basic subjects as grammar, spelling, and practical math. Parents protest that tuition costs have far outstripped the rate of inflation and their ability to pay. Meanwhile, growing numbers of professors receive huge salaries for teaching one or two classes a semester. Though constantly complaining about a lack of sufficient research opportunities and funds, they, as well as many administrators, have found ample time and resources to politicize the campus and to lead a frontal assault on the traditional liberal arts curriculum—all under the banners of "political correctness" and "multiculturalism."

Why has this happened? In scores of books and hundreds of articles, keen observers, analyzing all the relevant issues, have argued that the primary explanation is that the political and intellectual radicals of the 1960s became the Establishment on campus in the 1980s and early 1990s. Once in power, they took their liberal-left agenda on race, class, and gender and camouflaged it under a mantle of "diversity," like the nets of fake foliage used to disguise tanks in Operation Desert Storm. Thus concealed, the diversity troops launched an all-out campaign to displace traditional values and academic discipline. There is no denying that in their quest to "capture the culture," these radicals have enjoyed great success. They have fomented an intellectual revolution on campus—a revolution that is certainly one of the most critical events in modern times. But it is not the root cause of the current educational malaise. Like the academic ills it has encouraged, it is a consequence of something else.

That something else is government. Whereas once the dominant form of education in this country was private, the state now holds sway from kindergarten to graduate school. The effect of federal subsidy and control has been more profound, more direct, and more damaging than anyone has yet realized. It has led to a situation in which the entire system of American higher education is academically, morally, and, quite literally, going bankrupt.

Chapter 1

COLLEGES IN CRISIS

As the premier "brand name" in American education, Harvard University elicits visions of the finest in academic standards and financial solidity. Over its long history, the school has produced an honor roll of the nation's scholars, scientists, politicians, and business leaders. Yet many of Harvard's illustrious graduates, particularly in accounting, would find recent developments at their alma mater more than disturbing. In 1991–92, Harvard University ran a *$42 million deficit,* the biggest the school has ever reported, according to the *Chronicle of Higher Education.*[1] The university officials who claimed that this figure was nothing to worry about nevertheless admitted that it might take a decade to erase the deficit. Harvard has also lost hundreds of millions of dollars in speculative investments in the last several years.[2] And Harvard is far from alone; many of its peers are in far worse condition. One of the best-kept secrets in American higher education today is that many colleges and universities are teetering on the brink of disaster.

Of course, educators have been aware of the crisis for a long time, and, more recently, deep budget cuts in a number of state university systems have made national news. But the general public simply is not aware of the fact that, despite billions of dollars in federal and state support, hundreds of schools are spending more than they take in and are racking up huge deficits or eating up what is left of their endowments.

The *Educational Record* attests that "the 1990s dawned with higher education in perhaps its worst financial shape of the last 50 years."[3] Nearly half of the 807 college presidents polled by *U.S. News & World Report* in 1992–93 said their institutions would face continuing deficits, and nearly a third said they did not expect to balance their budgets until after the year 2000.[4] One or more private colleges close or merge each year, and now public campuses are being threatened; at least four have closed in the last fifteen years, but many more may follow in the near future.[5]

Colleges and universities have been known to misrepresent their financial condition, of course, showing deficits or surpluses whenever it suits them, but the drastic budget cutting going on right now indicates that the financial crisis is genuine and wide-reaching. *The Economist* notes that even schools that are not in any danger of going bankrupt are "trying to cope with a financial squeeze by cutting back on student numbers, closing down courses, increasing class sizes, reducing library acquisitions, freezing salaries, laying off staff, and putting off essential mainte-nance."[6] *Campus Trends*, an annual American Council on Educa-tion survey, confirms that nearly *60 percent* of the nation's colleges and universities were forced to cut their budgets in 1991–92. Thirty-four percent made cuts in 1992–93, and 38 percent expect to do the same in 1993–94.[7] Most have no endowment at all, or their endowments are comparatively meager; of the $64 billion in endowments for all of higher education, half belongs to just twenty-nine institutions.[8] Yet these—the nation's richest schools—also are in trouble.

Paradoxically, an institution can have a huge endowment and/or hundreds of millions of dollars in revenue in the form of federal research grants and still be starving for operating funds. The reason? The bigger the institution, the bigger the outlays. Harvard University, Stanford University, Columbia University, MIT, and the University of Michigan are just a few of the institutions that rack up bills of more than *$1 billion* a year. And little of what they spend can be called "discretionary"; they are overcommitted to entitlements in exactly the same way as is the federal government. Robert Baker, provost of Cornell University in 1990, confessed, "Each term I meet with the provosts of Stanford, Princeton, Columbia, Harvard, Yale, MIT, and Chicago. Despite enormous differences between the institutions, we all find ourselves in similiar financial situations—expenses outpace revenues. . . ."[9]

At Washington University in St. Louis, a $1.3 billion endowment did not keep it from closing down its dental school and an entire academic department because of "lack of funding" several years ago.[10] Johns Hopkins University is another prime example. Despite research grants in excess of *$500 million a year*, the university announced cuts of up to 10 percent among its arts and sciences faculty in the late 1980s.[11] Actually, the cuts turned out to be higher, since a number of professors saw the handwriting on the wall and resigned before things got worse. And they did; for one year an entire academic department was reduced to a single, untenured assistant professor. According to an anonymous administrative source, the university only narrowly avoided closing its undergraduate school; it was saved by an under-the-table "gift" of $25 million from its medical school and several large private bequests. Yet Johns Hopkins' troubles are far from over. It was forced to balance its 1992–93 budget by "imposing department cuts, salary freezes, delaying capital projects, delaying or downsizing department general funds, and decreasing assistance to graduate students."[12]

SIGNS OF CRISIS

It is not difficult to put together a random list of other recent signs of crisis in American higher education:[13]

- Yale University has deferred a total of *$1 billion* in maintenance. In 1992, it announced an 11 percent faculty cut and the probable elimination of at least two departments. It also admitted that it expected a $15 million deficit by the end of the fiscal year.

- Deferred maintenance on all college and university campuses amounts to a minimum of *$60 billion.*
- Columbia University is still in the process of making huge cuts in a desperate effort to reduce shortages it projected in 1992–93 ($50 million) and in 1993–94 ($87 million) to around $30 million.
- The City University of New York system was looking to cut $40 million in 1992.
- UCLA is closing four professional schools and must cut $38 million by 1994 on top of all previous cuts.
- The University of Maryland system is getting rid of fifty-six academic departments, is reorganizing fifty-nine others on its eleven campuses, and has closed one college.
- The University of Minnesota system has closed an entire campus.
- The University of Pennsylvania is closing its school of veterinary medicine.
- Drexel University put a freeze on all hiring in 1992.
- Spring Garden College (est. 1851), "the nation's oldest independent school of technology," closed its doors in 1992 due to a $10 million deficit.
- Duke University was only saved from a $2 million shortfall in 1991–92 by basketball-related commercial revenues.
- The University of Connecticut incurred a $2.6 million deficit, ironically enough, as a consequence of a fund-raising campaign during the 1980s.
- Loyola University of Chicago plans to close its dental school, which is some $3 million in debt. It is the fifth dental school to close in the past several years.
- San Diego State University laid off 147 tenured professors and announced the elimination of nine academic departments in 1992.

- The University of Wyoming was forced to cut $2.7 million in 1992.
- Michigan's Ferris State University had a $9 million deficit in 1992, and the faculty took a vote of "no confidence" in the last two presidents. Dozens of programs and hundreds of positions must be eliminated if the school is to remain in operation.
- The University of Bridgeport in Connecticut was saved from extinction in 1992 only by a last-minute infusion of $50.5 million from the Professors World Peace Academy (PWPA), which receives most of its funding from Rev. Sun Myung Moon's Unification Church.
- Arizona State University had a $15 million deficit in 1992–93, even after cutting hundreds of class sections and nearly two hundred teaching positions the previous year.
- The University of Arizona cut $16.3 million before the fall 1992 term.
- Towson State University in Maryland has slashed spending for more than three years in a row and has even resorted to tapping student government funds to help meet operating expenses.
- Southern Methodist University is trying to cancel a long-term debt of $84 million, but is still racking up annual deficits in the neighborhood of $11 million. One close observer says that the problem is that SMU "has always liked to do forward funding and for decades it [has] had a pattern of overreaching."
- Stanford University cut $22 million and 112 nonfaculty positions in 1990–91, but that was not the end of its troubles. In the last several years it has been compelled to make over $40 million in additional cuts. It even contemplated shutting down its prestigious academic press to save on costs, but under strong pressure decided to compromise by slashing its budget by more than 50 percent. Stanford also may have to terminate its multimillion-

dollar high energy physics program and lay off hundreds of university scientists in the next two years.

- Since 1991, Oregon State University has merged two colleges, eliminated twelve academic programs, and combined many more through what one faculty member calls "shotgun marriages." The most common joke on campus is: "What's the difference between the Titanic and Oregon State?" Answer: "The Titanic had a band." (The OSU band was one of the eliminated programs.) On top of an 11.5 percent cut between 1991 and 1993, all eight Oregon public four-year colleges and universities must cut 20 percent from their budgets between 1993 and 1995.
- Around the country, schools desperate for students are discounting tuition by as much as *$7,000* a year.

The state of Ohio offers a good example of what has been happening everywhere in higher education. There are about 650,000 students enrolled in the public and private systems, and higher education spending accounts for a "modest" (in comparison with other states) 12 percent of the total state budget. Governor George V. Voinovich cut the 1992–93 state budget by $316 million, which, in turn, cut $170 million from the anticipated $1.8 billion appropriation for higher education. Ohio State University was already in deep trouble, cutting $78.7 million and nearly five hundred positions. Kent State University faced $9.6 million and Youngstown State University $3.5 million in budget reductions. University of Cincinnati President Joseph A. Steger who, like his counterparts at other schools had called for budget increases, greeted the news by pronouncing melodramatically, "What we are witnessing is the abandonment of public higher education." The governor's education advisor Tally Krumm responded, "Almost every state in the country is having financial difficulty. The problems result because so much of the budget is entitled that there is little discretionary money left." Voinovich himself noted in defense of the cuts that since the 1980s state spending on higher education had increased 126 percent.[14]

The California State University system, which depends on the state for 95 percent of its budget, is also in dire straits. It lost $125 million, or 7.6 percent, of its state funds in 1992. The same year, it eliminated 743 nonfaculty jobs and left 644 vacant, declined to issue contracts to nearly two thousand part-time instructors, and slashed five thousand class sections along with seven thousand student enrollments.[15] And the University of California system has cut a massive sum—$900 million—in the last four years. Despite nearly doubling tuition and eliminating, through early retirement, layoffs, and other means, over 3,500 positions and over five thousand class sections, campuses still had to make 17–33 percent budget cuts in 1992–1993. UC officials have also turned thousands of students away from classes.[16] It is not uncommon now for crowds to queue up in front of campus administration offices the night before registration begins. Things were—and still are—so bad that whole departments on some campuses have been asked to sacrifice the telephones in individual offices. The head of one graduate division predicts that the situation will continue to worsen and the UC system will have to be privatized by the year 2000. Whether this is likely or not, his attitude, widely shared by his peers, is itself revealing. Privatization of an entire public university system does not sound all that far-fetched to those faculty and staff who always had taken it for granted that they would have such standard devices as telephones in their offices.

Campuses throughout the nation have also witnessed riots and protests, some involving thousands of students, over tuition increases and closed courses. In 1992 alone:[17]

- Five hundred students rallied at Lock Haven University of Pennsylvania, angry that the school had cut courses that they needed in order to graduate.
- At Rutgers University, students opposing tuition hikes and seeking more funds for campus lobbying disrupted a board of governors meeting and barred members from leaving.

- At California State University, several thousand students demonstrated against reductions in course offerings and increases in tuition and fees.
- At Bennington College in Vermont, students who tried to prevent faculty layoffs and other cuts made necessary by a projected $1.5 million deficit took over the president's office for seven days. Rather than confront the students, President Elizabeth Coleman and her staff slipped quietly away to other offices, thereby providing the usual display of daring and courage exhibited by today's educational leaders.
- At Louisiana State University, Chancellor William E. Davis actually suspended classes in order to allow four thousand students and faculty to participate in a protest rally against the 1992–93 state budget cuts of $129 million. As the crowd chanted, "No more cuts!" he took the podium to cheer them on and completed his performance the same day by testifying before the state legislature in support of a tax increase for higher education.

No Bailout

The good news is that, despite the recession, private donations to colleges and universities were up by 10 percent in 1989–90, to $9.8 billion; in 1990–91, they were up 4 percent, to $10.2 billion. But there are three important facts to keep in mind: First, since inflation was at 5 percent, the latest figure represents a decline. Second, it was the smallest increase in the last fifteen years. Even phenomenal fund raisers like Harvard University, for example, saw an 8 percent drop in gifts, and Stanford University suffered an 11 percent decline. And, third, we must realize that at best corporate and private giving only accounts for 8 percent of all higher education revenues.[18] It simply is not realistic to count on private sector charitable contributions to save failing public and private higher education *as it is presently constituted* or to do much at all to lessen the effects of the current financial crisis.

Combined federal, state, and institutional student aid is up to nearly $31 billion a year, an increase of 33 percent in a decade even after adjusting for inflation.[19] Research funds, capital support, and institutional aid account for billions more in revenue, but, given the gargantuan costs of education, even these sums aren't enough. And state support, the major source of income for public institutions and a significant source for private ones, has begun a gradual but irreversible decline. States were spending a quarter of their budgets on higher education two decades ago; now, on average, they are spending 18 percent or less.[20] The National Governors Association's "Fiscal Survey of the States" reports that twenty-nine states cut their budgets in 1991, and thirty-five states cut them in 1992.[21] Here are a few glimpses of what that meant for higher education:[22]

- The University of Maryland system's state revenues were reduced by 20 percent in 1990–1992.
- Roughly ten years ago, SUNY-Binghamton received 75 percent of its budgeted funds from the state; by 1992–93 it was down to 54 percent.
- Ten public colleges and universities in Vermont received less than 50 percent of their revenues from the state in 1992–93, down from 66 percent in 1988.
- Arizona State University lost $2 million in state funds in 1992–93.
- The state of Pennsylvania eliminated all institutional aid (over $75 million a year) to private colleges in 1992. A portion was restored later, but nothing near the previous figure.
- Faced with a $700 million deficit in 1993, Louisiana reduced higher education appropriations by $45 million, and its legislators immediately began debating cutting college and university expenditures by as much as 40 percent.

- California, which took in $1 billion less in revenues in 1993–94 than in 1992–93 and which ended the latter year with a whopping deficit of $4 billion, is cutting hundreds of millions of dollars in aid to higher education. There is no expectation that the funds will be restored.

The truth is that many similarly hard-pressed states just don't have any more funds to give. Over a three-year budget cycle, Maine is currently predicting a $1.3 billion deficit; Minnesota, $770 million; New Jersey, $1 billion; North Dakota, $150 million; Oregon, $1.2 billion; Texas, $6.5 billion; and Washington, $1.6 billion.[23] Such a state of fiscal emergency puts everything, including sacred cows like higher education spending, on the chopping block. One educator summed it up even more crudely: "[It's] like a family of twelve when there is only one pork chop on the table."[24]

The federal government is, if anything, even less well equipped to respond to this emergency, because it is in the throes of its *own* crisis, which dwarfs that of the states and of higher education— the national debt is over *$4 trillion*. Entitlements, out-of-control deficit spending, and the competing demands of special interests are eating up the supposed "peace dividend" of the post-Cold War era. Discretionary domestic spending, including higher education, was about 22 percent of the U.S. federal budget in the early 1980s, but it is currently down to 15 percent.[25]

Indeed, many education programs enacted in the last decade died at birth because they never received funding. Pell Grants have not been awarded at authorized maximum levels since 1979–80.[26] Research grants and grants to science and technology are also down by nearly $600 million, and, with all the hue and cry resulting from overhead scandals at major universities, they will likely continue to decline.[27] Even if they were to increase, such funds would be devoted to restricted purposes, usually involving big, costly research centers and hundreds of staff. They do not cover operating expenses or address the spiraling costs of undergraduate education.

Though President Clinton promised to pour billions of dollars into increased federal aid, the *Chronicle of Higher Education* says that in his first year of office, "virtually every area of the Education Department budget related to postsecondary education took a hit."[28] His 1994 budget for higher education even drew fire from lobbyists who warmly welcomed his presidency. Arnold Mitchem, executive director of the Council of Education Opportunity Associations, characterized it as "a real retreat" and remarked bitterly, "There's a lot of deep disappointment and shock."[29]

Educators also refuse to face the hard facts: Neither the states nor the federal government will be able to bail them out of the current crisis. Yet their only response seems to be: "Raise taxes!" Several years ago, C. Peter McGrath, chancellor of the University of Missouri system and president of the National Association of State and Land-Grant Universities, noted that this is just what their response ought to be. He added approvingly, "I see more university presidents and chancellors willing to engage on this issue, usually on a nonpartisan or bipartisan basis."[30] But even if taxes are raised at the state and/or federal level, the competition to expend the money (for health care, elementary and secondary education, highways, prisons, law enforcement, social services, etc.) will be fierce, and there is no guarantee that higher education will benefit significantly. One thing *is* certain. The crisis in American higher education goes beyond the current financial difficulties on college and university campuses.

DEFAULTS ON FEDERAL ───── STUDENT LOANS ─────

When government loan programs for college students were first proposed years ago, the loans were to be unsubsidized and the states were to be the guarantors. But the states were afraid of too much exposure, so the burden fell upon the federal government. The loans also were to be for the middle income students who were ineligible for most merit or need-based aid, but, relatively quickly, low income students and vocational students—in short, everyone—became eligible. This led to an explosion of federal student loans in the 1970s and 1980s and so overloaded the system that it never has recovered.

Defaults on federal student loans have also exploded. Contributing greatly to their unchecked growth have been huge increases in such programs as Parent Loans for Undergraduate Students, Perkins Loans (formerly National Direct Student Loans), Supplemental Loans for Students (originally intended as a last resort for a small number of needy students, now a primary source of funding for hundreds of thousands), and Stafford Loans (formerly Guaranteed Student Loans). PLUS defaults tripled between 1989 and 1991, from $18.9 million to $56 million. Perkins Loan default percentages have been in the double digits for years. SLS defaults jumped from $14 million to $533 million between 1987 and 1991.[31] Yet these sums are nothing compared to what Stafford Loan defaults have been costing. Defaults on these loans grew by over *300 percent* in the last decade.[32] Taxpayers forked over more than ever before—*$3.6 billion*—to cover them in 1991. The total went down to $2.9 billion in 1992, but this was largely due to an IRS crackdown on federal employees who had defaulted.[33]

The fly-by-night and diploma-mill practices of trade schools and vocational colleges have been the major reason for high Stafford Loan defaults. In the last several years, many of these institutions' default rates have ranged between 33 and 41 percent.[34] They and their representatives in Congress have lobbied strenuously against every effort to curb abuse. Most notably, they fought Secretary of Education William Bennett's reform proposals in 1987-88 and a Gramm-Dole bill in early 1990. Eventually, some mild restrictions (cutting off aid to schools with default rates in excess of 35 percent, then 30 percent, then 25 percent) took effect as a part of the November 1990 budget reconciliation measure and the 1992 reauthorization of the Higher Education Act.[35]

But there are so many loopholes and so few effective methods of supervision that the new restrictions will be difficult to enforce. Here, for example, is how one trade school that had run up high default rates took advantage of the last round of administrative reforms in the late 1980s: It "sold" all its new, DOE-required loan identification numbers to another school and got a single replacement number that it then used to obtain loans for students on all thirteen of its branch campuses. With the replacement number, the default rate on each campus was back to zero.[36]

The average default rate on Stafford Loans at all four-year and community public and private colleges and universities—16 percent in 1990, up from 12.5 percent in 1980—may not seem so high in comparison to the rate of the trade schools and vocational colleges, but in its own way it is just as disturbing.[37] Leaving aside the important question of the ethics of defaulting—for which the student defaulters must take 100 percent of the blame—a large part of the overall problem rests with the fact that schools, lenders, and guaranty agencies do not have any real incentives to collect on loans before they go into default. That, they claim, is the Department of Education's job. Nor do students have a real incentive to pay their loans. Many tend to regard them as an unimportant obligation, taking the same kind of contemptuous attitude that is regularly shown towards cheating the insurance industry: "There's no shame in it since everybody does it, and besides, those big companies will never miss it."

It also is nearly impossible to identify repeat offenders, especially defaulters who are reapplying for federal loans in another state. A General Accounting Office (GAO) investigation revealed that between 1965 and 1990 at least 32,000 students defaulted on $54 million in Stafford Loans only later to receive $109 million in new loans.[38] And another report by the DOE's own inspector general claimed that between 1990 and 1992 nearly $500 million in Stafford Loans was awarded to previous defaulters.[39] This problem exists mainly because there is no national data base for federal student loans. The records of each state, lender, guaranty agency, and school are, in effect, sealed off. The Department of

Education does have a noninteractive "tape dump" that collects information on about 30 million loans each year and that is maintained by an outside contractor for an annual fee of nearly $1 million.[40] But it is designed strictly for internal use and is monitored only to check that the information supplied is complete rather than accurate. The DOE's record on both counts is remarkably poor. In its partial search, the General Accounting Office found incomplete data fields on thirty thousand loans totaling $71 million.[41] There are, finally, plans to develop a data base that lenders and guaranty agencies will be required to use, but it is, in many ways, a case of too little too late, and the department has decreed that it will be too expensive and time consuming to weed out known inaccuracies in the information that will serve as a basis for the new system. This certainly does not inspire much confidence in a federal agency that subsidized and guaranteed a staggering *$93 billion* in loans between 1965 and 1989 and today is liable for nearly *$64 billion.*[42]

On the question of how many students received loan amounts in excess of the legal limits, the GAO acknowledged that while actual abuse was limited, the potential was huge. Analyzing DOE figures, it determined that as much as $5 million in excess payments might have been made in a single academic year. "At current interest rates," it added, "$5 million in excess loans could cost the government [again: the taxpayers] $1.8 million in subsidies over the life of those loans."[43] In one specific case, a student received the maximum Stafford Loan amount of $7,500, but also received loans from three different lenders for a total of $27,000 for one year. He had already defaulted on $20,000 by the time his scam was discovered.[44] Until 1992, a student did not even have to undergo a credit check when applying for a federally guaranteed loan. Some legislators still think that credit checks, to most minds a sensible and responsible measure, are a bad idea. When Sen. Paul Simon (D-IL) discovered that a credit check provision had passed, largely unnoticed, in an unemployment bill, he called it outrageous, and Rep. William Ford (D-MI) became angry enough to create a scene on the House floor. Both moved, fortunately without success, to repeal the requirement.[45]

A quick summary of how the actual loan process works reveals that protecting the taxpayers' financial interests is a low priority. First, a student applies for a Stafford Loan at his college or university's financial aid office. Because there are no longer any need requirements, the office does no more than make a cursory inspection to see that he has filled out the form properly. The office is also technically responsible for ensuring that students are not applying for too much money and that they have not defaulted on any other student loans, but it cannot perform these tasks very effectively, as it is not a credit-checking agency. (Even if it were, it could not access the necessary records, as has been pointed out.) The Department of Education only requires it to audit about 30 percent of all applications. How does it select which ones to audit? Mainly by chance. Some forms also have a computer-coded symbol that tells the office to audit the application because the student listed his family income or the number of family members inconsistently in different sections of the application. Students who earn untaxed income or business/farm income are also supposed to be audited. In 1992, the DOE informed every financial aid office that henceforth it should audit every Stafford Loan application, but few have complied. The main function of the college or university financial aid office, then, is to use a complicated and ever-changing set of federally mandated formulas (Stafford Loan formulas, for example, have been revised at least five times in recent years) to determine how much combined aid from federal, state, and other sources a student should receive.

In the next step, the actual loan application is submitted to a bank or other lending institution, which, before approving it, requests a guarantee from one of the nearly fifty state or private guaranty agencies around the country. Of course, the federal government is the real guarantor. It not only makes good on defaulted loans but reimburses the administrative costs involved in making and collecting on loans. While the student is in school, the federal government also pays the interest on the loan. When repayment begins, it is at less than the market rate, so Uncle Sam continues to pay a portion.

Should the student default, schools, lenders, and guaranty agencies are required to make minimal attempts to collect, but since this consists of mailing out a few written warnings, collection is often ineffective and sometimes, in violation of DOE regulations, is not carried out at all. Time and time again, schools, lenders, and guaranty agencies also have cheated the department by delaying notification of defaults; moreover, since the paperwork on federal loans typically is handled in slow, bureaucratic fashion, lenders also are able to get the Department of Education to pay them millions of dollars for unused student loans. The money is eventually refunded, but they can keep up to four months of subsidy payments and interest besides. This amounts to more than $16 million a year in added and totally unnecessary costs for taxpayers.[46]

In the late 1980s and early 1990s there were numerous accounts of loan corruption in the news. The FBI investigated Florida Federal, a savings and loan institution that was then the second largest Stafford Loan lender, for allegedly falsifying collection information on more than $100 million in loans. Fraud totaling $6 million was proven conclusively and the managers involved were convicted, but Florida Federal was not disqualified from participating in federal loan programs. A few years later, when it collapsed and the federal agency known as the Resolution Trust Corporation took it over, it was still the twelfth largest Stafford lender.[47] An affiliate of Sallie Mae, the largest secondary market that processes billions of dollars in federal student loans, was also found guilty of falsifying data, and the state of Kansas seized the Bank of Horton, the nation's fourth largest Stafford Loan lender, because of high defaults, corruption, and mismanagement.[48] But the real fiasco occurred when the federal government refused to make good on *$575 million* in defaulted loans because United Education and Software, a California student loan collection company, failed to follow proper collection procedures. This left the original lenders, including Bank of America and Citibank, liable and sent shock waves throughout the entire business community.[49]

Not only does most federal loan abuse go undetected, but the system itself encourages it. For example, a number of guaranty agencies also service loans and operate secondary markets for the loans they guarantee. This essentially means that they are allowed to audit and oversee their own operations—a clear conflict of interest, says the DOE inspector general. And a Senate probe revealed that, throughout the 1980s, "Low risks and high profits drove some financial players to handle loan volumes which far exceeded their capabilities."[50] In order to generate more funds to make new loans, many institutions also sold loans to secondary markets within hours of their origination. It is no wonder that the General Accounting Office has determined that defaults, mismanagement, fraud, and abuse due to "internal control weaknesses" within the Stafford Loan program are currently eating up in excess of *54 percent* of total program costs.[51] This means that less than half of the money allocated for Stafford Loans actually goes to pay for new loans.

The GAO has also gone on record that the Department of Education is "running a multibillion-dollar, commercial-type loan operation with a data system that contains incomplete, inaccurate, unreliable information, and that does not allow for even the most basic communications between schools, lenders, guaranty agencies, and the department."[52] In 1992, the U.S. Comptroller General declared in his own report:

> Over the years the federal government has tended to em-phasize access to loans at the expense of accountability. The structure of the [Stafford] loan program is inordinately complex and participants have little or no incentive to prevent defaults. Lenders and guaranty agencies bear little risk, and some use the program as a source of easy income, with little regard for the students' educational prospects or

the likelihood of their repaying the loans. Nearly all the risks fall to the federal government, whose only recourse is to pursue the defaulters. Yet as loan volume and federal financial exposure [has grown], the government [has] failed to establish adequate controls to minimize its losses.[53]

Stafford loan defaults were a "nuisance" to which nobody, least of all the Department of Education, paid much attention in the 1980s, when they were costing "only" a few hundred million dollars a year. Now that they are costing billions of dollars, they are a major scandal. Many in Congress and the bureaucracy have tried to excuse it by saying that the shift from grants to loans (80 percent of all students eligible for federal aid received grants instead of loans in the mid-1970s; now less than 50 percent do) is the real problem and that we have only to issue more grants to make it go away. (That is, they advise that we should spend a large fortune in order to save a small one.) Lobbyists and educators speaking on behalf of colleges and universities agree wholeheartedly with this recommendation, and they add, for good measure, that the federal government ought to throw trade schools out of federal aid programs. Trade schools and their lobbyists retort that those who want to throw them out are "trying to hoard scarce loan dollars at the expense of poor (and largely minority) students trying to learn a vocation."[54]

Representatives from all camps, but especially from within the Department of Education, have also advocated shifting entirely to direct loans administered by the Department of Education (see Chapter 2), even though this is the same agency that has been criticized for gross mismanagement of loan programs by Congress, the GAO, and its own inspector general every year since those programs were established. The *Chronicle of Higher Education* points out the irony of the situation: "The Education Department's new leadership acknowledges the department's shoddy history of managing large programs in one breath, while assuring members of Congress that the department can handle direct lending in the next."[55]

Pell Grants:
————Record Deficits————

In early 1992, it appeared as though the annual deficit for the $5.5 billion Pell Grant program was going to reach a record high of $1.5 billion.[56] The National Association of Independent Colleges and Universities, the National Association of College and University Business Officers, and the American Council on Education represented the universal reaction of the higher education establishment by urgently calling on President Bush to request an immediate "emergency appropriation" to cover the deficit.[57] The Department of Education was also alarmed, but its only action was to delay officially notifying Congress until June. By then, it was clear that the initial estimate of $1.5 billion was far too low, but it was the only figure discussed publicly. Months later, on the last day of the Bush presidency, Secretary of Education Lamar Alexander issued a statement admitting that the Pell Grant deficit would exceed *$2 billion.*[58]

Congress tried to "spread" the costs of this enormous shortfall without violating the 1990 budget agreement by cutting some programs and by funding grant awards at less than authorized levels. Imitating an old pattern, it also added hundreds of millions of dollars to the next year's budget that it then "borrowed" or "forward funded" to help pay for part of the old deficit. This was done despite the fact that critics pointed out that not only would such borrowing guarantee more borrowing the next year, and the next, and so on, but that it was exactly the same scheme that had gotten the federal government into trouble in its attempts to save failing savings and loan institutions.[59]

Why did the extremely well-funded Pell Grant program suffer a deficit in the first place? It was because the Department of Education underestimated the number of students who would be eligible in 1992 and was caught unaware when 300,000 additional students applied.[60] Although the program is not an entitlement, it functions in some respects as if it were, since by law any eligible student must be given an award. Underestimating demand has been a habitual problem since the inception of the program. The DOE has to estimate what it will spend two years in advance, and, according to a former chief financial officer, between 1990 and 1992 it was off by nearly $3 billion. Another factor that contributes to this chronic overdemand and undersupply is the high number of Stafford Loan defaulters who, though ineligible, also regularly apply for and receive Pell Grants—$102 million worth in 1992 alone.[61] Even convicted criminals may receive Pell Grants while they are serving time in state correctional facilities or federal prisons. Furthermore, some schools are reimbursed through the Pell Grant program for tuition fees that are higher than those actually charged to the prisoners.[62]

————— AN S & L STYLE CRISIS —————

Countless sources have predicted that the 1990s will be the worst years for higher education since the Great Depression, perhaps the worst in American history. Government subsidies have helped to create this crisis because they have shielded colleges and universities from the normal forces of the marketplace. They have also led to a situation in which public and private institutions are free to enroll students without regard to the true cost of their education (not to mention the academic preparation they need). And, at the federal level, there is little oversight of the billions of dollars expended on student grant and loan programs, despite the fact that the sums involved are larger than the budgets of most of the world's leading corporations. As Comptroller General Charles A. Bowsher put it in his final report to the Bush administration, the Education Department, like most other cabinet-level agencies, suffers from a "primitive case budgeting system—without satisfactory controls or audits; without accruals; without balance sheets; without a clear picture of assets, liabilities, returns on investments, or risks."[63]

Like the savings and loan industry prior to its collapse in the late 1980s, higher education appears thriving and prosperous on the surface. But vast instability and corruption lie below. The question is, how long can the veneer last? What finally broke the S & Ls was a combination of bureaucratic meddling, a credit crunch after years of "easy money," and the industry's own chronic mismanagement and massive overinvestment. That combination is precisely what threatens colleges and universities today.

Chapter 2

———————— 🏛 ————————

GOVERNMENT AND HIGHER EDUCATION

To understand fully the current plight of American higher education, one must delve into its past, especially its historical relationship with government. Today, of course, government intervention is a fact of life. It pervades every sector of our society, and nowhere is its influence felt more powerfully than in education. But such intervention has not sprung up over-night; it has advanced slowly, like a desert encroaching on once-productive agricultural land. This incremental approach, always under the banner of "Progress," has made its negative effects difficult to notice and even tougher to fight.

The first tentative step toward intervention in education came very early. Under the Articles of Confederation, the new United States Congress issued the Northwest Ordinances of 1785 and 1787, which went to extraordinary lengths to promote education. Over the next 150 years, these two acts would set aside more than 80 million acres of land and hundreds of millions of dollars from land sales and leases for the exclusive support of elementary schools, high schools, and colleges.[1] But Congress did not directly attempt to subsidize higher education until the Civil War when, under the provisions of the Morrill Act, it organized the first publicly supported colleges.

LAND-GRANT COLLEGES

These institutions began in a burst of good intentions. Their promoters intended to revolutionize higher education in an era when less than 2 percent of the population attended school beyond the twelfth grade. Rep. Justin Morrill (R-VT) initially introduced his bill in 1857, declaring loftily, "The role of the national government is to mold the character of the American people."[2] Exactly where he got this idea is uncertain, but it was not from the U.S. Constitution. The character of the American Founders certainly had not been so molded. In Morrill's vision, what would the government use to do the molding? He had a specific instrument in mind: public education. To rely on private education, he claimed, was not only unrealistic but undemocratic.

Subsidized public education naturally would attract thousands more students from every level of society—students who ordinarily would never think of going to college—and therein lay the ingenuity of Morrill's bold proposal. President James Buchanan disagreed with its soundness, however. In a sharply worded veto message, he condemned land-grant colleges as an unconstitutional extension of national power and a deliberate challenge to the principle of federalism, which reserved certain rights and responsibilities for the states, local governments, and individuals. The American Founders, Buchanan argued, had not made education a federal prerogative. But Morrill evidently knew what other politicians have since learned: that government power advances most easily in times of crisis. Momentarily defeated, but undaunted, he later reintroduced the bill as a wartime measure, and in 1862 it was signed into law. The foundation thus was laid for the transformation of higher education through federal legislation.

Despite the eager optimism of Morrill and other would-be education reformers, major changes came slowly. Even with the introduction of land-grant colleges, there were only 563 institutions of higher learning operating in the United States by 1870. They enrolled few students, many under the age of sixteen. They also had painfully modest means, and most teetered on the verge of bankruptcy. All told, they awarded only 9,371 bachelor's degrees, no master's degrees, and one doctorate that year.[3] In 1872, Harvard's freshman class of two hundred was the largest in the country. Yale, with 131, and Princeton, with 110, were next in size.[4] Many schools counted themselves fortunate to attract fifty entering students. A college education still was considered a luxury reserved for the rare few. But all was changing in the late nineteenth century as the spirit of the Progressive movement, with its twin faiths in activist government and trained professionalism, began to take hold among intellectuals and politicians.

PROGRESSIVISM AND THE ——— NEW DEAL ———

If modern society were to advance and prosper, Progressives argued, colleges and universities must abandon their old and inefficient methods. The new objective was not so much to impart learning and culture as to churn out competent, trained workers and citizens, just as factories produce goods. To attain that end, of course, the educators in charge would have to rely on help and supervision from "experts" in government. Washington, D.C., was more than ready to oblige; it had already staged a form of dress rehearsal during Reconstruction, when it used its bureaucratic powers to introduce a Northern political and cultural influence into Southern education. In 1867, it had also created the Education and Labor Committee in the U.S. House of Representatives and the U.S. Office of Education in the executive branch. After a slow start, land-grant colleges proved increasingly important vehicles for Progressivism as a rising standard of living and subsidized tuitions combined to attract new students. Implicit in the land-grant idea itself was one of the central tenets of Progressivism: "education for everyone at public expense."[5]

Private colleges did not especially welcome the attentions of zealous reformers any more than they welcomed the notion of becoming human production lines. They still clung to their supposedly obsolete, backward classical curriculum and retained their independent, idiosyncratic ways. They were not alone; most rural land-grant colleges were just as bent on retaining their own individual character and local autonomy. But as Progressive ideals filtered through their faculties and students, they, too, gradually came to believe that the curriculum must be made more "relevant" and that modern times demanded reexamination of the relationship between education and government.

By the mid-1930s, colleges and universities still were educating only a fraction of the adult population, and federal financing, including land-grant support, still totaled less than 5 percent of all spending on higher education.[6] Then came the New Deal, which the Progressives welcomed with unrestrained enthusiasm. The Works Progress Administration, the Public Works Administration, and the Civilian Conservation Corps channeled hundreds of millions of dollars to colleges and universities. In 1933, the National Youth Administration also established the first federal program of direct student aid, supplying work-study funds for more than 600,000 students over the next ten years.[7] This huge and artificial source of revenue finally led to the kind of expansion that Justin Morrill and, later, the Progressives had envisioned. By 1940, there were 1,708 colleges—more than triple the number seventy years before. The 186,500 bachelor's degrees awarded constituted a nearly twentyfold increase. Educators also awarded 26,731 master's degrees and 3,290 doctorates.[8] The human production line was picking up speed.

Though the New Deal spending programs were billed as a temporary response to the economic crisis of the Great Depression, they left a permanent mark on American higher education by bankrolling expansion of enrollment and facilities. They also made it much easier for the state to adopt new "emergency measures" as a response to the next crisis—World War II.

WORLD WAR II AND THE
———— G.I. BILL ————

The cataclysmic events that occurred between 1942 and 1945 welded government and higher education as never before. The urgency of war changed the minds of many independent campus leaders and anti-New Dealers who had previously fought against a closer relationship. Government contracts for research and personnel training—the main products of the new relationship—became routine. In the last two years of the conflict, the federal government also spent $3 million on student loans and passed the Servicemen's Readjustment Act and other veterans' legislation that became known as the "G.I. Bill of Rights."[9] Rexford G. Moon, Jr., a director of the College Entrance Examination Board, observed that this legislation, which would be amended and expanded twenty-eight times between 1944 and 1958, constituted another mammoth advance in the direction of higher education for everyone at public expense. It was basically the land-grant concept all over again, but with an important difference: This time there would be no limits to what kinds of institutions could participate—private as well as public colleges and universities were eligible for indirect aid through their students.[10]

Hundreds of thousands of former G.I.s immediately descended upon campuses around the country. Within a short time, veterans' entitlements were costing over $300 million a year.[11] But even more important, the resulting shock wiped away the last traces of the old system of American higher education begun hundreds of years earlier. Even as late as 1900, it had to contend with fewer than 250,000 students. By 1947, however, it was desperately trying to educate nearly *2.5 million* students. There was no doubt that immediate, massive federal aid created a whole new problem: immediate, massive demand. The answer? According to politicians, only more federal aid could help the new system of higher education cope. In less than fifty years, Congress went from spending a few million dollars to more than $2 billion a year on aid to higher education.[11] It also began to donate "surplus" land to colleges and passed the Housing Act of 1950, which established the College Housing Loan Program.

But ardent supporters of the "new and improved" government-subsidized system still did not consider these measures sufficient. President Truman's Commission on Higher Education published a six-volume report that revealed the statist mindset of those charged with drawing up the blueprint for postwar higher education. The commission recommended doubling the amount of annual federal spending and specifically called for: (1) free tuition for the first two years of study at any public college or university and drastically reduced tuition thereafter; (2) tens of thousands of federally financed scholarships and fellowships; and (3) over $1 billion in new institutional aid.[12] In the conclusion to its report, the commissioners stated that private colleges, which were enrolling about 900,000 students (less than half of the college population), were no longer the main or the most important form of higher education in America. To meet the nation's needs, they insisted, the federal and state governments must assume a permanent and dominant role in supporting and overseeing public colleges and universities.

THE COLD WAR AND THE NATIONAL DEFENSE ———————EDUCATION ACT———————

In 1957, the Soviets simultaneously launched Sputnik and a national panic among American politicians, who feared that the government was not doing enough to support higher education. Thus, another crisis—the Cold War—supplied a strategic reason to subsidize colleges and universities. In 1958, the National Defense Education Act announced:

> The Congress hereby finds and declares that the security of the nation requires the fullest development of the mental resources and technical skills of its young men and women.

The national interest requires . . . that the Federal Government give assistance to education for programs which are important to our national defense.[13]

True to form, Congress assured the public that National Defense Student Loans (later called National Direct Student Loans and then Perkins Loans) were only a temporary exigency and that government was not getting into the education business. Undergraduate scholarships had been proposed in the Senate and House committee drafts, but were eliminated from the final bill as they "ran into a deep congressional suspicion of giving students a 'free ride' to attend college no matter how needy or meritorious they might be."[14] But Congress had overcome its scruples in regard to federal loans, and NDSLs constituted the first really broad national program of student aid enacted in our history.

They also proved a big step toward an official federal policy that "no student of ability will be denied the opportunity for higher education because of financial need."[15] In *Congress and the Colleges,* Lawrence Gladieux and Thomas Wolanin see NDSLs as more than just a step; they characterize them as a quantum leap. The National Defense Education Act, which spelled out the provisions of these loans, "was styled a temporary, emergency program, and a program specifically aimed at producing scientific manpower. However, it became in fact a permanent and broader program well before its initial four-year authorization expired."[16]

By the 1950s at least forty-six different executive branch agencies were administering programs involving higher education.[17] These were granting 17,000 graduate fellowships and 25,000 research assistantships; the American Council on Education further estimated that 90 percent of all graduate students in science and 60 percent in public health fields also were dependent on federal grants. In addition, institutional research grants included what amounted to substantial sums of "covert" aid for graduate students: $80 million in research, $73 million in education and training, and nearly $23 million in international activities in 1960 alone. Add to that the $191 million in direct federal student assistance, and the total came to just under $367 million, with grants outnumbering loans by two to one.[18]

The mobilization of the academic community, initiated during World War II when the federal government began to issue grants and contracts to individuals as well as institutions, continued to grow apace. By 1960, the federal government was spending billions of dollars a year on university research, with nearly $1 billion going to just one hundred institutions. The main beneficiaries were the California Institute of Technology, Cornell University, Harvard University, MIT, Princeton University, Stanford University, the University of California (at Berkeley, Los Angeles, and San Diego), the University of Chicago, the University of Michigan, and the University of Texas. Notably, federal research grants had become so huge at some of these schools that they yielded three times as much income as student fees and endowment earnings combined.[19]

THE "GREAT SOCIETY" AND THE HIGHER EDUCATION ACT OF 1965

By fits and starts, federal responsibility for higher education had gradually evolved from a radical and revolutionary idea to an unchallenged reality. According to Gladieux and Wolanin, "There was a broadly shared perception of the need for federal assistance to help colleges and universities accommodate the boom in enrollments."[20] No one in Congress was willing to acknowledge, of course, that the boom was an artificial one created by federal assistance in the first place. Everyone was too intent on celebrating the 1960s as the golden years, when federal payments to land-grant colleges and universities passed the $100 million mark, and the Higher Education Facilities Act of 1963, initiated by President John F. Kennedy and signed by President Lyndon B. Johnson, earmarked $2 billion for new capital construction on public campuses.[21]

"Great Society" programs not only made education spending a top priority but, in Johnson's view, a strict necessity. "Every child," he declared, "has the right to as much education as he has the ability to receive." He rushed to take full credit for the Higher Education Act of 1965, a landmark bill intended "to give every American the opportunity to go to college."[22] Many since have regarded it as the cornerstone of modern higher education policies and another critical step in moving "the federal government further along the road to direct support of higher education."[23]

At an initial estimated cost of nearly $1 billion, the 1965 act created the Guaranteed Student Loan (GSL) Program, the first national undergraduate scholarships called Education Opportunity Grants, and huge, additional support for teacher education, academic research, facility construction, and education-related community service.[24] Alarmed by its broad scope, Sen. Barry Goldwater (R-AZ) warned that "control of education by Federal authorities" was becoming inevitable.[25] Few of his peers agreed, but what everyone in Congress freely acknowledged was that the Higher Education Act signaled, for the first time, federal aid for higher education "for its own sake" and not as a response to some perceived crisis.[26]

What had started as a means had become an end. But with the election of Richard Nixon, it appeared that the Great Society's grandiose dream of universalizing higher education through massive injections of federal aid was over. Whereas Johnson regularly had taken the initiative in proposing new domestic spending policies, Nixon vehemently opposed them, vetoing forty-one bills during his administration. In Congress and as vice president presiding over the Senate, he consistently voted against more federal involvement in education, and, as president, he vetoed the 1970 education appropriations bill, which called for nearly a half billion dollars in increased spending. But Nixon also faced a challenge that had not been posed for one hundred years: The opposition controlled both houses of Congress. Eventually, this would help force him to approve legislation that was destined to increase the government's role in higher education more than any other bill since 1965 or for many years afterward.

THE EDUCATION AMENDMENTS
—————— OF 1972 ——————

The Education Amendments of 1972 constituted one of the first "omnibus" bills in Congress. Although eventually boiled down to 146 pages, at one stage the measure bloated to more than six hundred pages and was dubbed the "Sears Roebuck Catalogue," the "Christmas tree," and the "grab bag."[27] Its purpose was to consolidate many previous regulations on elementary, secondary, and higher education, but some of its sponsors harbored more ambitious designs. The bill legalized institutional aid to colleges, something Kennedy and Johnson had tried unsuccessfully to achieve. In addition, it created another precedent-setting program called Basic Educational Opportunity Grants. Not long after, these would be renamed Pell Grants after their primary architect, Claiborne Pell, a Rhode Island Democrat who had chaired the Senate Subcommittee on Education since 1969 and previously succeeded only in securing passage of minor laws on railroads and seaweed.[28]

The House and Senate conference committee for the final bill read like an all-star lineup of liberals from both parties, including Pell, Rep. John Brademas (D-IN), Sen. Edward Kennedy (D-MA), Sen. Walter Mondale (D-MN), Sen. Alan Cranston (D-CA), Sen. Jacob Javits (R-NY), Rep. Carl Perkins (D-KY), and Sen. Thomas Eagleton (D-MO). The important thing to note, however, is that no one except the members of the relevant authorizing committees cared much about the bill's higher education provisions. It was the issue of forced busing that greatly agitated the public and Congress. As a consequence, there was no real debate about the provisions on institutional aid to colleges and universities, even though such provisions constituted a huge departure from all previous policies. Time and time again, they had been defeated. But the only expressed concern now was about what formula should be used to determine which colleges and universities received the most money. Over this issue, there *was* considerable disagreement, with some favoring basing aid on enrollment, others on graduation rates, and still others on the cost of instruction.

There was also almost no debate over Basic/Pell Grants, another controversial idea that had been shopped around the halls of Congress unsuccessfully for years. The explanation for this lack of interest may well be that they had been around for so long that everyone had come to accept them as inevitable. Senator Pell had been pushing for years for what he called a "G.I. Bill to help all high school graduates." As early as 1969, he had introduced a measure calling for a flat $1,000 award to every student in the country for the first two years of college. Unable to gain support, he came up with a plan for automatic grants of $1,400 a year to needy college students, announcing, "It is my philosophical belief that the federal government must play a major and ever-expanding role in support of higher education." Many congressional critics objected that there weren't sufficient funds in the federal budget, but Pell huffed that "they have lost sight of the true significance of this bill. If the American people want universal opportunity, and the Senate obviously thinks they do, then this bill is going to be funded."[29]

The passage of the Education Amendments of 1972 appeared to vindicate his belief. The Basic/Pell Grants the amendments created differed from other grants and loans, wherein college and university financial aid offices dealt with individual students and worked out aid packages to meet individual needs. These new awards allowed for no discretion; if a student qualified, acceptance was automatic, and a complex "needs test" formula determined the size of the grant. Basic/Pell Grants stopped short of being an entitlement, however, since funds were appropriated from year to year and could go up or down depending on the size and distribution of the federal budget.

Like the Education Act of 1965, the new amendments were not a temporary answer to a crisis but a deliberate and permanent foray into social legislation on a vast scale. Their sponsors intended them to effect profound changes regarding who attended college and who paid for it. They also greatly enhanced the powers of the Department of Health, Education and Welfare and the U.S. Office of Education and paved the way for the elevation of the latter to cabinet-level status. But the White House, which had vainly attempted to introduce its own watered-down version, reasoning that this would be the lesser evil, had a last-ditch opposition strategy. President Nixon announced that the state of the economy demanded budget cuts and that he would veto any appropriations bills that dramatically increased spending on higher education. Initially, this strategy looked as though it would succeed, and the "social programs and liberal traditions of the New Deal and the Great Society seemed to be destined for the chopping block."[30] But soon, the Watergate hearings landed Nixon in a struggle for his political survival, and he was forced to abandon the fight.

JIMMY CARTER AND THE DEPARTMENT OF EDUCATION

The Higher Education Amendments of 1976 and the Middle Income Student Assistance Act of 1978 basically reauthorized the same structure of federal student assistance created in 1972, but there were three critical revisions: broadened eligibility requirements, increased maximum grant awards, and removal of all income restrictions on Guaranteed Student Loans. The effects of these revisions were as dramatic as they were immediate. Pell Grant spending soared to unbelievable levels, and the number of GSL borrowers rose from one million to about *2.5 million* in just two years. Interest rates were so favorable that *House and Garden* actually featured an article on "how you can make a substantial profit from a student loan."[31] Overall, federal need-based aid, which only a few years earlier had been costing $200 million, jumped to $3.5 billion and, by the end of the Carter presidency, to more than *$5 billion* a year.[32]

Beset by a troubled economy and increasing demands on the public purse, the administration did make attempts to limit education spending in the late 1970s. But this only resulted in a long and bitter struggle between those who sought to scale down federal aid programs and those who wanted to protect, maintain, and even expand them. Ronald Reagan, waiting in the wings, already was making his education battle plan clear in countless speeches delivered around the nation, declaring forcefully: "We must halt the growth of the education bureaucracy which has done so much to harm the strength of our once-independent educational system." When Carter elevated the U.S. Office of Education to the cabinet-level Department of Education, Reagan vowed that if elected president he would do everything in his power to dismantle it. His landslide presidential victory in 1980 gave him the opportunity to back his words with action.

THE REAGAN REVOLUTION

Reagan chose not to mount a frontal attack. Instead, he targeted the Department of Education's number-one program, federal student assistance, and in the Budget Reconciliation Act of 1981 he made some limited, but nonetheless important, gains. The new law reinstated the needs test for Guaranteed Student Loans for students with family incomes over $30,000. It also set limits on Pell Grants. But Congress reached a stalemate over the prospect of additional cuts, and Secretary of Education Terrel Bell, no great advocate of conservatism, was reluctant to do much of anything to influence the outcome.

It was Reagan's vocal and influential second secretary of education, William Bennett, who threw down the gauntlet before Congress in the mid-1980s by calling for a 25 percent cut in the higher education budget. He suggested that capping undergraduate grant and loan packages at $4,000 per student would achieve most of this proposed reduction.[33] He also argued that taxpayers were financing the education, at minimum, of hundreds of thousands of students who could pay a greater percentage of their tuition or afford to take out loans from private sources. But the educational establishment and many members of Congress, both Republican and Democrat, denounced any limits on aid as an attack on the poor and on middle income students who were being crushed by "a growing burden of debt." The educational establishment heaped invective on Bennett and condemned him as the enemy of "the very community which counts on his leadership."[34] He did succeed in privatizing loan collection services, consolidating loan programs into one division, and reducing the number of employees at the Department of Education from 7,700 to 4,500. In terms of employees, the DOE became the smallest cabinet-level agency, but education spending and new programs continued to grow.

Terry Hartle, then education staff director of the Senate Committee on Labor and Human Resources, who fought ceaselessly for such growth, understated the case when he said, "The 1980s turned out to be a pretty good decade for America's colleges and universities." Guaranteed Student Loans increased, in real terms, by *57 percent* and Pell Grants increased by *48 percent*. As noted earlier, federal, state, and institutional student aid grew, in real terms, by 33 percent.[35] Liberal Democrats and Republicans in Congress gleefully claimed that the Reagan administration had won some initial skirmishes but lost the war.

THE HIGHER EDUCATION AMENDMENTS
——— OF 1992 ———

In mid-1991, Congress began debating reauthorization of the Higher Education Act (HEA) of 1965 and subsequent amendments. William D. Ford (D-MI), chairman of the Education and

Labor Committee, saw this principal legislation as a grand opportunity to extend the size and scope of federal spending and authority. The draft bill he introduced in the House of Representatives increased eligibility for grants and loans to include at minimum hundreds of thousands of middle income students. It also nearly doubled the size of Pell Grants and made them an entitlement in order to assure that Congress would be required to fund the maximum awards regardless of annual budget constraints. In addition, it scrapped federally guaranteed loans and substituted a revolutionary new program in which the Department of Education would bypass some thirteen thousand lending institutions and, for the first time, make direct loans to college students.[36] The government would raise capital for this purpose by selling securities. Colleges and universities would handle the actual disbursements and most of the paperwork. All students would be eligible, and interest rates would be subsidized well below market rates. The government also would pay the interest on the loans of needy students while they were in school.

Representative Ford's plan was a flagrant violation of the 1990 budget agreement, but he argued that this was irrelevant since it would not take effect until 1994, when, presumably, gigantic defense cuts would leave plenty of budget surpluses for education. Lobbyists were ecstatic. "It's a real vision for higher education; the biggest rewrite ever," gloated Charles B. Saunders, Jr., senior vice president of the American Council on Education.[37] But Rep. Tom Coleman (R-MO) protested that abandoning the pay-as-you-go system for Pell Grants for yet another mandatory spending program was wildly irresponsible: "It's just absolutely incredible," he said, "that Congress would be willing to tie its hands when we have a budget deficit of $350 billion." Even education spending advocates like House Budget Committee Chairman Leon Panetta (D-CA) and Appropriations Committee Chairman William Natcher (D-KY) expressed reluctance to cash in prematurely on the supposed peace dividend. "The entitlement is important to keep hope alive," shot back James B. Appleberry, president of the American Association of State

Colleges and Universities. "Without that, [students] are subject to the whims of the budgetary process."[38] Senator Kennedy also spoke up in favor of the provision, pointing to huge entitlements for agriculture and arguing that education deserved the same.[39]

Rep. Pat Williams (D-MT), chairman of the House Education Subcommittee on Postsecondary Education, offered an amendment, adopted by voice vote, "that would require Congress to borrow from the following year if it did not have enough money to fund the maximum on Pell Grants set by the appropriators."[40] Weighing in on the provisions in the House bill that liberalized grant and loan eligibility, he said, "The heart and soul of this bill is what it does for middle income working families."[41] Rep. Tom Petri (R-WI) likewise intoned, "Tuitions keep rising and the middle class in particular is increasingly hard pressed to foot these bills, despite the fact that education should pay off economically for most students."[42] The *Congressional Quarterly* noted that during the reauthorization proceedings Republicans eagerly lined up with Democrats "to expand the education pot, regardless of administration wishes." Ford himself expressed the opinion that a majority of his peers in Congress believed that expanding educational aid to the middle class was a top priority: "The people who pay America's bill should also enjoy some of the benefits." Secretary of Education Lamar Alexander complained with justification, "The general disposition on the Hill is to give more money to everybody."[43]

But the Bush administration's greatest objection to the House draft bill concerned direct loans. Early on, the president sent a personal letter to Ford, warning that he would veto reauthorization of the Higher Education Act if a direct loan program was part of the package. The nation's banks and secondary lenders like the Student Loan Marketing Association (Sallie Mae) were also in an uproar. So, too, were Harvard University, Yale University, Brown University, and Northwestern University—institutions which, coincidentally, owned hundreds of thousands of shares in Sallie Mae stock and profited handsomely from the student loan business.[44]

When the government first began its student loan programs, the idea was to have outside entities administer the entire operation. Federal agencies would not actually lend money; they would simply guarantee loans against default and pay the interest while students were in school. Because interest rates on these loans were artificially low, the government also would make up the difference and pay an additional handling fee. Sallie Mae was created by the Education Amendments of 1972 to serve as a "representative interest" for government, buying student loans from banks so that they could make more loans.[45] Because it is a federally chartered, for-profit corporation with special advantages over other lenders, Sallie Mae always has been criticized as a monopoly, but it was never seriously challenged until the reauthorization debate began in the early 1990s. Direct loan advocates like Ford, Sen. David Durenberger (R–MN), Sen. Paul Simon (D–IL), Rep. Robert Andrews (D–NJ), and even the Bush White House for a short time before it reversed its position, held that cutting all lenders, including Sallie Mae, out of the picture would save anywhere between $1 and $2 billion a year in interest subsidies and fees.[46] They backed up their case with several well-publicized scandals surrounding lending and collection agencies around the country and the $2.1 million annual salary of Sallie Mae President and CEO Lawrence Hough.[47]

Hough responded by asking where Congress was going to get the money—$75 billion or more—to launch a direct loan program and warned that it would be political suicide for any member to try to extract it from U.S. taxpayers.[48] Tom Scully, then associate director of the Office of Management and Budget, added that the many hidden costs involved would cancel out any potential savings created by direct loans: "It doesn't take too much math to figure out we're going to be putting out $150 billion in ten years without getting any money back. It's like starting up a bank with nothing, from scratch."[49] Others, while not defending Sallie Mae or the cushy, no-risk relationship many student loan lenders had developed with the federal government, expressed serious doubts about whether the Department of Education would be capable of monitoring more than 6 million loans. The department's past record of mismanaging Pell Grants and GSL/Stafford Loans seemed to indicate clearly that not even added manpower and outside contractors would help. Opponents also objected that direct loans would let the people with the least interest in properly handling and administering federal funds—bureaucrats on the government payroll and in the financial aid offices of tuition-hungry college and university campuses—wield significant and largely unsupervised control. Several years later, William F. Buckley Jr. would offer them more ammunition:

> To say that fees earned by banks are "excess profits" is sheer anti-capitalist attitudinizing. The planted axiom is that if government takes over an operation previously handled by the private sector, the operation becomes more efficient and cheaper. In fact, the weight of experience tells us that it is an almost unfailing rule that the absorption of responsibility by the government a) adds cost to the transaction, and b) pitches the transaction onto a political rather than an economic plane. [One] might as well say that since government buys a lot of airplanes, tanks, and automobiles, it should produce them in order to avoid excess profits from the middleman.[50]

But in 1992 the general attitude of members of Congress was favorable towards the direct loan program, and despite strong opposition from the White House and the banking community, it seemed likely to succeed. According to an informal poll by *Congressional Quarterly*, most Democrats and Republicans agreed with about 90 percent of what Ford had proposed in the House of Representatives' draft bill. With some political wrangling that led to the elimination of the Pell Grant entitlement provision, the House version passed 365–3 in the last week of March. The three "nays" were issued by Philip M. Crane (R-IL), John T. Doolittle (R-CA), and Robert Stump (R-AZ).[51] The Senate bill, a more modest imitation, had already sailed through with only one opposing vote by Jesse Helms (R-NC).[52] It also expanded grant and loan eligibility to include middle income students, but it kept existing loan programs intact and gradually rather than immediately transformed the Pell Grant program into an entitlement.

The approved bills were then taken up by a conference committee made up of delegates from both houses of Congress. In the reconciliation process, the entitlement provision was defeated. Direct loans were limited to a pilot program for three hundred to five hundred colleges, but this was still counted a victory since federal pilot projects inevitably develop into full-fledged programs. The maximum dollar amount for individual grants and loans went up, in some cases nearly 50 percent. And under the new broadened eligibility formula adopted, total borrowing limits increased by one-third for many students, and family home and farm equity and college savings were exempted from the asset column. For a second time, financial need requirements were abandoned for GSLs, now known as Stafford Loans. This effectively made all students eligible.[53] The final reauthorization also created the Unsubsidized Loan Program, which, according to the topsy-turvy logic of Washington, *is* subsidized. It guarantees automatic federal loans for students who are ineligible for other programs. Creditworthiness is not a requirement, and interest rates are below market rates.

For months, President George Bush repeatedly promised a veto of the final reauthorization bill, but, faced with mounting pressure from Congress and a fizzling reelection campaign, he signed the six-hundred-page, $100 billion, five-year law in a special White House ceremony in July 1992.[54] He and his advisors hoped that this would bolster his image as the "education president," but they were sadly disappointed. Conservatives on Capitol Hill, and especially rank-and-file political appointees within the Department of Education, felt bitter that Bush had gone back on his word and approved a bill that would result in billions of dollars of new debt. They cited Congressional Budget

Office predictions that under the new rules of eligibility established by the amendments there would be at least 1.1 million new
borrowers and 1.4 million new Pell Grant recipients.[55] "Where,"
they asked, "would the money for these students come from?"
Finally, they denounced the reauthorization as a blatant attempt
to buy off middle class voters worried about rising tuitions.

Liberals were equally bitter. They had been adamant that Pell
Grants must be made an entitlement if new federal aid was to
have any impact at all. Their worst fears were realized less than
two months later when Congress admitted that it would not have
the budget money to pay for increases in the Pell Grant program
and that full awards would actually have to be cut to $2,300 per
student—$100 less than the previous level and $1,400 less than
the new legal maximum. Work-study grants and Stafford Loans
would not be cut, but the budgets for these programs would only
rise by 3 percent.[56] Furthermore, the federal government would
not be able to fund any of the new programs created by the
reauthorization. One lobbyist fumed: "The administration and
Congress part company on education when it comes to funding,
but the leadership appears reluctant to push those differences and
put some money in education."[57] Neither he nor his peers was
appeased when Secretary of Education Lamar Alexander pointed
out that, during the Bush presidency, overall spending on higher·
education had actually risen *52 percent*.[58]

CLINTON AND "EDUCATION FOR EVERYONE
———— AT PUBLIC EXPENSE" ————

While still a candidate, President Clinton vowed to seek full
funding for the 1992 reauthorization and to budget billions of
dollars in additional spending on "national service" and other
new education schemes. Four months after his inauguration, he
declared that the Department of Education budget would be
increased by 25 percent over a five-year period.[59] Accordingly,
his new appointee, Secretary of Education William Riley, pre-

sented a 1994 budget request to Congress that was so huge that it even dismayed staunch prospending Democrats. House Appropriations Committee Chairman William Natcher pointed out that it was several billion dollars above the legal spending limits, and in the Senate, Tom Harkin (D-IA) complained, "The President's budget for this subcommittee just doesn't add up." When pressed to say where he thought cuts ought to be made in other departments to pay for the increases in education, Riley responded, "I'm in the education business. I wish that I could tell you exactly how OMB and the White House intend to deal with [cuts]. All I can tell you is what I was told."[60]

It is becoming increasingly clear that Clinton may not be able to deliver on his grand promises. By the end of his first year in office, he was being severely criticized by the education establishment for failing to persuade Congress to approve substantially higher education appropriations in the fiscal 1994 budget and for his policy of shifting much of the current financial and administrative burden onto the states. One disgruntled Harvard educator characterized the president's actions as "an impoverished campaign strategy in education in a situation where there's no new money."[61]

But this may turn out to be the good news for higher education, after all. The system has grown too big and too fast through the financial steroids of government aid. While only 2 percent of the population attended college in 1870, by the beginning of World War II, the figure had mushroomed to 15 percent. By the the 1960s, it more than doubled to 33 percent. In raw numbers, the 1960s saw enrollment increase from about 3 million to nearly 9 million students, and, by the end of the 1970s, there were over 11 million. In the 1980s, the college population finally peaked at 12.5 million and has remained at roughly that level ever since. The nation's two-thousand-plus, four-year colleges and universities are granting well over a million bachelor's degrees, over 300,000 master's degrees, and nearly forty thousand doctorates every year.[62] Some may survey this record and call it progress. But is it *education?*

Chapter 3

GOVERNMENT FUNDING
TODAY

In the 1950s, the federal government devoted most of its higher education spending to research. By the 1960s, however, when spending had increased over 400 percent, it was student assistance that accounted for the biggest gains.[1] Today, this single federal budget item costs taxpayers nearly *$22 billion* a year.[2] Between 1970 and 1992, the number of students receiving federal grants *doubled* and the number receiving federal loans *tripled*.[3] Since then, the 1992 reauthorization of the Higher Education Act has made thousands more middle income students eligible for grants and loans.

Incredibly, many in Washington are indignant that the government is not spending even more. In particular, they demand an increased emphasis on federal grants since loans allegedly create "an intolerable burden of debt" for middle income students (as though such grants would not increase the nation's already intolerable burden of debt). They take little comfort in the fact that over 4 million students received Pell Grants in 1991-92—18 percent more than the year before—or that between the 1990-91 and 1991-92 academic years, total student aid from combined federal, state, and other sources increased 7.9 percent to a record-high $30.8 billion. As the College Board reports, this amount is 33 percent higher than a decade ago, even after adjusting for inflation.[4] (In case anyone is missing out, the Department of Education is developing a free software package for prospective college students that will teach them how to apply for bigger and yet bigger amounts of financial assistance.)

Student assistance was once for the needy, but that is no longer true, as a look, once again, at Harvard University confirms. At that prestigious upper-class bastion, nearly two-thirds of the undergraduates receive some form of financial assistance. At some private and public institutions, the figure is as high as four-fifths. It is not at all uncommon, in fact, for students with annual family incomes in excess of $60,000 to be eligible for government aid. What is more, of all available college financial aid, nearly *75 percent*—an astonishing three out of four dollars—comes from the federal government.[5]

———— NATIONAL SERVICE ————

Despite overwhelming evidence to the contrary, President Clinton has expressed deep disappointment in what he has characterized as the slow growth in the size and scope of federal student assistance. He has promised to shower higher education with still more billions of dollars by raising taxes and by exploiting the "peace dividend" in the post–Cold War era. He has also championed income-contingent repayment plans on all federal loans and proposed a new, massive spending program devoted to "national service."

National service is a bandwagon that has been rolled out regularly ever since Franklin D. Roosevelt launched the Works Progress Administration and the Civilian Conservation Corps. Presidents John F. Kennedy and Lyndon B. Johnson sold VISTA and the Peace Corps to the public as national service programs. In the 1970s, Sen. Claiborne Pell floated the idea of a national service youth corps. It surfaced again in the late 1980s under the sponsorship of Rep. David McCurdy (D-OK) and Sen. Sam Nunn (D-GA), and, in an elaborate, televised ceremony in 1989, President George Bush officially unveiled it as a proposed solution to the "tuition crisis" in higher education. The idea was to allow middle income as well as needy students to exchange volunteer service or time spent in service-oriented careers (as teachers, policemen, drug counselors) for a free college education. But Bush's plan gained little besides glowing endorsements; there was simply no money to fund it. (Congress did come up with $63 million in 1990 for a Commission on National and Community Service, which was to supervise various demonstration projects.)[6]

Nevertheless, Governor Bill Clinton was determined to make his "National Service Trust Fund" a central issue in the next election race, ranking it among his top five political goals. Throughout 1992 he declared that he wanted to see a half million students participating annually, and, after winning the presidency, he chose to make one of his first public addresses on the theme of national service at Rutgers University on March 1, 1993, the thirty-second anniversary of the establishment of the Peace Corps. Joined by Sens. Edward Kennedy, Claiborne Pell, Christopher Dodd, John D. Rockefeller IV, and Harris Wofford and Reps. William Ford and David McCurdy, he invoked the memory of the Morrill Act and the G.I. Bill and promised that there would be at least 100,000 national service "volunteers" by the end of his first term.[7] Needless to say, there was no real discussion in the Rutgers speech of where the money would come from to pay for this new program, though one of the first official White House estimates released in February 1993 stated that it would cost "only" $6 billion a year. By March, the official figure hovered between $7.4 billion and $9.5 billion, and some independent analysts were predicting that $12 billion was more realistic.[8]

Then in June the administration announced that it would no longer seek $10,000-$12,000 a year in college loan forgiveness for each national service participant but would settle for $5,000 a year. This cave-in was a response to critics who pointed out that students would be paid twice—to attend school and to perform service—and to angry veterans who protested that those who served as civilian volunteers should not be better compensated than those assuming the risks of military service. Currently, the total two-year national service "package" is designed to offer, roughly: $10,000 in loan forgiveness; $18,000 in "volunteer" wages; and about $10-$12,000 in medical care, child care, tax exemption, and other benefits. The organizations that accept national service participants are allowed to chip in an additional $9,000 in wages.[9] Because of the $5,000-a-year limit on loan forgiveness, this may not be much of a tuition assistance program, but it certainly is a great pork-barrel jobs program, says Bruce Chapman, president of the Discovery Institute in Seattle. Chapman also notes that it will automatically create a demand for increased benefits as more students sign on. It is, in effect, like a "Social Security entitlement for young people."[10]

Whether any of the latest estimates on individual or total costs of the program are correct (and there are good grounds to believe that all are too low, since proposed federal programs invariably end up costing more than anticipated), there are a number of philosophical and practical arguments against national service: (1) It will not achieve any meaningful social reform or raise the level of public-spiritedness among our citizens. As William F. Buckley Jr. has pointed out in defense of a different plan of national service, you cannot vitalize the idealism of young people by buying their time. In fact, it will denigrate real voluntarism and humanitarian service. As Chapman wryly points out, "hired volunteer" is an oxymoron. (2) It will create another artificial boom in enrollments in higher education by placing most of the burden of rising tuitions on the taxpayers rather than students. (3) It will encourage more of the entitlement mentality that presupposes that all students have a right to taxpayer-funded education. (4) It will invade and politicize the private philanthropic community, leading organizations to compete for volunteers they couldn't or wouldn't normally attract. (5) It will leave the decisions about which institutions and which students will be eligible up to bureaucratic commissions appointed by state governors. These commissions are likely to have a vested interest in favoring public college-affiliated organizations and public college student applicants in order to shift more of the financial burden of higher education from the states to the federal government. (6) It will leave private organizations that accept national service participants as volunteers and private colleges and universities that enroll them as students open to the charge of accepting federal subsidies. (7) It will encourage colleges to try to get the government to subsidize existing programs, which, with cosmetic changes, can be made to look like national service programs. (8) It will create "make-work" instead of genuine jobs and delay thousands of individuals' entrance to the workplace at an untold cost to the nation's economy. (9) Finally, it will make big government even bigger. "Imagine," says Doug Bandow, senior fellow at the Cato Institute, "the bureaucracy necessary to decide which jobs are 'service,' sort through labor objections to 'unfair competition,' match thousands of participants with individual posts, and monitor the quality of people's work. The incredible fraud, misuse, and waste endemic to other so-called public service programs hardly augur well for yet another, even larger, federal effort at social engineering."[11]

Any of these objections alone is enough to condemn national service, but the Clinton administration remains obstinate. It launched the pilot program with one thousand students in the summer of 1993 and plans to jump quickly to twenty thousand students by the end of 1994. A variation on national service is "service-oriented grants" to institutions. This is becoming an increasingly common method of covertly funneling more taxpayer money into federal student assistance and into controversial projects. Georgetown University's Equal Justice Foundation, for example, recently received $50,000 from the earlier cited Commission on National and Community Service. The grant, which included a $3,000 fellowship for one of the university's law students, was to research gay civil rights for the American Civil Liberties Union. The fellowship recipient admitted frankly, "If it weren't for grants, we wouldn't be able to do this." The commission's ongoing task of "encouraging community service" is being accomplished mainly, reports the *Chronicle of Higher Education,* by funding a liberal agenda on AIDS, homelessness, illiteracy, pollution, and minorities.[12]

—————— INSTITUTIONAL AID ——————

Congress has long awarded millions of dollars in direct federal subsidies to schools with recognized "special" missions such as Gallaudet College and the National Technical Institute for the Deaf, the University of the District of Columbia, and the nation's historically black colleges. In 1935, the Bankhead-Jones Act legalized direct appropriations for land-grant colleges, and, in the 1950s, colleges and universities with qualifying programs in teacher education and the sciences also became eligible. It was in the 1960s that education spending advocates began pushing for national institutional aid. But what they meant by this term was something far different from funding built into existing federal programs. This new form of national institutional aid was to be "undesignated 'free' money available to a more or less comprehensive range of colleges and universities to be used by the institutions at their own discretion, not necessarily in any one expenditure category or for any predetermined purpose."[13]

The groups who pushed hardest were the newly empowered higher education lobbies in Washington. In 1969, the American Council on Education (ACE) declared that "the principal unfinished business of the federal government in the field of higher education is the necessity to provide support for general institutional purposes."[14] Even the Association of American Colleges (AAC), which in the 1950s had come out strongly against direct aid out of fear of federal control and potential church/state conflicts, reversed its position as "financial necessity overcame suspicions of federal support."[15] Virtually all these groups publicly declared that all previous aid to colleges and universities was insignificant compared to the new goal of national institutional aid. The American Council on Education prepared a report basically dictating the language and terms that Rep. Albert H. Quie (R-MN) would introduce into the House in 1970 as the Higher Education General Assistance Bill. But it was defeated, as were other similar bills with institutional aid provisions in 1972, 1976, and 1980.[16]

Congress was willing to spend billions of dollars on expanding student aid, university research, and capital construction, but it shied away from unrestricted institutional aid. One observer noted that the real reason for this was not so much Congress's preference as it was the inability of the higher education community to agree on a basis for equitable distribution of institutional support, i.e., how to divide the spoils. Even though he was a zealous promoter of federal aid to education, Rep. John Brademas (D-IN) was frustrated by the greed and acrimony that prevailed in academe when it came to institutional aid: "We turned to the citadel of reason—we said, 'Tell us what you need,' and they answered, 'We need $150 per student because that is what we've been able to agree upon.' "[17]

However, when "cost of instruction" allowances finally were approved as the first direct, across-the-board aid to colleges and universities, they turned out to be only very minor compensation for each Pell Grant recipient on campus. Today, there are other more lucrative kinds of institutional aid for many schools: "bonuses" for those that enroll certain quotas of Pell Grant students and special awards for any that are "financially struggling" or "developing institutions." Current federal appropriations for this latter category total nearly $90 million a year.[18] Federal agencies like the National Endowment for the Humanities and the Department of Education can also issue institutional aid in the form of "challenge grants" in which federal dollars match between every $1-$4 in private donations.

FEDERALLY FUNDED RESEARCH AND
———— "FEDERAL FOUNDATIONS" ————

But the lobbies were wrong when they predicted that institutional aid would make all other forms of assistance appear insignificant. There would be an even bigger cash cow for higher education in the form of federally funded research. For a long time, of course, the United States had no national scientific policy, and there was not much of a federal presence in scientific research. There existed, in fact, a strong American intellectual tradition opposed to European-style state involvement. But between 1900 and 1939, Progressives and New Dealers managed to establish more than forty fledgling federal scientific agencies.[19]

Limited initial budgets and projects were expanded dramatically with the advent of World War II, which meant that research had strategic importance. After the war, the head of one of these agencies, Vannevar Bush, published an idealized account called *Science: The Endless Frontier,* arguing that subsidies for peacetime research were also vital. The report was widely accepted, and by 1949, the Department of Defense and the Atomic Energy Commission accounted for 96 percent of all federal money spent on campus research. The Korean War sent university R & D spending into the stratosphere. Between 1951 and 1953, it jumped from $1.3 billion to $3.1 billion. In the 1960s, there was a new war on, this time in Vietnam. The government's role in university research had become so unquestioned by then that the federal budget for this activity soared to *$15 billion* a year.[20]

Thus, in the space of a single generation, federally funded research exploded. While the overall budget of the U.S. government rose elevenfold, its R & D budget rose some *two hundredfold* between 1940 and the late 1960s. In the 1970s, it reached *$19 billion* a year.[21] The degree to which federal dollars have come to dominate research on college and university campuses is indicated by the example of the University of Michigan. U of M funds about $42 million of research each year out of its own budget; nonfederal sources account for another $78 million or so; and federal agencies supply $227 million, or almost double the first two sources combined.[22] Education philosopher Jacques Barzun notes that federally funded university research has become symbolic of an activity at once mysterious and sacred. When we judge its results, we are expected to suspend our skepticism and express universal confidence.[23] We also are supposed to open our wallets—to the tune of billions of dollars—to support it.

One grants advisor to higher education has likened the federal agencies that spend our tax dollars to wealthy charitable foundations in the private sector. They are basically independent operations that have huge resources to dispose of at their own discretion. And, just like their private sector counterparts, they have mission statements, annual reports, guidelines for grantees, and peer review evaluation for proposals. Apart from the Department of Education, the agencies that distribute most of the money and that constitute a major source of funding for American higher education include the Department of Agriculture, the Department of Defense, the Department of Health and Human Services, the Department of Energy, the Environmental Protection Agency, the National Science Foundation, the National Institutes of Health, and the National Endowment for the Humanities. A brief look at the last three is warranted, since their central focus is higher education:

• *The National Science Foundation*: Together with the Department of Defense, NSF has made the federal government "the chief patron of academic science." Within ten years after its founding in 1950, it was funding three-fourths of the basic research conducted on campus.[24] According to former Deputy Director John T. Wilson, the 1966 Daddario-Kennedy Amendment changed the agency in both form and substance by designating the social sciences as eligible for NSF funding and by broadening its financial commitment to basic research and education as well as international activity. In addition, the amendment changed five senior positions from career to political appointments.[25]

The NSF has been under fire for over a decade for its careless review of projects. To cite just one instance, in 1987 a draft of an NSF report to Congress was supposed to be approved by nine reviewers, but eight provided no formal review, and one could not recollect even seeing the report.[26] Congressional oversight committees have responded with investigations and have even rescinded funding for peer-reviewed projects they deemed unworthy, rescinding $2 million in grants in 1992 alone.[27] Many within the education community, however, oppose congressional oversight and claim that Congress is overstepping its authority. Vartan Gregorian, president of Brown University, expressed the general attitude of educators recently when he stated that, except in extraordinary cases, "there should not be any intervention into the peer-review process." But Rep. Ralph Regula (R-OH) countered, "Somebody must be accountable for how tax dollars are expended." The reality, says the *Chronicle of Higher Education,* is that under the current system, in which peer reviewers only meet once or twice a year to review huge numbers of grants, nobody really is accountable.[28]

The current annual budget of roughly $3 billion is spent primarily on science education and scientific research, but, over the last four decades, NSF has also provided vast sums for student and faculty assistance as well as new facility construction on college campuses and at off-campus laboratories under university management. Significantly, it has adopted many "investigator-initiated projects" in which researchers are "spared the administrative regulations that encumber other federal contractors."[29]

Public support for big spending on NSF projects has always been relatively high, since people tend to think of scientific research as vital to the future of the nation. But many NSF grants are of dubious value. Recent budget cuts mandated by Congress, for example, forced the agency, reluctantly, to renege on *three* grants to the National Institute of Dental Research "being used to study ways in which people can overcome their fear of dentists," and a university grant to study the "life history of the swallow-tailed butterfly."[30]

Federal support for defense-related scientific research on college and university campuses (which comes mainly from the Department of Defense) is also a big-ticket item and should be mentioned at least briefly here. Between 1981 and 1986, it grew over 100 percent. But as this field declines in the post–Cold War 1990s, do not look for big cuts in federal spending on university research. Other areas will take up the slack. NSF and NIH have done exactly this in the past whenever defense spending has shrunk. Today, in real dollars, NSF supplies colleges and universities with 20 percent more research funds than in 1967, and NIH supplies them with 80 percent more.[31]

• *The National Institutes of Health:* The largest biomedical research organization in the United States, NIH traces its roots as a government agency back to the late nineteenth century. In the 1930s, it began to take the shape we know today, with over twenty member institutes ranging from the National Cancer Institute to the National Institute on Aging. In the 1960s, its budget for research grew faster than that of any other agency, including the Department of Defense and the National Science Foundation.[32] The trend toward more and more bureaucratic control of scientific activities can be seen clearly at NIH. Hundreds upon hundreds of new regulations have been passed or proposed on research, products, and collaboration with industry. The institutes' boards see their role as science police. Any outside interference is considered taboo, as evidenced by the recent fight that broke out over the agency's 1992 reauthorization. The boards, along with the Department of Health and Human Services, attempted to halt the reauthorization because, they claimed, the House and Senate had been micromanaging NIH; they wanted an express provision stating that this was unacceptable. (Congress refused and approved the reauthorization.)

The national media and the Democratic leadership made much of the fact that in the same year Congress "cut" the proposed 1993 budget. But in Beltway parlance, of course, a "cut" means less than the requested increase—the NIH budget actually rose $312 million to $10.4 billion. This was about $196 million less than requested, however, and as a result the agency is currently able to support only one in five proposed grants; it had been supporting *one* in *three*.[33] (This is NIH's idea of "hard times.")

• *The National Endowment for the Humanities*: NEH was founded in 1965 along with its more notorious twin, the National Endowment for the Arts. During those boom times for the education industry, the sciences were "awash with money," but the humanities seemed to be suffering from neglect.[34] Sen. Claiborne Pell and Rep. John Brademas once again successfully led the "Great Society" campaign for federal intervention and yet another new taxpayer-supported program. NEH funds a wide variety of academic projects, seesawing between elite academic scholarship and "popular appeal" in languages, religion, literature, history, sociology, philosophy, and education—all for $177 million a year. In the past, NEH has been noted for supporting such research as:[35]

- a project "to help youth understand how the sky has influenced the humanities disciplines";
- a project "to study the impact of Cicero's jokes on Renaissance France and Italy";
- a project to study "raccoon hunting and hand fishing, two vanishing skills";
- a project to study "the significance of cultural artifacts of neon tube advertising in Texas";
- "The Romantic Poetry of Karl Marx";

- "Folk Rituals of Birth, Marriage, and Death Among Urban Polish Americans";
- "The Contribution of the Gay Experience to American Visual Arts";
- "Prizefighting in Boston's Irish Community";
- "The Americanization Process of Syrian Americans";
- "The Life and Times of Rosie the Riveter";
- "Mothering in Three Generations of Orthodox Jewish Women";
- "The Harp Tradition in Uganda"; and
- "Medieval Doctrinal Attitudes Toward Male Sexual 'Aberration.' "

About eight hundred reviewers pass judgment on nearly nine thousand applications every year.[36] Though it has dispensed "only" a few billion dollars in the last few decades, and its financial resources are small compared to many other "federal foundations," NEH has exerted a profound influence on the direction of higher education. It is, in fact, the largest single patron of the humanities in the nation. And an NEH grant bestows an official stamp of approval on many projects, which then and only then can attract other public and private support. It can even make the difference in whether a grantee receives tenure or promotion at his college or university.

Under the recent leadership of William Bennett and Lynne V. Cheney, there was a concerted effort to cut the agency's budget, to institute more rigorous intellectual standards, to defend Western culture, and to battle the "political correctness" and unabashed socialist propaganda found in a number of previous NEH-funded projects. But the new NEH chairman is former University of Pennsylvania President Sheldon Hackney, who managed to turn the recent "water buffalo" name-calling incident between racially mixed students on his campus into a "political correctness" issue and a national public relations fiasco. Combine Hackney's record with the leftist tilt of the dominant forces in academe, and we are sure to see a resurgence of ideology-based, gender-based, and race-based grantmaking, as well as bigger and bigger budgets at NEH.

───────── AGENCIES WITHIN AGENCIES ─────────

Neatly tucked away like nesting Russian dolls, one finds a number of "agencies within agencies" inside the Department of Education's Office of Educational Research and Improvement (OERI), formerly known as the National Institute for Education (NIE), which was created by the Education Amendments of 1972.[37] With a staff of over 450 and a budget in excess of $426 million, OERI is intended to operate on "the cutting edge" of educational research and program development. But, from the start, the office has been handicapped by an ill-defined mission and mismanagement. In the 1980s, almost one-third of the staff was comprised of "visiting scholars." The idea was to attract the brightest and the best academics for temporary service, with a maximum stay of three years. But, according to a former deputy director, more than half of those recruited stayed much longer, and at least one lingered on for fourteen years, a stint that might be better described as permanent residency. Once entrenched, these "visitors" wielded a strong enough influence on programs to control the agenda, promoting such controversial approaches as the "New Social Studies" and the "New English," at the elementary and secondary level, as well as an anti-Western curriculum under the guise of encouraging diversity and multiculturalism at the college level.

Typically, little oversight has been applied at the nineteen centers and ten labs OERI runs around the country. In the 1980s each of these had budgets ranging between $2 and $6 million; today, they range between $1.5 and $3 million. One early GAO report found that a center in St. Louis spent a significant portion of its budget on a dance studio, a trip to Egypt, and travel that had little or nothing to do with educational resources or curriculum development. But neither GAO reports nor violations have had much effect on whether funds are cut off or on how future funding decisions are made. It can take an inordinately long time just to get such reports approved by all the relevant departments; in some cases it has been a full *year* before they reach the secretary of education.

There are other "agencies within agencies" in the DOE which, while virtually unknown to the public, supply hundreds of millions of dollars to education. The Fund for the Improvement of Postsecondary Education (FIPSE), for example, gives away almost $16 million a year. Another office in the department has, according to a confidential internal memo, awarded funds for "drug education," mostly at the precollege level, to "support projects that provide services to gay and lesbian youth in New York City ($595,000 awarded, 1988 to 1991), San Francisco ($12,000, 1991) and Columbus, Ohio ($70,000, 1991)."

My own experience was with an "agency within an agency within yet another agency," as the presidentially appointed chairman of the National Council on Educational Research (NCER), the policy arm of the then $51-million-plus a-year National Institute for Education (est. 1972) within the Department of Education. NCER's specific task is to formulate policies governing all federal grants for education research in the United States. My tenure, from June 1982 to May 1985, confirmed my fears that such agencies are part of the problem plaguing education rather than part of the solution. NIE and NCER by then had spent about $800 million on pet projects of the education lobby while education standards and student performance at the elementary, secondary, and college levels were falling. Most of the career officials with whom I had contact expressed thinly disguised contempt for the notion that schools, teachers, and parents knew best how to educate, for the "three Rs" and traditional pedagogical methods, and for any efforts to roll back federal intervention in education.

——————CONGRESSIONAL EARMARKS——————

Just as peer-reviewed federal agency grants for academic research constitute a multibillion-dollar business, so, too, do congressional "earmarks" over time. These are pork-barrel appropriations made by Congress that bypass the normal budget and peer review process. There is no competition or merit basis for such appropriations. Typically, they are hidden in huge annual spending bills for energy, agriculture, and defense, but they crop up in other bills, too. For instance, one massive trade bill that passed in the late 1980s contained $1.7 billion in education spending, a substantial portion of which was earmarked for colleges and universities.[38] Procuring these funds has become one of the major ways for politicians to "bring home the bacon" to their states and one of the highest institutional priorities for money-hungry public and private colleges and universities.

On top of hundreds of billions of dollars in "competitive" grants, Congress earmarked $2.5 billion for higher education between 1979 and 1992. One-third went to just ten schools. Seven of these were also among the top ten contending for federal research grants, despite the fact that earmarks are intended to address "funding inequities" among institutions.[39] Between 1988 and 1992, moreover, congressional earmarks *tripled*. Even lobbyists like Association of American Colleges President Robert M. Rosenzweig have opposed this rampant growth. He said recently, "I think it's a lousy way to do business." But just how common are earmarks? In 1991, to cite one average year, the only state in the union that did not have one or more colleges receiving earmarks was Delaware.[40]

Congress set aside $684 million in earmarks in fiscal year 1991–92, a 39 percent increase over the previous year, making it "the most lucrative year on record," according to the *Chronicle of Higher Education*. Later, worry over the deficit caused Congress to rescind some $100 million of this total, but in 1992–93, earmarks increased again, this time to a record-high *$763 million,* even as members of Congress complained "about tight spending limits and their struggle to deal with the deficit." In 1993–94, they have been reduced significantly, but as the states cut back on general higher education spending in the years ahead, earmarks are bound to become politically attractive again.[41] The more intense the earmarking, in fact, the greater the signal that colleges are in trouble, says Michael M. Crow, associate vice-provost for science at Columbia University. He should know. Crow, reports the *Chronicle,* is renowned for his ability to convince politicians to earmark funds for his own hard pressed institution.

In their quest to get on board the gravy train, leaders of many colleges and universities seek allies in Congress. Marywood College in Pennsylvania enlisted Rep. Joseph M. McDade (R-PA) to insert $10 million in a defense appropriations bill to construct an on-campus facility for the Institute for Family Support Services, which studies "stress in the families of military personnel." These earmarked funds were equal to one-third of Marywood's annual operating budget. Some institutions band together to increase their chances. The Massachusetts Biotechnology Research Institute, for example, consists of two research institutes plus Worcester State College, Worcester Polytechnic Institute, the College of the Holy Cross, Clark University, and Tufts University. Rep. Joseph Early (D-MA), a member of the House Appropriations Committee, has helped this group win earmarks totaling more than $2 million.[42]

Pork-barrel money rises faster than aid based on merit, concludes the *Chronicle,* offering, among hundreds of others, the following samples of congressional earmarks in 1992:[43]

- American Samoa Community College: $647,000 (shared with four institutions) from the Department of Agriculture for agricultural research in the Pacific region.
- Atlantic Community College: $300,000 (shared with twenty-eight colleges and the Philadelphia Academy of Natural Sciences) from the U.S. Coast Guard for fishing vessel safety.

- Auburn University: $8 million (shared with three universities) from the International Trade Association on textiles; $398,000 from the Department of Agriculture for water management. Also from Agriculture: $200,000 for rural health and $157,000 (shared with two universities) for research on home sewing.
- Bethune-Cookman College: $300,000 from the Department of Education to build the Mary Bethune Memorial Fine Arts Center.
- Boston University: $29 million from the Department of Defense for research.
- Carnegie Mellon University: $10 million from the Defense Advanced Research Projects Agency.
- Clark Atlanta University: $2.5 million from the Environmental Protection Agency for Superfund research.
- Colorado State University: $3.5 million (shared with twenty-two universities) from the Department of Agriculture for urban gardening programs. Also from Agriculture: $437,000 (shared with four universities) for research on Russian wheat aphids and $412,000 (shared with eleven universities) on barley gene-mapping.
- Daniel Webster College: $3 million from the Federal Aviation Administration for facilities and equipment related to its airway science curriculum.
- Drake University: $1.3 million from the Legal Services Corporation for facilities and equipment related to its National Trial Advocacy Institutes.
- Florida State University: approximately $8 million from the Department of Energy for its Supercomputer Computations Research Institute.
- George Mason University: approximately $750,000 from the Department of Defense for research and $750,000 from the Department of Transportation for its Center for Suburban Mobility.
- George Washington University: approximately $1 mil-

lion from the Department of Health and Human Services for its Native American Policy Center.

- Georgetown University: $20 million (to be shared with community colleges and foreign students) from the Agency for International Development for its Central American Scholarship Program; $3 million from the Department of Housing and Urban Development; and $400,000 from the Department of Transportation.
- Indiana State University: $1.5 million from the Small Business Administration for its Center for Interdisciplinary Science Research and Education.
- Iowa State University: nineteen earmarks (eight shared), mainly from the Department of Agriculture, the Department of Energy, the Federal Aviation Administration, and the Environmental Protection Agency. The amounts were: $3 million; $2.9 million; $2 million; $1.9 million; $1.7 million; $1.5 million; $1.5 million; $750,000; $750,000; $750,000; $700,000; $500,000; $500,000; $275,000; $237,000; $237,000; $210,000; $150,000; and $100,000.
- Kansas State University: ten earmarks (three shared) from the Department of Defense and the Department of Agriculture: $7.7 million; $2.9 million; $1.9 million; $1.6 million; $159,000; $125,000; $100,000; $100,000; $94,000; and $50,000.
- Lehigh University: $50,000 for soybean ink study.
- Louisiana Tech University: $10 million from the Department of Energy for its Institute of Micromanufacturing.
- Michigan State University: eighteen earmarks (ten shared) from the National Aeronautics and Space Administration, the Department of Defense, the Department of Agriculture, and the Environmental Protection Agency in the amounts of $28.4 million; $1 million; $900,000; $750,000; $10.4 million; $4 million; $3.6 million (urban gardening); $2.9 million; $2.9 million; $2.4 million; $1.4

million (potato research); $531,000; $283,000 (studying stone fruit decline); $189,000 (bean and beef research); $120,000 (animal waste disposal research); $94,000 (apple quality research); $94,000 (asparagus research); and $39,000 (celery research).

- Navajo Community College: $148,000 from the Bureau of Indian Affairs to increase its operating budget.
- New York University: $6.7 million from the Environmental Protection Agency for a new center for neural science and $3.1 million for neural science equipment.
- Oregon Health Sciences University: $10 million from the Department of Energy for ambulatory research and a new building.
- Oregon State University: $46,000 from the Department of Agriculture for mink research (in addition to fourteen other earmarks).
- Pittsburgh State University: $4 million from the Department of Energy to restore its Technology Complex.
- Prairie A & M University: $75,000 from the Department of Agriculture for dairy goat research.
- Rutgers University: $260,000 from the Department of Agriculture for blueberry and cranberry research (in addition to seven other earmarks).
- Seton Hall College: $1 million from the Small Business Administration for its Center for Entrepreneurial Opportunity.
- University of Arkansas: $3 million from the Department of Agriculture for its Poultry Center of Excellence and $50,000 for research on seedless table grapes (in addition to eleven other earmarks).
- University of Arkansas-Monticello: $200,000 from the Department of Agriculture for fire ant research.
- University of California-Davis: $1.6 million for a grape-importing facility.
- University of Colorado: $504,280 from the Department of Justice for the study of juvenile delinquency.

- University of Maine: $185,000 from the Department of Agriculture for blueberry research.
- University of Michigan: six earmarks (all shared) from the National Aeronautics and Space Administration, the Environmental Protection Agency, the Department of Agriculture, and the Department of Defense in the amounts of $28.4 million; $1 million; $900,000; $750,000; 3.2 million; and $2.9 million.
- University of Notre Dame: $3 million (shared with five universities) from the Department of Energy for the Midwestern Superconductivity Consortium.
- Wake Forest University: $1.8 million from the Department of Agriculture for its medical school.
- Western Michigan University: $1.3 million from the Environmental Protection Agency for research on recycling office waste.

Remember, these are just earmarks, not peer-reviewed research grants, and as such they are a relatively minor portion of federal funding of higher education. Thus, schools like Clemson University (which received $8 million to study competition in the textile industry) and the University of Missouri-St. Louis (which received $10 million for its Center on Molecular Electronics) look upon earmarks as an "add-on" rather than as a main source of federal revenue.[44]

But if these projects are so worthwhile, why aren't they being funded through the regular peer-review process, or better yet, by the private sector? Those opposed to earmarks, like University of Dayton senior research scientist Joseph P. Martino, believe that once the pork-barrelers saw that they could get away with awarding huge sums to higher education in such a surreptitious way, they were bound to do it regularly. It is, he says, "merely a symptom of the overall corruption of the congressional appropriations process." But those who favor earmarks agree with Rev. Paul S. Tipton, president of the Association of Jesuit Colleges and Universities: "It is the classic American way. The

Congressman goes to Congress to help his district out. . . . This is why these guys and ladies are elected—to help a local university—that is what they do. I am personally quite supportive of it."[45]

—————— STATE AID ——————

The American Founders made education a function of the private sector and, to a lesser extent, the individual states. But the states, as more than one educator has noted, are starting to regard themselves as mini-nations and have built educational establishments to match, with vast bureaucracies increasingly entangled with those of the federal government. The Education Amendments of 1972 began State Student Incentive Grants, which were part of a new federal/state matching funds program for needy students.[46] They also began federal funding for state higher education commissions. Many states welcomed the new federal role, but others feared it would lead to greater intervention and centralization, especially since the law was very vague as to how much authority these commissions would possess. Schools rightly feared they would have less control as the states and the federal government drove for more centralization, regulation, and standardization.

Meanwhile, state governments have not been merely augmenting federal aid to higher education; they have been surpassing it. All told, they appropriate about *$40 billion* a year to support students and to provide institutional aid to colleges and universities. Says one education writer, "The big money, without question, is at the state level." Only a small amount is for need-based aid; 95 percent is, in effect, to subsidize the education of all students.[47] A State Higher Education Executive Officers (SHEEO) report notes that there are about a dozen "mega-states" that appropriate $1 billion or more in any given year for higher education. In 1991–92, the biggest of these were California ($6 billion), New York ($3 billion), and Texas ($2.6 billion),

Florida, Illinois, Michigan, Minnesota, New Jersey, North Carolina, Ohio, Pennsylvania, and Virginia (each with $1-$1.7 billion). The top ten per-capita spenders were Alaska, Hawaii, Wyoming, New Mexico, Ohio, Minnesota, North Carolina, Nebraska, Iowa, and Alabama.[48]

But in 1991 and 1992, for the first time ever, there was a two-year drop in state appropriations. The 1992 total was about $300 million less than in 1991, or about $200 million less than in 1990, an overall decline of 1 percent.[49] One percent may not sound like much, but it has colleges and universities running scared. Their precarious financial condition does not allow *any* room for decline in state revenues, and, indeed, they had been counting on large increases to offset rising costs and mounting deficits. According to SHEEO, during the 1960s and 1970s, state appropriations rose 20-30 percent every two years. In the 1980s, they rose 10-20 percent. Up until 1991, they had at least doubled every decade.[50] So colleges and universities could claim to have sustained a loss of billions of dollars of potential revenue.

Edward R. Hines, professor of education at Illinois State University and director of the SHEEO report, comments that the figures are "pretty shocking" and that they indicate a worse situation than existed even during the Great Depression.[51] More than likely, it is a situation that will not improve either, at least not in the near future. States simply have too many fiscal obligations (a result of their own profligate spending), too many special interests competing for scarce resources, and too many debts to heed higher education's urgent pleas for more money. Says the *Chronicle of Higher Education:* "States have to reserve larger and larger chunks of their budgets for such things as Medicaid and prisons, for which courts or laws require certain spending levels. That leaves higher education and other 'discretionary' services to fight for an increasingly smaller plate of scraps."[52] Hines confirms: "I never heard really in higher education the term 'discretionary' come up before two years ago. All of a sudden, the contrast between 'discretionary' and 'mandated' crept in. States [are] really going after higher education because it [is] discretionary."[53]

THE BIG BUSINESS OF HIGHER
———— EDUCATION ————

Higher education is big business. It is in fact America's top growth industry. In 1960, the total budget for all U.S. colleges and universities was $7 billion, but in the next decade it had leaped to $25 billion. By 1980, it had nearly tripled to reach $62 billion, and by the early 1990s, it had nearly tripled again to reach over *$172 billion*.[54] Though that figure is going down rather than up because of state and federal budget cuts, it is still staggering. Many universities, as Hoover Institution Senior Fellow Martin Anderson and others have noted, are "huge enterprises in themselves."[55] Quite a few have annual budgets in excess of *$1 billion* (see Chapter 1). Yet we seldom think of them as corporate giants or expect them to be accountable as such. Worse, we do not question their massive subsidization by taxpayers. Anderson concludes in his book, *Impostors in the Temple*:

> The product the university sells is education, but curiously little of its revenues come from the sale of what it produces. Public universities receive only about 15 percent of their monies from student tuition and fees. Fully 60 percent of the funding comes from government—most of it from state governments, a substantial chunk from the federal government, and a little from local government. The other 25 percent is derived from gifts, endowment and miscellaneous sources, including various enterprises run by the university. To a very large extent—some 60 percent worth—you are watching your tax dollars at work when you look at today's public universities.[56]

He also notes that private colleges and universities "draw a significant amount of their incomes from the government checking account"—about 20 percent.[57] Some of this is perfectly legitimate indirect income, through state and federal aid dollars students receive and choose to spend on campus, but increasingly it is also in the form of direct subsidies.

In view of this mountain of evidence, it is impossible to maintain the position that government plays only a peripheral role in higher education. To paraphrase an observation once made about welfare, government aid to education may have begun as an ambulance in a dire emergency, but it has now become the entire transportation system. And it is, moreover, a top-heavy, bureaucracy-ridden system run by groups that like to make their own rules. To them, we now turn.

Chapter 4

THE POLITICS OF FUNDING

LOBBYISTS

"We as a nation should call a halt at this time to the introduction of new programs of direct federal aid to colleges and universities. We also believe it undesirable for the government to expand its scholarship aid to individual students."[1] That was the *unanimous* conclusion of a commission of the American Association of Lobbies in the 1950s. It is hard to believe, but forty years ago these higher education associations actually *opposed* federal aid. Despite their warnings, federal student assistance programs and other kinds of aid flourished during the Great Society of the 1960s, forcing education associations to reassess their own basic mission.

When asked by a judge why he robbed banks, the notorious criminal Willie Sutton is said to have answered, "Because that's where the money is." Education lobbyists also have learned where to find the loot: Washington, D.C. Most of them took the first tentative step toward political activism by moving their headquarters to Washington in the 1960s; prior to that, only a few had branch offices in the nation's capital. Today, you can find almost all of them at a single address that has become synonymous with the education lobby: One Dupont Circle.

In the 1970s, increasing federal regulation and congressional oversight of higher education combined with the rise of the student activist and consumer movements to create a demand for even more aggressive action. Though education associations had made a 180-degree turn to support federal aid, they were chastised for not doing enough to persuade Congress to pass the Education Amendments of 1972. Colleges and universities threatened to withdraw their association memberships, students protested, faculty wrote indignant letters, and the media featured sharply critical reviews of their performance. The message was duly received; from then on, education associations began to take on a new attitude, changing from largely informational groups to tooth-and-nail fighters for more federal money for higher education.

They have become part of a rapidly growing army. Today, in the 1990s, there are more than 7,500 registered lobbyists in Washington, up from three thousand in the 1970s.[2] Significantly, many education lobbyists are also former federal employees (and vice versa). Take, for example, Charles B. Saunders, Jr., longtime vice president for government relations at the American Council on Education; he was formerly assistant secretary for legislation at the Department of Health, Education and Welfare. When he left the lobby in 1993, Terry Hartle, education staff director of the Senate Committee on Labor and Human Resources, took his place.[3] And then there is Sharon Robinson, former National Education Association executive, who is now assistant secretary for the DOE's Office of Educational Research and Improvement. This revolving-door system benefits scores of individuals who use their positions of influence on both sides of the legislative fence to call for more spending and "a closer relationship" between Uncle Sam and higher education. While recent regulations supposedly prevent lobbyists from soliciting the departments where they once worked for a period of five years, there are plenty of loopholes, according to Washington insiders.

The American Council on Education has long been the most powerful higher education lobby, but it has been joined by many new, even larger organizations. Their direct mail tactics, mass demonstrations, national letter-writing campaigns, and seasoned professional lobbyists create a considerable impact. They also frequently bring to Washington "visible campus leaders," i.e., professors and administrators who favor more federal spending, to speak for their positions. Education associations even supply the actual language for legislation. A congressional staffer will get a "script" from his lobbyist counterpart and then take it to the relevant Senate or House legislative council for a minor rewrite and work with other staffers to get co-sponsors. Senators and representatives are hardly involved; later on, they will get a one- or two-page brief on what to say about the bill. Many agencies like the Department of Education also routinely engage in prohibited activity by leaking proposed department regulations and policies to congressional staffers for advance clearance. They do this with full knowledge that the staffers will then pass along everything they have learned to lobbyists. One must break the rules or no one will play ball, goes the reasoning. So congressional staffers and lobbyists end up privy to a great deal of confidential information and possess what amounts to a veto at every stage of lawmaking.

A former deputy assistant secretary at the DOE has complained that "the 1992 reauthorization of the Higher Education Amendments was a lobbyists' creation from start to finish," and that "lobbyists had more to do with HEA than the Department of Education." Several other former senior staffers who worked at the DOE during the 1980s and early 1990s claim that lobbyists have almost complete access to sensitive data in key areas such as the Office of Postsecondary Education (OPE). One former assistant secretary has even charged: "Within OPE there is more allegiance to lobbyists than to the President of the United States or to the nation's taxpayers. The mentality is that lobbyists—and the colleges and universities they represent—are OPE's real clients."

Just who are the lobbyists in question? A complete treatment of this endless catalogue of organizations would require a separate book, but here is a partial list:[4]

American Association of Colleges for Teacher Education—The AACTE has a network of more than seven hundred nationally or regionally accredited member institutions and forty-four state affiliates.

American Association of Community and Junior Colleges—More than 90 percent of all public community, technical, and junior colleges and over one-third of all independent two-year colleges are members.

American Association of School Administrators—The AASA has eighteen thousand members in elementary, secondary, and higher education.

American Association of State Colleges and Universities—The AASCU represents more than 370 institutions enrolling 2.5 million students.

American Association of University Professors—The AAUP represents faculty in federal, state, and university relations. It has 43,000 members, thirty-four state affiliates, and 980 campus chapters.

American Council on Education—Already mentioned as the most important education lobby, the ACE represents 1,200 accredited postsecondary institutions and national and regional higher education associations.

American Educational Research Association—The seventeen thousand-member AERA promotes funding for university research.

Association of American Universities—The AAU consists of fifty-six American and two Canadian universities. Research funding is among its major concerns.

Association of Independent Colleges and Schools—The AICS represents more than 850 schools and colleges enrolling over half a million students a year.

Association of Research Libraries—The ARL is comprised of 119 libraries and is primarily concerned with research funding.

California Community Colleges—The CCC represents California's 107 community colleges.

California State University, City University of New York, Georgetown University, New York University, Princeton University, University of California, University of Miami, University of Michigan, and the University of South Carolina—All these schools maintain permanent offices of "federal relations" in the nation's capital.

The College Board—Membership consists of more than 2,800 colleges, school systems, and educational associations. Lobbying interests relate to testing, evaluation, student grants, as well as loans, research, and admissions.

Council of Chief State School Officers—The CCSSO includes fifty-seven public officials who head departments of public education in every state and territory and represents its members before the federal government.

Council of Graduate Schools—The CGS has nearly four hundred member universities.

National Association of Admissions Counselors—More than five thousand admissions officers, counselors, and financial aid officers belong to this group.

National Association of Independent Colleges and Universities— The NAICU represents private colleges and universities on public policy issues.

National Association of State Scholarship and Grant Programs— The NASSGP represents fifty state agencies responsible for administering student financial aid programs.

National Association of State Universities and Land-Grant Colleges—This organization includes 149 public and land-grant institutions in the United States.

National Association of Student Financial Aid Officers— NASFAO represents over 3,500 postsecondary institutions and individuals.

National Council of Educational Opportunity Associations— NCEOA is exclusively devoted to race, gender, and other minority issues.

National Council of Higher Education Loan Programs, Inc.— NCHELP represents state and private guaranty agencies, secondary markets, lenders, servicers, collectors, and others.

United States Student Association—With 3.5 million members, the USSA boasts increasing clout on student-related issues.

You can add dozens more organizations, including the American Association of Educational Service Agencies, the Association of Urban Universities, the California State Department of Education, the Council for Educational Development and Research, the National Association for Equal Opportunity in Higher Education, the New York State Education Department, the Ohio Department of Education, the University and College Labor Education Association, and the Washington State Education Agency, as well as offices within the AFL-CIO, the American Federation of Teachers, and the National Education Association, and various political action committees (PACs) controlled by the student loan and banking associations or affiliated indirectly with colleges and universities. Ironically, since most lobbies are registered as nonprofit institutions, they can and do receive federal funding for their activities. And if the chair of a congressional committee or subcommittee requests testimony from a lobbyist, it is not counted as lobbying activity. Since testifying before Congress is a major part of what lobbyists do, the advantages are obvious.

Many colleges and universities also resort to employing a more specialized kind of lobbyist, the "hired gun." This has been a popular strategy since 1983, when Schlossberg-Cassidy and Associates, a Washington, D.C., lobbying firm made up mostly of former congressional staffers, helped secure earmarks of $5 million each for Catholic University and Columbia University through an amendment introduced on the House floor. Though widely condemned as pork-barrel politics that bypassed the normal processes of peer review, the bill passed, and in the next six months Schlossberg-Cassidy and Associates signed up a dozen other universities and opened the way for others to seek congressional earmarks using the same methods of aligning clients' interests with those of politicians. Early winners in this new game were Boston College (library, $7.5 million), Oregon Health Science University (information center, $20 million), the University of New Hampshire (space/marine science building, $15 million), and Tufts University (center on nutrition and aging, $32 million; veterinary school, $10 million; intercultural center, $7.5 million; and toxic waste research, $2 million).[5] In 1989, the same lobbying firm helped a number of schools that had "almost given up hope of winning major federal grants" because of media exposés about "questionable influence exerted on their behalf in Congress" to win big. Four of the firm's clients—Lehigh University ($15 million), the University of Scranton ($13 million), Loyola University ($8 million), and the Medical College of Ohio ($5.2 million)—divided the spoils with three other institutions—Auburn University ($6 million), the Minnesota Supercomputer Center ($12 million), and the Charles R. Drew University of Medicine and Science ($2 million).[6]

There is no doubt that higher education profits enormously by depending on political lobbying of all kinds. A few years ago, Michael O'Keefe, president of the Consortium for the Advancement of Private Higher Education, said ingenuously, "Members of Congress and their staff regularly look to One Dupont Circle for reliable information about federal programs."[7] He also advised that colleges and universities should spend more money on actively trying to gain political influence; higher education, after all, must compete for federal funds in an environment in which, by the end of the decade, political action committees will have spent $1 billion on lobbying. As their financial condition worsens, colleges and universities' number-one priority will be expanding student aid to the maximum limits set by Congress in the 1992 reauthorization of the Higher Education Act, but they and their lobbyists will push for anything that will result in more money for higher education. "We must fight to 'get our students their piece of the pie,' " says Bruce Foote of the Midwest Association of Student Financial Aid Administrators, adding, "We have to stop believing, and more importantly, get the public to stop believing, that 'education costs too much.' "[8]

EDUCATORS

"Educator" conjures up the image of someone dedicated to the life of the mind, the cultivation of truth, and the imparting of knowledge and culture to eager students. While many in academe still fit that description, more often than not the term now denotes a politically savvy power player. This is especially true in the empire of big education, where universities function as individual fiefdoms. Their presidents, chancellors, and provosts, reminiscent of a medieval court, are rewarded accordingly.

In 1990–91, at least three universities paid their presidents more than $400,000 a year in salary and benefits, and twelve paid more than $300,000.[9] Nonsalary compensation is unbelievably generous for relocation, housing, automobiles, travel and entertainment, family tuition benefits, housekeeping staff, spousal reimbursement for social duties, and so on. Several years ago, for example, one former president at Georgia State University, John A. Palms, received $500,000 just to renovate his home.[10] And while slashing the budget by $255 million and laying off 4,000 employees, the University of California awarded outgoing president David P. Gardner (salary $243,500) a severance and retirement package worth approximately $2.4 million in 1992.[11] Another UC executive recently retired with a $204,000 "golden parachute."[12] The California State University system provided Chancellor W. Ann Reynolds (salary $195,000) with rent-free use of a $2 million mansion in the Hollywood suburb of Bel-Air. Reynolds raided an employees' benefit fund to purchase new automobiles for her six vice-chancellors. She also secretly alloted herself a $58,000 raise. A public scandal ensued, but she merely decamped to another lucrative position as chancellor of City University of New York.[13]

There have been dozens of other state systems in which educators profit royally. Those who occupy these lofty positions, at large institutions in particular, maintain little if any contact with those for whom they presumably work—the students and their tax- and tuition-paying families. But they do understand that maintenance of the current system requires *a lot* of money. Accordingly, many have become very polished professional panhandlers. One former legislator who served on his state's appropriations committee says, "Lobbying by educators is just incredible. We're talking about incessant wining and dining and other forms of attention from well-placed administrators as well as trustees and alumni. Not surprisingly, those representing large institutions are the most aggressive, and it pays off. They receive favor after favor."[14] Lobbying has even taken some new forms. One Michigan school, Saginaw Valley State University, recently went so far as to create a music video to win an extra $3.25 million from state legislators.[15]

Hats in hand, educators will try any stunt as they regularly travel to Washington, D.C., and their state capitals to argue that the future of the nation depends on increased government aid to colleges and universities. It does not matter how much aid their institution already receives; it is never enough. The reasoning is inevitably circular: Government funding is needed to boost enrollments. Bigger enrollments create added demands on colleges. Government funding is needed, therefore, to expand campus facilities and operations. Expanded facilities and operations require bigger enrollments. . . . University of Illinois President David D. Henry expressed precisely this view when he wrote an article on federal aid to higher education in the 1960s which argued that "unprecedented anticipated enrollments . . . require unprecedented assistance."[16]

The 1993 annual meeting of the National Association of Independent Colleges and Universities entitled, "Financing Higher Education: Reshaping National Priorities," opened with the comment, "It's no secret that this is an exciting time to be in Washington . . . the voices of independent colleges and universities must be heard now perhaps more than ever in the . . . new administration." These were the major themes articulated by current and former college presidents and chancellors:

- Why the deficit should not be allowed to restrict funding for higher education.
- Why the federal government and the states should supply more funds (without any strings, it was insisted) to private institutions.
- Why higher taxes to support education spending must be sold to the public as an answer to the crisis of American learning and as a necessary "investment in the future and the economy" rather than as a way to gain more subsidies for a failing system. A college education is, in other words, to be represented as a "public good" rather than a "private benefit."
- Why Pell Grants must be made an entitlement and more grants than loans should be offered to students.
- Why "universal access" to higher education can only be achieved through more "selective admissions" (quotas) and more "selective distribution" (more money for middle as well as low income students, but especially for "politically correct" minorities).
- Why, as the congressionally appointed National Commission on Financing Postsecondary Education recommends in its recent official report, all college students should be guaranteed $14,000 a year in government aid.
- Why, as the Carnegie Commission argued back in 1973, the states should "give more money to all of higher education in order to close the gap between public and private institutions."
- Why students and parents should not be made to bear the major burden of the costs of college education.

One private college president notes approvingly that today most institutions have full-time staff whose primary responsibilities center on "government relations." They coordinate their strategies with national and regional associations that represent their interests to policymakers and grassroots advocacy groups that, in turn, share their message with the general public.[17] Of this new breed of administrators, grants officers are the ones who most often develop the closest ties to the federal branch. Here is some advice to rookie campus grants officers offered by the Federal Resources Advisory Service (FRAS) of the Association of American Colleges: "As far as your office is concerned, Mecca is also referred to as Washington, D.C. Depending on the number of faculty, their special interests, and the proximity of the college to Washington, you may go there monthly, quarterly, or semi-annually."[18] Once a college is successful in obtaining a grant, FRAS advises, grants officers should always be sure to fulfill only the minimum cost-sharing requirement; otherwise, they will be "wasting" money their college could spend on other projects. Faculty release time, secretarial labor, teaching assistant tuition, "consulting services," travel, conferences, printing, postage, duplicating, and computer time are all to be counted as cost-sharing. So are salary increases to persons named to direct grants, and these are referred to as a great "incentive system to encourage faculty and staff participation in the grants process."[19] Colleges and universities can even recover the full cost of applying for federal funds, notes FRAS, if they word their requests in the proper legalese. Until recently, they also could use federal funds to lobby for more federal funds!

The quest for easy money has even taken hold of the professoriate. Goodbye, Mr. Chips: Faculty members have shed their old image as unworldly eccentrics to become increasingly ambitious, sophisticated grant seekers who can submit identical proposals to multiple federal agencies in seconds via computer and fax machine. As suggested earlier, their success in securing federal grants often has a big impact on their chances for promotion, raises, tenure, and other kinds of career advancement. It also guarantees less time in the classroom and more time pursuing their own research interests, which hold the promise of even higher income.

POLITICIANS AND ———— BUREAUCRATS ————

It is easy to understand why educators are eager to solicit government funds for colleges and universities. But why are politicians and bureaucrats so willing to serve the cause? Even a casual look at the structure, operations, and philosophy of the powerful federal agencies and congressional committees that oversee higher education reveals that the liaison has not been a one-way relationship.

One reason already has been suggested: It has been widely accepted that higher education is a federal responsibility and that college students should not be obligated to pay for more than a fraction of what their education really costs. This is certainly the view of politicians like Rep. William D. Ford and Sen. Claiborne Pell. As noted earlier, Ford serves as chairman of the House Education and Labor Committee—a committee of which he has been a member since 1965. Pell became chairman of the Education Subcommittee of the Senate Labor and Public Welfare Committee (now Labor and Human Resources) in 1969 and was responsible for the establishment of the multibillion-dollar federal grant program that bears his name. There are many other careerists—Republican as well as Democrat—who have regularly promoted the expansion of federal spending on education and who have served on key committees for years. These committees came into their own and gained an important influence over the budget process in the 1960s when, as one of their number notes, "the conditions of legislative life put a premium on leadership as bargaining."[20]

Politicians also promote such spending for political gain. In closed door sessions to "protect the guilty," members of Congress vote for hundreds of millions of dollars in awards to colleges and universities in their home states. And repeatedly they attempt to buy off their constituents by increasing broader forms of federal aid. The student assistance provisions of the 1992 reauthorization of the Higher Education Act, for example, were deliberately calculated to appease middle class fears about escalating college costs. This was done by raising maximum awards and by watering down, and in some cases even eliminating, financial need requirements for federal grants and loans.

A desire to be directly involved in "landmark decisions" also plays a role. Every major education bill in the last three decades has been described by its proponents as "historic legislation" in the tradition of the Morrill Act and the G.I. Bill.[21] And personal ambition must be accounted as a factor. Bureaucrats at the Department of Education (which has more political appointees than any other agency) and at other education-related agencies see increased spending as a way to enlarge their own programs and the scope of their own power and influence. Politicians see it as a way to further their careers. This is also why Congress has burgeoned from thirty-four committees and a handful of subcommittees in the 1940s to 295 standing, special, and select committees and subcommittees today.[22] They are vehicles of power, not democracy, and they are useful mainly for playing politics, dispensing favors, settling scores, and extending federal jurisdiction into new areas.

John Brademas, former U.S. representative from Indiana, Democratic majority whip, and chairman of the House Select Education Subcommittee who, in a perfect example of the revolving door later surfaced as president of New York University, described himself while in office from 1958 to 1980 as a "vigorous champion in Congress for federal support of research on education." On the Education and Labor Committee for twenty-two years, he helped craft, in his own words, "nearly every major piece of legislation" on education passed during that period. Even after he was voted out of office in what he called "the wicked rebellion of 1980," he was able to incite strong opposition in Congress to the Reagan/Bennett proposed cuts in higher education, warning that such a "savage assault" would "spell disaster. . . . Political decisions are being made right now that could threaten an entire generation of scholars and imperil the direction and scope of educational inquiry for generations to come." He urged colleges and universities to use all the political influence they could muster to fight against any and all reductions, but added, "[this] is not so much a call to political activism as it is a call for intellectual activism in the service of politics." (This is the same man, incidentally, who wrote in his recently published political memoirs: "At times part of the lawmaker's task is to obscure the importance of a policy change, to downplay its impact, so as to keep legislative options open as long as possible and thereby enhance the chances of passage.")[23]

Arguments by politicians and bureaucrats in favor of increased federal spending on education typically have been alarmist. Here are some samples (in quotations) from the 1980s by Representative Ford, who has assumed Brademas's mantle as the leading defender of federal education spending in the House. Ford and his peers are still making essentially the same kinds of arguments today. (1) Claiming huge shortages in the academy: "There are 16,000 unfilled engineering faculty positions. . . ." (2) Citing the technology gap: "Most of the job growth in the 1980s and 1990s will be in occupations requiring high levels of competency. . . ." (3) Exploiting guilt: "The doors of opportunity are being narrowed. . . . Low income and minority students are . . . being denied the opportunity for economic and social mobility." (4) Enumerating the cost to America: "The nation will be denied the best use of our best minds. . . ." (5) Providing an "easy" solution, while taking a last swipe at any potential opponents: "There must be a renewed commitment to education . . . . Unfortunately, however, the Reagan administration has met the need for a vigorous federal education policy with tired slogans about the responsibilities of state and local government and the traditional role of the family in paying for higher education. . . ."[24]

But the most important political tactic is "log-rolling," which has been around forever. In order to secure bipartisan support, politicians simply pack a bill with pet provisions for everyone. Congressional earmarks are a perfect example; through intention rather than coincidence, they are usually designated as shared awards to colleges and universities in different districts and states. But it was the Education Amendments of 1972, the first omnibus education bill, that developed educational logrolling into a fine art. In the Senate, all seventeen members of the Labor and Public Welfare Committee not only voted in favor of the bill but were listed as co-sponsors. Why such unanimity? Here is how one congressional staffer summed up the motivation of the key members who persuaded everyone else to go along:

> Pell [D–RI] was dedicated to the Basic Grants provision and had a stake in the bill because it came out of his Subcommittee.
>
> Williams [D–NJ] had the community college title.
>
> Kennedy [D–MA] had Indian education, plus the knowledge that S.659 was in broad outline much like the "Higher Education Bill of Rights" he had sponsored in 1969.
>
> Mondale [D–MN] could also find much in the bill that was consistent with his own thinking, and he gave it his full support, even though he had been unsuccessful in putting across a different version of the Basic Grant in Subcommittee.
>
> Javits [R–NY] personally contributed the state scholarship incentives plus several other provisions, and he persisted in behalf of the administration's Foundation proposal.
>
> Prouty [R–VT] was responsible for the Prouty amendment to the cost-of-instruction allowance program.
>
> Dominick [R–CO] had nailed down the Student Loan Marketing Association [Sallie Mae].
>
> Schweiker [R–PA] had ethnic heritage studies.
>
> Beall [R–MD] had the emergency bail-out provision.[25]

House members had similar incentives and pet provisions in their draft bill. These ranged from mineral conservation education and youth camp safety to sex discrimination prohibitions and land-grant status for the College of the Virgin Islands and the University of Guam.[26]

In the Clinton administration, educators, politicans, and bureaucrats have even more reason to work together to achieve "mutual aims." Even before assuming office, the president named fifty educators to fill key appointments in various federal agencies and offices, and he made it clear that he would name many more. The link between the "ivory tower" and the Beltway thus has been reestablished to a degree that rivals the days of the Great Society and even the New Deal.[27] Whether the link is strong or not, so long as there are ways to redistribute the public wealth to their own advantage, politicians and bureaucrats will exploit them. The army of educators and lobbyists in Washington, D.C., works three shifts to make that exploitation possible. The result is a huge, wasteful, and corrupt system which bears the appearance of being adversarial but is in fact nothing of the kind. Free-spending politicians, bureaucrats, educators, and education lobbyists ultimately serve the same end: government dominance of higher education. They are different sides of the same coin.

PRIVATE COLLEGES

In 1949, Charles F. Phillips, president of a small Maine school called Bates College, made an impassioned plea for private educators to withstand the growing temptation of federal aid. He declared, "I believe that the private college can make its greatest contribution to a free society if it does not become dependent on government for its financial support." But, he acknowledged, "As a matter of fact, the majority of the presidents of our private colleges want this to happen. . . . The trend is clearly toward increased participation of the federal government in the daily lives of our citizens, a trend to which the majority of the presidents of our private colleges have already bowed, by urging the establishment of federal scholarships."[28]

By this time, less than half of all college students in the nation were attending private institutions. Poorly endowed, facing steeply rising operating costs, and seldom able to win out against subsidized competitors for talented students and faculty, Bates and hundreds of other small schools were in what seemed an untenable position. President Phillips conceded that he soon would be forced to pursue federal aid just as assiduously as any other college president in order to save his own institution. Reluctant or eager, nearly all his peers would do the same. Many already had accepted government research contracts during the war, and they could not (in terms of public relations or finances) afford to refuse students on the G.I. Bill. And since such "giants" of academe as Harvard were graciously willing to accept what Uncle Sam had to offer, why should they be the ones to stand on principle? As time went on, most of them even began to count on such sources of revenue as their due.

Special Presidential Assistant McGeorge Bundy, a vocal advocate of federal subsidies to private education, remarked with satisfaction in a speech to the American Council on Education in 1962: "The anguished prophecies of earlier decades are heard less often—and from less respectable sources. One incidental benefit has been that the representatives of private colleges, as their annual accounts began to show large admixtures of federal money, have somewhat muted the warnings against the 'low standards' and 'political pressure of public institutions' with which they have too often sought to attract private funds."[29] In other words, private colleges and universities had been bought off, and it was a damned good thing, in Bundy's opinion. An educator summed it up more tactfully: "The three traditional sources of funding for private colleges were tuition dollars, gifts from alumni, and funds from private benefactors. After the 1960s, which brought increased numbers of students and programs to campus, these three sources proved insufficient. Three new sources were added: the large philanthropic foundations, industry, and the federal government (through funds for research, new facilities, and programs to help minority and low income students)."[30] Though these new sources were often short term and unpredictable, private colleges and universities began to place increasing dependence on them; by the 1970s, they represented 31 percent of total revenue.

During the same period, nearly 30 percent reported that they were in serious financial trouble. Total enrollments at all private college and universities had already dropped to under 50 percent after World War II; now they were down to 22 percent. Between 1975 and 1984, ninety-three private institutions closed, merged, or shifted to public control. In a national survey, more than half of a group of 126 private college and university presidents responded that their institutions had narrowly missed closing or merging due to financial pressures.[31] Under such circumstances, it hardly is surprising that federal aid was welcomed and even solicited by its once-staunch opponents.

Today, in addition to what the federal government awards, there is also direct and indirect state funding; forty-one states provide hundreds of millions of dollars a year in student and/or institutional aid to private colleges and universities.[32] Up until recently, Pennsylvania, on the high end of the scale, for example, was spending more than $75 million a year at just eleven private colleges. Illinois, on the low end, spent some $30 million.[33] Most of the states spend at least $50 million every year, and in a number of cases the funds are "unrestricted," which means that they can be spent at the institution's discretion. One of the most common forms of aid, however, is a "bounty" paid for every resident who graduates from a private, independent, nonprofit college or university within the state. In 1992, the Michigan "general degree reimbursement" was $422 per student. To take one instance, the University of Detroit Mercy, with 1,130 eligible students, raked in nearly half a million dollars in reimbursements that year, courtesy of the state's taxpayers.[34]

Often aid is also meant to bridge the gap between public and private tuition, as in states like Georgia, which spends about $17 million annually on private tuition subsidies.[35] In South Carolina, where a state tuition program provides need- and nonneed-based aid to low and middle income students who wish to attend private colleges within the state, Furman College recently bragged that it had reaped $26 million for eleven thousand students since 1970. In one typical year, 1992, 452 Furman students were awarded $1.7 million, for an average state award of $3,756 per student. But now, with state budget cuts looming, the tuition program is in jeopardy. Furman has issued an urgent call for its alumni to contact their state legislators immediately to demand that the program be saved. "When you're in a financial crunch, your priorities become more crass. . . . We need to focus on the high ground, and understand the implications that severe cuts in the program might have," explained the Furman staff member who authored the appeal to alumni.[36]

High ground, indeed.

From coast to coast, there have been many similar appeals from private institutions desperate to increase state and federal aid. Ithaca College President James J. Whalen insists, "The state and federal government must take a stronger stance in support of independent colleges and universities." What, in his opinion, constitutes a stronger stance? More government subsidies. He bemoans the fact that state governments have spent less on higher education for the last several years and says, "Most of my colleagues at independent colleges and universities across the nation are lobbying to maintain their share of state support." And he concludes, without any apparent trace of irony, that reduced state subsidies are a disturbing symbol of a "faltering commitment to a strong and viable independent sector."[37] But as Martin Anderson points out, federal, state, and local funds— your tax dollars and mine, indirectly through student assistance and directly through grants and budget monies—account for about 20 percent of the annual operating costs of private colleges and universities.[38]

THE ALLOCATION OF
——————STATE AID——————

The allocation of state aid for public higher education shows how thoroughly political the funding process has become. Most people assume that a state legislature agrees on a total budget amount that is then divided up proportionately among all public colleges and universities in the state based on the number of full-time equivalent (FTE) students enrolled at each. But this isn't the way it works. Legislators, state agencies, and the schools actually "negotiate" funding, and political clout is the only factor that ultimately counts. Even in states that claim to base allocations on FTEs or other objective formulas, the truth is that there are dozens of ways to get around them by factoring in other "data," such as the "special mission" or "special needs" of a particular school, or through the ordinary politicking that goes on when bills are marked up in committees or amendments are added on the floor. In the majority of state legislatures, appropriations committees have extensive involvement in the administration of funding for public colleges and universities. They routinely dictate specific line item spending amounts on individual campuses (a level of intervention that creates a wealth of potential for abuse). Further, they connive with educators to fund many nonessential programs established solely to secure federal matching grants.

But it is true that formulas have been the usual starting point for determining education spending in the majority of states for nearly forty years.[39] This is to give at least a semblance of fairness and equity to the budget process. As competition has increased for state resources, formulas have also given legislators a convenient shield against angry schools claiming that they deserve more, and, as the costs of education have soared, formulas have given them another shield against angry voters claiming that all schools are getting too much.

In addition, formulas tend to be useful shields against everybody because they are so complex. One South Carolina educator speaks for virtually all formulas when he complains, "Around here, it's asserted that no one still living understands them." Some states have as many as twenty-five separate mathematical calculations for the number of full-time students, part-time students, the number of students taught in different disciplines, the number and academic ranking of faculty, the number of credit hours taught, the square footage of buildings, campus acreage, the number of fleet vehicles, and so on. Specific budget areas are also analyzed: undergraduate and graduate instruction, academic research, lab research, public service, library facilities, academic support, student services, institutional support, maintenance, physical plant, scholarships and fellowships, and auxiliary enterprises.

The ostensible goal of formulas may be the equitable distribution of state funds, but it is a goal seldom achieved, since funding is not determined by those who follow formulas but by those who follow political winds. "No formula is worth anything," says the same South Carolina educator, "if the legislature ignores it at appropriation time." Lobbyists and political pressure exerted by the institutions themselves have a far more important influence on actual funding. But even in cases where formulas are heeded, serious problems can arise. In Minnesota, for example, the state used an average rather than marginal cost formula based on the number of FTEs in 1980 to predict enrollment for the next several years. Despite the shrinking number of college-age students, enrollments went up sharply, leaving colleges short of funds. Then enrollment declined, so colleges lost even more money and demanded emergency relief from the state legislature.[40]

Since most state revenues are not granted on an FTE basis, a school can actually cut its enrollment and reap the same benefits—who is going to complain? Not the taxpayers, since they don't even know what is going on. Not the legislators, since they are happy so long as they are not being pestered for additional funds. For decades, many public colleges and universities have also employed a sleight-of-hand trick by channeling all corporate, charitable, and alumni donations through private foundations. These funds do not appear on a school's annual financial report except as a footnote disclosure, which helps enormously in lobbying for more state support.

"Front-Loading," "Forward Funding," and —————— "Enabling Legislation" ——————

Besides these slippery tactics, there are several classic shell games that have been practiced for years. One of them is commonly referred to as "front-loading." Suppose University A is allocated $120 million in state funds for the state's fiscal year, which runs from October to September. But the state gives it $13 million a month for nine months, totaling $117 million. This leaves only $3 million to be paid over July, August, and September, but University A has received an enormous advantage because if spread conventionally, monthly payments through the first nine months would have totaled only $90 million, and the institution would not have received an extra $27 million in advance. It has also gotten 98 percent of the allocation by the end of *its* fiscal year, which runs from July to June.

Michigan is one of the states that has exploited front-loading. In fiscal year 1992, a change was made so *total* allocations were actually paid in the first nine months, in effect telling University A (and all other Michigan public colleges and universities) that all revenues would be received and recognized by then. For the transition year, University A would have appeared—on paper, at least—to have received total revenue of *150 million*. (All public colleges and universities in Michigan have been beneficiaries of this deal, but amounts, of course, have varied according to their total appropriations.) State tuition grants and scholarships also have been front-loaded in similar fashion in Michigan and other states.

The greatest advantage of front-loading is that politicians actually can cut education spending but, because of the difference in the state's and its colleges and universities' fiscal years, they can pretend that no cuts have been made. Colleges and universities can also misrepresent their true financial condition by papering over cuts with the same accounting technicalities. And they profit handsomely by receiving their total appropriations over nine months rather than over the full course of the fiscal year. No other recipients of state aid ever receive appropriations in advance—it is a sign of how incestuous the relationship between government and higher education has become. Imagine if we gave all recipients of state aid, or even just one agency like the state welfare department, the same deal, and you will have some idea of the irresponsibility of front-loading.

On the state as well as federal level, politicians and bureaucrats also use what is known as "forward funding" to rescue programs that are perpetually in debt. What the term means, simply, is using funds from the next year's budget to pay for this year's budget shortfall. On numerous occasions in recent years, the Department of Education has "borrowed" hundreds of millions of dollars in "forward funds" to help reduce deficits in its grant and loan programs. If this sounds familiar, it is because it is essentially the same kind of check-bouncing scheme that Congress indulged in until news of the scandal made headlines in the early 1990s. With forward funding, federal and state agencies can and do overspend their budgets at will and plunge the system into even greater debt. The *Chronicle of Higher Education* has criticized the practice, arguing that it has repeatedly allowed Congress to bend its budget rules on behalf of failing higher education programs just as it had in the past to provide assistance to failed savings and loan associations. But even if forward funding were abolished, there are still subtle ways of achieving the same effect by passing "enabling legislation," i.e., laws that create decade-long plans and programs without appropriating any money. Since the proposed bills do not call for immediate spending and have no impact on the budget, they are relatively easy to pass. Later on, the same crew of legislative sponsors and lobbyists can argue in favor of large appropriations based on the "mandates" of the enabling legislation. The ensuing tax increases can be conveniently blamed on the actions of the past which are associated, naturally, with some other group.

Chapter 5

FEDERAL FUNDING AND
FEDERAL CONTROL

For a number of private colleges and universities, the first step was simple enough. All it required was accepting students who received federal tuition assistance such as the G.I. Bill. This was regarded as a limited, one-time-only repayment for military service on behalf of a grateful nation in the wake of World War II, and, as such, even stubbornly independent schools felt duty-bound to allow their students to receive such assistance. Few saw any potential for harm. But in the 1950s and 1960s, many schools went one giant step further and began accepting *direct* aid from Washington, D.C., for capital construction, special programs, and research. A few, like Harvard, had already been accepting such funds for years and had even set up separate administrative offices just to process all the research grants, contracts, and other revenues that poured in from government sources.

Incredibly, many of the nation's most prestigious academic leaders went along with this, even though from the start they realized that federal funding inevitably would bring federal control. In 1952, a blue-ribbon commission comprised of the presidents of Johns Hopkins University, Union College, the California Institute of Technology, the University of Missouri,

Stanford University, and Brown University, the former president of Columbia University, and the provost of Harvard University jointly declared: "We are convinced that it would be fatal were federal support to be substantially extended. Power means control. Diversity disappears, as control emerges. Under control, our hundreds of universities and colleges would follow the order of one central institution, and the freedom of higher education would be lost."[1] Of course, the funding they were already accepting from the government didn't count. Most of it was devoted to scientific and technological research and development, so they felt that they could confidently assert, as did Harvard President Nathan M. Pusey in 1962, that the independence of private universities was "virtually untouched by this very large flow of Federal money."[2] Special Presidential Assistant McGeorge Bundy declared, "American higher learning is more and not less free and strong because of federal funds," and he added, "generalized hostility to federal money is as senseless as tilting against a windmill. The windmill is there to stay, and it is no man's enemy." He did admit, however, that "nothing is plainer about the partnership between government and the higher learning than the simple fact that most Americans are deeply unaware of it."[3] For his part, University of Illinois President David D. Henry scoffed that federal control was:

. . . a straw man, an irrelevant oversimplification. Instead, we should be asking the American people, "Do you want teachers in your classrooms, doctors at your bedside, lawyers in your courts, scientists in your research laboratories? Are you in favor of having the federal government help in the war on cancer and in the evolution of new ideas in the exploration of space? Are you willing to ask the federal government to help assure that there will be room for your son or daughter or your grandson or granddaughter on some college campus?"[4]

Even when some leaders confessed that some forms of federal funding could have a profound impact on the institutions that accepted them, they shared a common attitude that the only regard in which such impact was of concern was how it affected further funding. College and university presidents even went so far as to encourage various federal agencies to maintain separate and inconsistent policies on higher education because, says former University of Chicago President and National Science Foundation Deputy Director John T. Wilson, they "took the position that it was better off to live with a highly disorganized federal 'system' than to take the risk of potential interference and perhaps reduced availability of funds that a more coordinated and better-managed government effort might bring."[5] In this context, he quotes educator Homer Babbidge: "The 'economic royalists' of higher education did well under conditions of organizational deficiency in government programs, and they were quick to use the cover of academic freedom in opposing a more systematized effort that would allow less favored institutions to fare somewhat better."[6]

Most educators paid no attention to warning signs indicating that there was a price to be paid for the Faustian bargain they had struck. They did not demur, for example, when President Truman's Commission on Higher Education proclaimed matter-of-factly that the federal government possessed "sufficient regulatory powers" to withhold appropriations from any institution it judged as engaging in "unacceptable practices," or when the commission went on to make an even more sweeping claim: "In the sense that all private institutions are nonprofit-making, they receive indirect subsidy through tax exemption."[7] (By this logic, all individuals who claim any exemptions on their tax returns are wards of the state.)

Ironically enough, the first time educators publicly began to protest against federal control was in 1968 when Congress passed legislation stating that students and faculty convicted of "crimes connected with disruptive campus activities" could not receive federal funds.[8] National Science Board member Robert Morison complained: "The point is that we have moved with great (some would say frightening) rapidity towards the time when virtually all scientific research [is] supported by public funds. . . . These developments mean, among other things, that scientists are in a very real sense wholly dependent on government for their means of livelihood and the pursuit of happiness."[9] Then, in 1969, there was another uproar among academics when Rep. Edith Green (D-OR), chairman of the House Subcommittee on Higher Education, proposed requiring colleges and universities to "file formal plans for dealing with campus disturbances or forfeit their right to receive any federal funds."[10] Her motion launched a bitter committee fight and ultimately failed, but it was a telling incident, and a number of attempts to pass a campus unrest bill followed in the 1970s.

In 1972, during the Senate discussions of the Education Amendments, Birch Bayh (D-IN) offered a floor amendment that would use the threat of withholding federal funds to bar discrimination on college campuses. Dubbed the "Bayh-sexual amendment," it was set aside on a technicality, but, as a harbinger of things to come, it continued to worry those who feared future challenges to higher education's autonomy through the arm-twisting instrument of federal funding. They were also worried, say Lawrence Gladieux and Thomas Wolanin, by certain provisions that did make it into the final legislation and moved federal policy in the direction of cost accounting standards, i.e., in the direction of direct fiscal accountability on the part of all colleges and universities to the federal government. These were hidden away in an obscure passage requiring institutions to provide "as a condition of receiving federal or institutional aid, data on how much it costs them to educate students."[11]

The floodgate opened gradually, but it opened steadily. By the mid–1970s, there were dozens more laws and hundreds more regulations on higher education. A diverse assortment of educators and organizations began sounding the alarm:[12]

- Lobbyist Charles B. Saunders, Jr.: "Is regulation strangulation? The question conveys our uneasy awareness that government legislation and court decisions are increasingly influencing the shape of higher education in America."
- Economist Earl Cheit: "Review procedures, regulations, litigation, and demands for information now command so much of the energies and attentions of college and university officials, it is easy to forget that for most of its history higher education in the United States was a movement, not a bureaucracy."
- Rep. James O'Hara (D-MI): "Nowhere more than in the field of education have we seen bureaucracy run rampant."
- Future HEW Secretary David Matthews: "[Regulations are] threatening to bind the body of higher education in a Lilliputian nightmare of forms and formulas."
- Yale University President Kingman Brewster: "[We must oppose] the use of spending power as a lever to extend regulations."
- *Change* magazine headline: "Will Government Patronage Kill the Universities?"

AFFIRMATIVE ACTION
———— AND QUOTAS ————

Many saw their worst fears confirmed with the rise of "affirmative action."[13] Originally, this term was little more than a political slogan used by President Kennedy to urge correction of civil and economic handicaps experienced by minorities in federal employment. By the Johnson years, it began to appear with greater frequency and scope during the debate on the Civil Rights Act, but not always in a positive context. In hearings a number of congressmen and witnesses expressed the fear that the proposed regulatory powers, rather than *outlawing* all forms of discrimination, might in fact be used to *enforce* particular forms of discrimination. Advocates responded (just as they did when proposing any kind of federal aid to higher education) that affirmative action would only be a temporary expedient, and their arguments won the day; the landmark act passed in 1964.

Though the final draft did not mention affirmative action or quotas, both continued to crop up in discussions of enforcement tactics. It was suggested that overall racial proportions should be used as evidence measuring intent and performance of institutions. Presumably, such "evidence" would allow the enforcing officials to bypass the slow process of individual court cases and thus deal directly with discriminatory situations. But even the most outspoken proponents of the concept saw racial proportions as only one indicator of possible discrimination. Equal opportunity and equal protection under the law were still the ultimate ends, and affirmative action and quotas were regarded as merely the means. As the 1960s wore on, however, that distinction became increasingly obscure. In 1967, President Johnson issued his executive order calling for an end to discrimination among federal contractors and the Department of Labor followed with its Revised Order No. 4. Overnight, these measures transformed nondiscriminatory intent into compulsory discrimination based on race and sex. Moreover, the new regulations established percentage hiring goals that applied to all colleges and universities accepting federal funds. By the government's estimate, that included more than two thousand campuses around the country.

In the early 1970s, the Department of Health, Education and Welfare (HEW) and its Office of Civil Rights (OCR) began a series of even more active attempts to mold the hiring and enrollment practices of America's colleges and universities along blatantly discriminatory lines. Since the federal government was by then dispensing billions of dollars in contracts and research funds to private as well as public institutions, it was no real surprise that they decided to use economic sanctions as a weapon. One of their first victims was Columbia University, which received half of its $175 million annual budget from federal sources. The assault astonished Columbia officials, who felt that they "had been making serious efforts during recent years to keep the university abreast of rapidly moving patterns of social change in New York City. . . ." As President William McGill put it, "In all respects Columbia's record in the field of affirmative action to remove employment discrimination seemed to me to be an outstanding one. Nevertheless the government chose to move against us. . . . No one likes to be in the position of negotiating for his survival with Uncle Sam sitting at the other end of the table. Our instincts in such circumstances were to promise almost anything in order to get the government off Columbia's back."[14] That was the special irony of the situation: Nearly every one of the colleges labeled as suspect or singled out for economic sanctions was already trying every means to increase minority representation among its faculty and in its student body. But this would prove to be "not good enough," according to federal bureaucrats.

Here is a revealing explanation issued by one of the primary architects of affirmative action, J. Stanley Pottinger, then assistant attorney general for civil rights:

> The concept of affirmative action requires more than mere neutrality on race and sex. It requires the university to determine whether it has failed to recruit, employ, and promote women and minorities commensurate with their availability, even if this failure cannot be traced to specific acts of discrimination by university officials. Where women and minorities are not represented on a university's rolls, despite their availability (that is, where they are "under-utilized") the university has an obligation to initiate affirmative efforts to recruit and hire them. The premise of this obligation is that systemic forms of exclusion, inattention, and discrimination cannot be remedied in any meaningful way, in any reasonable length of time, simply by ensuring a

benign future neutrality with regard to race and sex. This would perpetuate indefinitely the grossest inequities of past discrimination. Thus there must be some positive action, along with a schedule for how such actions are to take place, and an honest appraisal of what the plan is likely to yield— an appraisal that the regulations call a "goal."[15]

Pottinger was quick to reassure that "goals" were not quotas, but this was, and still is, a distinction without a difference. "Goals" are bureaucratic Newspeak for quotas, and anyone who argues otherwise is, to put it mildly, being untruthful. The federal government says, "No quotas," with a wink and a nudge at institutions that are faced with proving that they don't discriminate almost solely on the basis of statistics regarding the race and gender of their faculty, staff, and students and whether these are in line with the acceptable numerical "goals" set by affirmative action bureaucrats.

As it happens, numerical disparities are a fact of life. Further, proving a negative, like proving one's innocence, is a daunting— some would say impossible—task. In a postscript to his earlier statement, Pottinger proved that, along with Newspeak, he had also mastered the subtleties of Doublethink: "While HEW does not endorse quotas," he said coyly, "I feel that HEW has no responsibility to object if quotas are used by universities on their own initiative."[16] With the implicit consent of educators, he and other bureaucrats have redefined the aim of higher education, which once was to treat and teach all students equally. That principle has been stood on its head. The demand is now that we treat and teach students differently, not based on the content of their character, the quality of their mind, or the effort they put forth, but on the color of their skin, or their sex, or their other particular "disadvantage." Equality of result, not equality of opportunity, is the new ideal.

Where once the blindfolded goddess of justice was supposed to view all who came before her with impartiality, now she is encouraged—nay, compelled—to peek: "Tell me your race and your sex," today's goddess whispers, "and then I will tell you how I plan to treat you." And as a result, says former Education Department official Lawrence A. Uzzell, colleges and universities must be prepared to hand over detailed race and gender data "on demand to OCR's army of field inspectors. The agency's tacit assumption is that any 'disparity' must be due to racism or sexism."[17]

Many institutions comply gladly. In fact, they have been so anxious to increase minority representation on their campuses (5 to 10 percent are the most commonly cited goals, although most do not attain anywhere near these figures) that they have raced beyond the federal guidelines placed upon them and pushed reverse discrimination to shocking levels. Justice Harry Blackmun rationalized their bias in the now-famous 1978 *Bakke* v. *Board of Regents of California* decision in which the Supreme Court ruled that Title IV of the Civil Rights Act of 1964 did not apply to whites. "In order to get beyond racism," Blackmun explained, "we must first take race into account,"[18] even though such a move is equivalent to suspending *habeas corpus* as a "temporary measure" until a crime wave passes—a measure neither he nor any other member of the high court would have endorsed.

Bakke stipulated that race may be a "plus factor," but not the only factor taken into account in admissions and hiring. Nevertheless, colleges and universities routinely ignore the law. Until 1992, when it halted the practice (and some sources claim it has made only cosmetic changes to avoid prosecution), the University of California-Berkeley's law school divided admissions candidates into segregated groups ranking races (Hispanics above whites, blacks above Hispanics, nearly everybody above Asians, etc.) in order to reach specific numerical "goals," i.e., racial quotas for each. It even had the audacity to inform some students of their status, says the *Wall Street Journal*. Several Asian-Americans, for instance, were told: "You are in the bottom half of the Asian waiting list."[19] Dinesh D'Souza notes in *Illiberal Education: The Politics of Race and Sex on Campus* that at the undergraduate level at Berkeley, "Blacks and Hispanics are up to twenty times (or 2,000 percent) more likely to be accepted for admission than Asian-American applicants with the same qualifications." Former San Jose State University President John Bunzel says that at Berkeley race was and is an overriding factor in admissions; in the late 1980s, for example, only about 40 percent of the freshman class was selected on the basis of academic merit.[20] He wrote at the time, "Asian-American and white students usually will not be admitted to Berkeley without a grade point average of at least 3.7 or 3.8 (4.0 is 'straight A'). However, virtually all other minority students who apply to Berkeley and meet minimum UC requirements automatically get in."[21]

Berkeley is not an anomaly. All the "best" schools rely on de facto quotas. At some, like the University of Wisconsin-Madison, administrators have even figured out a way to take quotas to their ultimate limit: All minority applicants who have what U of W's Director of Admissions Millard Storey calls "a reasonable chance of academic success" are admitted automatically. Nonminorities must compete for the remaining slots.[22] And at Pennsylvania State University, says D'Souza, "preferential treatment for black students extends beyond admissions; the university offers financial incentives to induce blacks to maintain minimum grades and graduate. All black students who maintain a grade average of C to C+ during the course of the year get checks from the school for $580; for anything better than that, they get $1,160."[23] This is not a need-based award, and no other races are eligible. In addition, D'Souza points out that while virtually all universities and most medium- to large-size colleges have changed their admissions rules specifically to attract "certified minority groups," they are also extending their affirmative action programs to "other groups claiming deprivation and discrimination, such as American Indians, natives of Third World countries, women, Vietnam veterans, the physically disabled (now sometimes called the 'differently abled' or 'physically challenged'), homosexuals, and lesbians."[24]

Regarding hiring quotas in higher education, there are literally hundreds of examples that could be cited. In 1989, the *Columbia Law Review* announced that it would henceforth offer preferential hiring for homosexuals and lesbians, and it would create five new editorial positions to promote "diversity," especially in regard to "sexual orientation."[25] And Wayne State University offered another model a few years ago when its sociology department issued a memo that stated that its two faculty openings must be filled by minorities, or they would not be filled at all.[26] Indeed, "Males need not apply," and "Whites need not apply," have become the basic messages of most faculty job advertisements today, making a mockery of the inevitable disclaimer that the college or university in question is an "Equal Opportunity Employer." When an occasional editorial or investigative article reveals beyond any doubt that educators are brazenly violating civil rights laws, they claim, like the Vichy captain in *Casablanca*, to be "shocked, shocked" that quotas have been enforced and promise never to use them again—which means until the next term begins.

Just how are alleged discrimination cases handled on campus? Here is how it works at one typical institution, the University of West Florida: When an employee files an allegation of, say, sexual harassment, it goes straight to the desk of the Equal Opportunity/Affirmative Action officer. (Do not pass the president's or dean's office, do not collect $200.) The officer then makes a unilateral decision that is binding only on the defendant; the plaintiff is entitled to request an appeal. Appeals are heard by an "impartial" committee composed of a member chosen by the Equal Opportunity/Affirmative Action officer, a member chosen by the plaintiff, and one other member chosen by the first two. The committee's ruling then goes to the president, who functions as a mere messenger and informs both parties of the decision.[27] Defendants in Stalinist show trials stood a better chance of vindication than the victims of this arrangement, in which, contrary to our legal tradition, guilt is often assumed.

But the real tragedy of affirmative action and quotas is that they hurt the very groups they are supposed to protect. At the

University of Michigan in the late 1980s, Deane Baker, a "dissident" on the board of regents, challenged other members to defend the separate admissions criteria used for minority students. He pointed out that U of M was rejecting nonminority students with a 3.5 grade point average and a total of 1,100 on the SAT (a perfect score is 1,600), while accepting minority students with a grade point average of 2.8 and 800.[28] In the 1970s, he added, the standards for minorities were even lower; 2.5 and 600 were good enough scores to gain admittance. Was Baker simply concerned about reverse discrimination against qualified white students? Not at all. He went on to remind the board that even though most minority students were receiving 100 percent aid, special tutoring, counseling, and other significant forms of financial, academic, and emotional support, they were not staying in school and, therefore, minority enrollment was going down rather than up.

Minority students, especially blacks, were in reality the victims in the university's headlong pursuit of equality; they had been landed in a highly competitive, academically rigorous world where, as a result of poor academic preparation, they just couldn't cope. In the process, they had also been branded as what Stephen Carter, a black professor of law at Yale University, has called "affirmative action babies," i.e., students considered incapable of getting into a good school on their own merits. What could be a more cruel cheat than plunging an eighteen-year-old (by definition, a walking bundle of insecurities), and especially a black eighteen-year-old (who may be haunted by countless slurs and abuses against his race) into such a situation?

The University of Michigan's case is typical of the rest of higher education, in which well-intentioned but misguided administrative schemes to achieve racial diversity have actually institutionalized racism, doomed thousands of minority students to failure, and taken no account of the human cost of misguided attempts at social engineering. Predictably, however, the only response of affirmative action advocates has been to blame all failure on racism and to call for even more quotas, more aid, and more special treatment for minorities. Meanwhile, to cite Berkeley again, more blacks are dropping out in a three-year period than are graduating in a decade.[29] And the national drop-out rate among black students has reached epidemic proportions. The latest estimate is that *nearly 75 percent* will not complete their college education.[30] This is a bitter harvest to reap, but it is one we will keep on reaping until we gather the courage to reject affirmative action and quotas.

Does that mean that black students who are struggling academically should abandon any hope of attending competitive colleges and universities? Of course not. But they must first receive sound preparation in elementary and secondary school. (That is why I support private education at every level—public schools have simply done a rotten job of teaching basic academic skills, especially to minorities.) Then, when they get into good colleges on their own merits, look out—the sky is the limit. Thousands of black students have the potential to succeed; what is holding them back is not too little opportunity but too much government.

THE HILLSDALE AND ——— GROVE CITY CASES ———

In the mid-1970s, HEW decided to mount a new offensive against higher education by using the Title IX provisions, originally part of the grab-bag Education Amendments of 1972, which prohibit sex discrimination in education programs that receive federal financial assistance. The department sent a letter to all colleges and universities in 1975, informing them that they were required to sign an "assurance of compliance" form stating that they agreed to abide by Title IX and all other civil rights statutes. The fact that Title IX had become the law of the land was not enough—colleges and universities must acknowledge it in writing, in effect, as a kind of loyalty oath.

HEW also informed them of two startling new changes: (1)

Although the actual language of Title IX limited the definition of federal coverage to institutions that directly "received" federal assistance, HEW's revised interpretation would be that institutions that indirectly "benefited" also would be covered. (2) While Title IX limited federal coverage to the particular programs or activities receiving aid benefits, from now on, as far as HEW was concerned, the entire institution would be defined as the relevant "program." In conclusion, the department threatened not only to cut off federal aid to institutions that refused to sign the compliance form but to cut off all federal grants and loans to students. Later on, it reiterated its warning that colleges and universities that accepted federal funds or students with federal funds must keep detailed records of all student and employee applications, enrollments, academic records, personnel files, suspensions, hirings, firings, promotions, denial of promotions, and so on—all broken down by race, age, sex, and ethnic origin—and submit them upon demand to federal authorities. There were no exceptions for colleges and universities in states that expressly forbade asking employees and students for information on their race, age, sex, and ethnic origin or for institutions that had their own alternative policies of non-discrimination.

All but a handful of colleges and universities dutifully signed and returned HEW's compliance form. Of that handful, all but one simply filed it away unanswered, hoping that no one would notice and that they would fall through a crack in the Byzantine federal bureaucracy. Hillsdale College, a small Michigan liberal arts school of a little over a thousand students, was the only institution in the nation to send the form back, unsigned, with the message that it felt HEW's new interpretation of the law was dead wrong. This launched a mammoth and costly legal battle that would last more than a decade.

Hillsdale's position was that since it did not accept direct aid from government, it was under no obligation to divulge proprietary information or to sign what amounted to a blank search warrant authorizing widespread bureaucratic intrusion into its records and decision-making processes. The college was by no means objecting to the principles of civil rights; in fact, Hillsdale had a long history as a pioneer in equal opportunity since its founding in 1844. It opened its doors to all, as its mission statement records, "irrespective of nation, color or sex." It was the first college in the nation to have a written policy of non-discrimination incorporated into its state charter. It accepted blacks and women on par with all other students almost two decades before the Civil War and was one of the first colleges to enroll American Indians. It awarded the first B.A. degree in Michigan and the second in the nation to a woman. During World War I, it successfully challenged the War Department's policy of segregating ROTC units. And it had consistently maintained that commitment ever since. If anything was clear, it was that Hillsdale was in the "equal opportunity" business more than a century before the government even discovered there was such a thing.

But this was not a battle over equal opportunity; it was a battle over power, and little Hillsdale was forced into defending itself in a David vs. Goliath struggle. It stood alone for nearly three years. Then, in late 1977, HEW lawyers dug up the fact that a church-affiliated school in Pennsylvania, Grove City College, did not sign a compliance form, and it, too, was compelled to fight. From that point on, many points within the original Hillsdale brief were used by both colleges in different federal appeals courts.

Hillsdale eventually won a partial victory in the Sixth Circuit in late 1982. The court agreed with the college that the entire institution was not the program as far as Title IX was concerned and that the regulation requiring it to sign a compliance form was invalid because it was overly broad. However, it concurred with the recently established Department of Education (DOE) that Hillsdale was a "recipient institution" under Title IX and that it was subject to federal control on a program-specific basis. This finding was reached because 204, or less than one-fifth of its students, received federal grants or loans *as individuals*. Finally, the court ruled that the DOE could legitimately cut off funds to students *without finding that the college had actually discriminated.*

The government decided to accept defeat on the "program specificity" issue, but Hillsdale wished to continue the fight for total independence and petitioned the Supreme Court to hear its argument. However, the justices decided to hold the *Hillsdale* case in abeyance pending their decision regarding *Grove City.* (Grove City College had lost in the Third Circuit on all counts and had also petitioned the Supreme Court. It continued to use the same defense as Hillsdale.)

The case was called *Grove City College* v. *Bell.* Again, the government never showed or even alleged that the "defendant" was discriminating against anyone or violating any laws. The only point of this exercise was to determine whether private colleges and universities must knuckle under to federal bureaucrats. In the first part of the decision handed down in 1984, the Supreme Court ruled in accordance with the *Hillsdale* case that Title IX was program-specific. Thus, if a single college department was found guilty of violating federal regulations on discrimination, only that department, not the entire school, would have to forfeit federal funding. But the second part of the decision wiped out the distinction between indirect and direct aid by determining that if a single student received a federal loan or grant, the entire school would be considered a "recipient institution" and would be subject to the full weight of federal control.

Under this tortured reasoning, colleges and universities that accept one student with a federal grant or loan are no different from schools that take hundreds of millions of dollars in direct and indirect federal aid. And private schools are no different from public schools. Clearly, there is no sense in such a position. The educational monies given to students are not the same as direct federal funds given to a college or university. Federal student assistance funds may be used to defray food, lodging, and all sorts of personal expenses as well as tuition. And when federal funds are co-mingled with personal funds, it is difficult to trace from which source tuition is drawn. While the college or university does ultimately benefit, it is no more a "recipient institution" than the corner grocery store that accepts food stamps, or the hospital that accepts Medicare patients, or the bank that accepts Social Security checks. But by the Supreme Court's logic, every place of business in America—down to the last lemonade stand— is a "recipient institution."

Hillsdale's response to the *Grove City* decision was to announce that it would no longer accept students with Pell Grants, Supplemental Educational Opportunity Grants, National Direct Student Loans (now Perkins Loans), or veteran's benefits. Henceforth, eligible applicants would be offered private grant and loan alternatives to replace these funds. The college would still accept students with Stafford Loans and PLUS loans, which were not affected by *Grove City.* (Although these are nominally called "federal loans," the government only acts as the guarantor of an agreement between banks and students or their parents. No taxpayer money goes to the college, and Hillsdale students' default rate on these loans is near zero.)

In 1992, the college had to raise more than $6 million to cover its total annual student aid obligations, $1.4 million of which replaced federal grants and loans. The figures are going up every year, since it is competing not against other schools but against the federal government. (It is impossible to make money as fast as a counterfeiter.) Let me give you a down-to-earth example of what this means. Not long ago, as president of Hillsdale, I had to report to the board of trustees about twenty-seven students whom we had accepted and who were strongly committed to coming to Hillsdale. They were all top quality students with good academic credentials. We offered them the best aid packages we could afford—and lost them. Other schools, some without chipping in a dime of their own money and most without committing significant support, could offer them so much more because they were willing to be "recipient institutions." Hillsdale, by contrast, can only afford to replace a portion—typically 41 percent or less—of the maximum set for federal awards (and that was before the 1992 reauthorization raised them yet again). I have to make similar reports to the board of trustees every year. It is the students, then, who are making the real sacrifice—those who have to go elsewhere and those who choose to attend Hillsdale despite the severe financial penalties imposed on them by the federal government.

But this was not the end of the story. Many politicians and bureaucrats who wished to see Hillsdale College and Grove City College defeated were unhappy with the *Grove City* decision because in their opinion it did not go far enough. In early 1988, largely at the instigation of Sen. Edward Kennedy (D-MA) and Sen. Lowell Weicker (R-CT), Congress overrode a presidential veto by 73–24 in the Senate and 292–133 in the House to enact the Civil Rights Restoration Act, a breathtakingly awesome exercise of federal power that eliminates the "program-specific" restraint, stretches the principle of nondiscrimination to cover virtually any group regulators decide is "minority," and extends the legislation well beyond higher education to affect virtually every organization and business in the United States. Now every lemonade stand *is* under the bureaucratic thumb of the United States government.

——————CIVIL RIGHTS——————

Another assault upon the independence of higher education came in 1983 when the Supreme Court ruled on a case involving Bob Jones University. Nearly all the headlines and editorials about this case focused on the university's pernicious policy banning interracial dating and marriage. But they ignored the equally pernicious decision of the Court that the IRS, on its own authority, had the right to yank the tax-exempt status of the university. As columnist George Will warned, from now on, the IRS would be free to "make its own assessment of whether any particular group's activities are or are not "contrary to public policy."[31]

In June of 1992, the Supreme Court also ruled that Mississippi's colleges and universities were unlawfully segregated, even though whites and blacks were at liberty to attend the schools of their choice and were not being coerced into attending one institution or another.[32] It is only a matter of time before the related issue of race-based scholarships, which caused both an internal struggle at the Department of Education and a national furor in the early 1990s, also comes before the Supreme Court. The trouble started when Michael Williams, an assistant secretary within the Office of Civil Rights (OCR) who happens to be black, declared that race-based scholarships were illegal. Civil rights groups protested that the law was meant to prohibit whites-only scholarships, not minorities-only scholarships, since past discrimination against minorities required special redress. Finally, OCR decided to compromise and stated that its revised interpretation of the law was that private donors could endow race-based scholarships, but colleges and universities receiving federal aid would be prohibited from using their own funds for such purposes. Under the Clinton administration, OCR has made yet another about-face and now fully supports race-based scholarships.[33]

There are dozens of thorny problems that arise when considering this issue, and not all are linked to race. What if a former football star wants to establish an athletic scholarship for a male student? May a female or a disabled male apply? What if a Florida businesswoman wants to establish a scholarship for female students from Florida? May an in-state male or an out-of-state female apply? I am willing to bet that most people would readily respond in the negative to these questions. But once a legal precedent is established that some restrictions on admissions are not legitimate, all restrictions become vulnerable. For instance, a quadriplegic student rejected by ten medical schools recently was accepted under strong pressure at Yeshiva University even though his handicap makes his ability to function as a doctor extremely limited if not nonexistent. Yet Pennsylvania, for one, has changed its state laws on discrimination in education precisely to ensure that colleges and universities cannot legally refuse such students.[34]

Whatever the specifics of a future Supreme Court decision on race-based and other designated scholarships and on admissions eligibility, there is likely to be an enlargement of bureaucratic powers at the expense of colleges and universities and minorities as well as nonminorities.

Liberty University offers a further indication of how the same ill wind breathed by an inconsistent government policy on civil rights blows for religious institutions. In 1993, the Virginia State Council of Higher Education decreed that LU students would be eligible to receive state tuition grants only if the university (in serious financial straits with a debt of over $70 million) agreed to eliminate mandatory chapel attendance and its policy of requiring students and faculty to sign broad statements of faith. Moreover, in exchange for continuing the grants, which amounted to $1.2. million a year, the council wanted proof that "total academic freedom" would be preserved. (Read: If a faculty member publishes atheist or satanic views, this would not be sufficient cause to deny him tenure or to terminate his contract, even though LU is an expressly Christian institution.) "Liberty has basically agreed to exchange its unique religious character for a government handout," crowed the school's main critic, Barry Lynn, executive director of Americans United for Separation of Church and State. He announced after the council's ruling that his group's next targets would be Regent University in Virginia Beach and Christendom College in Front Royal.[35]

Further, as the result of the Supreme Court's refusal in 1993 to examine an appeals court ruling, the Virginia Military Institute and the Citadel are now facing the prospect of giving up a 150-year-old tradition of single sex education. They will lose federal and state aid unless they accept women or their states come up with hundreds of millions of dollars to fund "parallel opportunities" for women.[36] The principal argument against these two schools is that the mere fact of being all-male violates the constitutional rights of females. This perversion of such ideas as choice, equal opportunity, and exclusion, as well as federal intrusion (yet again) into academic affairs, is bound to wreak havoc in the next decade—and not just in higher education.

CURRICULAR DECISIONS AND
———— ACCREDITATION ————

The power of the bureaucracy to affect even curricular decisions is gradually becoming established. Rockland Community College in Suffern, New York, for example, is being forced to repay $9.8 million in tuition assistance to over three thousand students who attended between 1983 and 1987 because government auditors decided that the Judaic studies courses in which they enrolled "did not meet the criteria for a liberal arts degree."[37] Colleges and universities of all sizes and descriptions continue to come under fire from federally certified accreditation agencies because they have not surcharged their curriculums with "modern" subjects and academic fads ranging from relativism and deconstructionism to gender- or race-based teaching disguised as multiculturalism, and because they have shown "insufficient sensitivity" in their hiring and enrollment policies. They have been warned to "get with the program" or receive low or failing marks during their next evaluation.

In 1990, the Middle States Association of Colleges and Schools (MSACS) demanded that Philadelphia's Westminster Theological Seminary show just cause for not ordaining women and not having women among its trustees. It made its own position in opposition to Westminster's perfectly clear: "An institution must have a governing board which includes diverse membership broadly representative of the public interest. . . ." Secretary of Education Lamar Alexander intervened and forced MSACS to rescind its demand, but he was subsequently hauled before a subcommittee of the House Government Operations Committee to explain, amazingly enough, why *he* had been "improperly interfering with the traditional independence of colleges and universities."[38]

In the same year, one of New York's model affirmative action schools fell afoul of the thought police in the "politically correct" movement and, as a result, was nearly denied accreditation by the same agency. MSACS declared that Baruch College was "an excellent academic institution," but objected that it "emphasized academic values without exhibiting equal concern for the values of social justice and equity critical to serving working people in a multicultural urban environment."[39] When Baruch pressed for specifics about its supposed failure to measure up to the agency's vague, unwritten standards, MSACS was evasive. Finally, it was only the intervention, again, of Secretary Alexander, which saved the college. He threatened to yank the agency's *own* accreditation because of its high-handed behavior.

But help came too late for President Joe Segall. He resigned his position and in so doing characterized accreditation investigations as "a Kafkaesque trial process because the institutions are not made aware of explicit charges nor are they presented with evidence." The case against Baruch was mainly based on what was referred to as the "paucity of minority representation on the faculty and in the administration" and "low student retention rates." But what, Segall asked, constitutes "paucity"? Of Baruch's full-time faculty in 1990, 18 percent were minorities. This was much higher than the national average and was particularly impressive at a time when, as he pointed out, only 3.5 percent of all new Ph.D.s were black and universities were competing desperately to hire them. And as for "low student retention," what about Baruch's record of 40 percent for blacks, which also was higher than the national average? Segall charged that MSACS was more concerned about "social justice" than equal opportunity or academic excellence and concluded, "What is more horrifying is that colleges across the country are quick to accommodate the demands of those who would call them racist if the demands are not met."[40]

Under pressure, MSACS backed off, but only temporarily. The Clinton administration has given it much freer rein to investigate in the future. MSACS also has more than a dozen other schools currently on its "suspect" list, and all accreditation agencies are beginning to enforce "diversity" standards like the Western Association of Schools and Colleges', which requires each candidate for accreditation to "demonstrate its commitment to the increasingly significant educational role played by diversity of ethnic, social, and economic backgrounds among its members by making positive efforts to foster diversity."[41] No one, least of all the colleges and universities whose fate rests on fulfilling this "commitment," knows precisely what that entails.

In the hands of hostile bureaucrats, accreditation is a powerful tool for intimidation. Schools that receive a poor ranking or lose their accreditation also stand to lose students, faculty, and donors, as well as all federal aid. Their students lose loans and grants. And their graduates may not be eligible for many advanced degree programs or teaching certification. Some schools, either preparing for this latter possibility or simply responding to the rigid and costly nature of the current system, have withdrawn from the National Council for Accreditation of Teacher Education and set up their own alternative forms of teacher accreditation. In Iowa, for example, the list includes the four largest schools: Drake University, Iowa State University, the University of Iowa, and the University of Northern Iowa. In Arizona, the University of Arizona, Arizona State University, and Northern Arizona University have dropped out.[42] Colleges and universities around the country are following suit, and there has even been discussion of alternative academic accreditation agencies among the members of the National Association of Scholars and other organizations that are opposed to the ideological litmus tests conducted by the current agencies and to the prejudice of those agencies in favor of big research universities.

FEDERAL AGENCIES AND FEDERAL —————REGULATION—————

The Department of Education, created under President Jimmy Carter, is leading the way in creating new, costly, and ever-expanding bureaucratic rules for colleges and universities. Lawrence Uzzell observed in the 1980s that "the Department of

Education regulation-writers openly dictate to schools," and he added, "The department enforces a total of more than one thousand pages of fine-print laws and regulations—a standing refutation of the 1950's claim that federal aid would not promote federal control."[43] Although President Reagan vowed to abolish the Department of Education, he was fighting a losing battle from the start. The Democratic-controlled Congress perceived any plan, even if it was merely to cut spending or to curb the influence of the newly established cabinet-level agency, as an all-out attack on education and promptly blocked it. Worse yet, instead of shrinking, the DOE's budget rose from $10 billion to $22 billion, and it continued to amass money and power under the Bush administration.[44]

Today, says the *Educational Record*, "the number of regulations with which colleges and universities must comply has increased tremendously." And these regulations are not just the products of Congress and the Department of Education since, once passed, legislation "is typically routed to executive agencies for the attachment of appropriate regulations. . . . Moreover, regulations pertaining to a single area may be issued by any number of executive departments."[45] These are frequently contradictory or overlapping, but it does not matter; they are all binding. Here are just a few samples of areas in which federal agencies routinely interfere in higher education:

- The Department of Agriculture: animal research, commercial research, audits, biotechnology, black and land-grant colleges, student grants, research grants, challenge grants, lobbying, and even student eligibility for food stamps.
- The Department of Commerce: commercial and marine research, research grants, audits, liability, lobbying, consumer protection, auxiliary enterprises, and patents.
- The Department of Defense: all defense-related grants and research as well as overhead, audits, security, lab procedures, health and safety, hazardous substances, patents,

commercial development, technology transfer, and minority issues, including race, gender, sexual orientation, age, disability, or other discrimination or harassment.

- The Department of Education: campus security, consumer protection, health and safety, student services, graduation requirements, career placement, athletics, drugs, alcohol, hazardous substances, admissions, tuitions, scholarships, student grants and loans, defaults, vocational education, special education, research grants, institutional grants, overhead, audits, academic requirements, and minority issues, including race, gender, sexual orientation, age, disability, or other discrimination or harassment.

- The Department of Health and Human Services: AIDS and biomedical research, scientific misconduct, health and safety, audits, research grants, institutional grants, athletics, drugs, alcohol, hazardous substances, student grants and loans, training grants, volunteer work, and minority issues, including race, gender, sexual orientation, age, disability, or other discrimination or harassment.

- The Department of Interior: adult education, grants, research grants, audits, lobbying, patents, tribal colleges, and minority issues, including race, gender, sexual orientation, age, disability, or other discrimination or harassment.

- The Department of Justice and the Department of Labor: antitrust cases, student grants and loans, foreign students, campus security, drugs, alcohol, hazardous substances, employment practices, commercial research, liability, audits, work/study grants and other student aid, and minority issues, including race, gender, sexual orientation, age, disability, or other discrimination or harassment.

- The Department of the Treasury: charitable contributions, property, defaults, investments, partnerships, overhead, audits, commercial research, grants, and scholarships.

• The Department of Veterans Affairs: reservists and veterans' benefits, health and safety, employment practices, and minority issues, including race, gender, sexual orientation, age, disability, or other discrimination or harassment.

"Much of the current regulation," James Davis, president of Shenandoah University, has observed, "appears to be a result of a malaise that has fallen upon the nation. Legislation is intended to be a quick solution to issues confronting campuses, but it might be better were campuses allowed to work through some of the issues on their own."[46] Yet according to a recent poll by the American Council on Education, some other college and university presidents say they actually welcome federal regulation. They see it as a healthy way of keeping their institutions on their toes and guaranteeing accountability. (This, if anything, tells you all you need to know about the sad decline of educational leadership.) Of course, most of them have little to do with the actual implementation of regulation and fulfillment of requirements about reporting data, compliance, and so on. The average college president spends less than five to ten hours a month on regulatory or legal issues.[47] And few are accustomed to even thinking of the true financial costs of implementing regulations, since they have come to rely heavily on greater and greater infusions of government aid.

But in most cases the truth is that colleges and universities bear a heavy regulatory burden. As noted earlier, they must hire on-campus "supervisory personnel" whose full-time job is to make sure that the school paying their salary is complying with all federal regulations and to be on the lookout for any sign of alleged discrimination. One affirmative action planning officer's smug and self-serving explanation for the rising level of college support staff is, "They have to hire more people like me." And it's no wonder: Educational bureaucrats pile on new regulations year after year—in the areas of civil rights and alleged discrimination, student loan reporting, environmental impact, indirect costs and overhead, tax and nonprofit status, conflict of interest disputes, lab research, patents, and commercial development—and these are piled on top of thousands of other "standard" regulations in health, safety, licensing, hiring, liability, and so on that apply to all businesses, not just colleges and universities. And after several record decades of skyrocketing tuition increases, student loan defaults, and cases of institutional corruption, federal and state legislators are more than ready—they are positively eager—to make the 1990s an era of record regulation. "In retrospect," laments one college administrator, "we may come to see the 1980s as the good times."[48]

The American Council on Education agrees that in the next several years the 1992 reauthorization of the Higher Education Act will result in more "vast regulatory changes." Though it is a lobby that is supposed to be looking out for its members' interests, the ACE has noted with approval that these changes will virtually guarantee more staff time and/or additional funds spent by colleges and their bureaucratic overseers to ensure full compliance.[49] Even more worrisome is the fact that new provisions regarding grant and loan programs recommend that the states hire more staff in order to start monitoring and investigating campus financial aid offices. This does not just expand an existing form of intervention—it creates a whole new category. Some lawmakers also want the federal government to pay the states "to operate agencies that would set standards for reviewing an institution's financial and administrative capacities, facilities, curriculum, student services, and admissions policies."[50]

The Student Right to Know and Campus Security Act of 1990 also deserves mention. It requires colleges and universities to disclose to prospective as well as current students detailed information about minority representation, retention rates, graduation rates, job placement, loan default rates, financial aid, athletic scholarships, campus safety, emergency policies and facilities, campus law enforcement, campus relations with local, state, and federal law enforcement, crime prevention, counseling, drug and alcohol education, disciplinary procedures, and a host of other issues.[51] The law is very vague about how to collect this information, about how much is enough, about reporting in comparable terms (there are contradictory instructions in different sections), and about how this information may be used in the future by accreditation or federal agencies. Still, colleges and universities are held accountable for compliance; whatever compliance means will be determined whenever the bureaucracy gets around to it.

And coming on the heels of this major federal intrusion in the name of "consumer protection" and "the right to know" is another recent ruling in which the Department of Education forced Harvard University, the University of Pennsylvania, Stanford University, and Wesleyan University to show students (and, of course, their lawyers) confidential records and notes made about them by admissions counselors and other staff.[52]

——— REGULATORY "GOALS" ———

Here are some additional regulatory "goals" on which the bureaucracy is working:

• *A requirement for tax-exempt organizations with revenues of $100,000 or more a year to publish full, public financial disclosures.*[53] Regulators already contend that tax exemption is a government subsidy rather than a recognition of independent status. Over the last several decades, they have curtailed and even sought to eliminate tax-free educational benefits for graduate students and the families of college and university employees and tax breaks for other businesses that offer to pay for the education of their employees and employees' families. Reducing the tax deductibility of charitable contributions to higher education is also a persistent aim, and in 1988, the IRS published a highly controversial manual stating that new private schools applying for tax exemption must first prove that they do not discriminate.[54]

• *Eliminating tax exemption for all college and university enterprises not directly related to the classroom or administrative operations.* Already schools must pay taxes on "activities not 'substantially related' to their primary missions,"[55] and there have been repeated attempts to get a bill through Congress to tax, in addition to the "usual targets" (campus bookstores, college presses, conference centers, and sports programs), a number of new ones (dormitories, cafeterias, computer sales, student services, and even investment income and royalties from scientific and technological research).

• *Greater intervention in commercial/academic research and technological development.* Congress is openly hostile to the close, historic ties between industry and academe. Although a number of recent ethical scandals involving individual faculty with clear conflicts of interest indicate that there is a need for reform, there is no basis for the contention that both industry and academe are inevitably corrupted by the "profit motive." (It is exceedingly rare, by the way, to find members of Congress worried about the ties between government and academe or the corrupting influence of public sector subsidies on the nature of research.) Particularly troubling is a proposed Commerce Department regulation that would prohibit colleges and universities from owning some patents and limit publication rights on much of their own research. If made law, licensing to industry would become nearly impossible.[56]

• *More federal investigations by the U.S. Office of Research Integrity, various congressional committees and federal agencies in cases of alleged scientific misconduct in higher education.* In 1992, the Department of Health and Human Services held a public "trial" in one such case that will, in all likelihood, spawn other significant extensions of federal authority in the areas of science and research.

• *A requirement for all schools to report directly to the Department of Education as well as to students proprietary information and race- and gender-based statistics on athletics.* This means athletic scholarships, broken down by race and sex; athletic graduation rates, broken down by race and sex; and comparisons with the rest of the student body—you guessed it, broken down by race and sex.[57] Already member schools must report these statistics to the NCAA, which indirectly shares them with the DOE.

• *Legal enforcement of absolute gender equity in athletics.* This is what is known as a "hot" regulatory issue. Seldom does a week go by without a major dispute involving the alleged violation of women's rights at colleges and universities that spend more on men's than on women's sports. As little as 6 percent disparity between scholarships for male and female athletes is enough to constitute a violation of the DOE's new guidelines for "gender equity" in collegiate sports.[58] Predictably there have been numerous lawsuits, but not always filed by women; two male athletes currently are suing their colleges for violating Title IX and "equal protection" under the Constitution because the men's swim teams at their schools have been eliminated in order to free up funds for women's programs.[59]

• *Use of antidiscrimination statutes to extend the "rights" of "new" minorities.* As has already been pointed out, the Civil Rights Restoration Act has opened a Pandora's box when it comes to antidiscrimination. Almost anyone can qualify as a victim and get access to the courts in order to make someone else (preferably with "deep pockets") pay for it. In mid-1992, the *Chronicle of Higher Education* reported that forty-one schools were at the time charged with violating the rights of the physically disabled.[60] Homosexuals, lesbians, and pedophiles claim that they, too, have been discriminated against in higher education, and some have succeeded in winning lawsuits. Now, they want federal legislation to give them special, enumerated legal protection for their "sexual orientation."

• *More federal and state control over academic standards.* The U.S. Task Force on Assessing the National Goals Relating to Post-secondary Education, established in 1990, has called for a government-enforced set of uniform standards for all college students with special, federally funded "assessment teams" to evaluate the results.[61] By the end of the 1980s, twenty-four states had academic "assessment requirements," and twelve more states had begun to debate implementing them.[62] The National Governors Association declared recently that such requirements ought to be the "central strategy for improving the quality of undergraduate education," and also recommended that they be made federal law. The Department of Education has already stuck its camel's nose under the tent by requiring a number of individual campuses to prove that their student bodies are making "satisfactory academic progress."[63] Several years ago, one lobbyist, who had also been an educator and a regulator, told the House Subcommittee on Postsecondary Education that the DOE ought to decide which schools are not merely eligible but are "fundamentally worthy" to receive federal aid.[64] That is certainly where the trend in regulation is heading: academic evaluation as yet another means of control.

• *Using the threat of withholding federal funds to control tuition.* In early 1993, a *Washington Post* editorial laid it all out quite plainly: "Since colleges and universities are apparently unable to get their budgets under control themselves, perhaps it is time to begin applying public sanctions to the high flyers. How about a rule that reduces eligibility for federal student aid, at least among the most expensive colleges, when their tuition rises more than inflation costs?"[65]

• *Using the threat of withholding federal funds to protect academic freedom.* In an understandable but misguided reaction to "political correctness" and the anti-free speech movement in higher education, even staunch conservatives have expressed their willingness to use federal funds to influence campus affairs. They did not condone the *Grove City* decision in the 1980s, but, they say, turnabout is fair play, and it is high time to begin using the law to extend rather than limit freedom.

Specifically, they have promoted an amendment "that would

prohibit private colleges from receiving federal funds if they took any action against individuals for offensive speech."[66] The problem, as the *Wall Street Journal* has pointed out, is that "such legislation would protect free speech by removing the broader freedom private universities have had from government control and federal lawsuits."[67] There are better ways to fight; ultimately, "political correctness" will not be defeated in the courts but in academe. It is a war of ideas, not of legalities and regulations, that is being waged.

THE LINK BETWEEN FUNDING ——— AND CONTROL ———

Despite the earnest promises of Congress when aid to higher education was first debated, it is evident that federal funds have indeed brought federal control. In fact, federal funds have become the *primary* tool of an increasingly meddlesome bureaucracy in which a single, unelected official can threaten to withhold millions of dollars in funds not because a university has been found guilty of specific acts of supposed wrongdoing, but because it has committed the unforgivable sin of refusing to acknowledge federal hegemony. Title IX regulation, the *Hillsdale* and *Grove City* decisions, and the Civil Rights Restoration Act have given bureaucrats all the excuse and legal ammunition they need not only to try to micromanage the day-to-day affairs of public and private campuses, to conduct vague antidiscrimination fishing expeditions, and to operate in a climate of perpetual suspicion, but also to redefine radically the terms on which all colleges and universities must operate. "Toe our line, or we will take away your funds," the regulators say. It is scarcely possible to pose a more naked threat. They might as well announce, "You take our money, so we own you," to colleges and universities. What is especially galling about this is that "our money" means money that really belongs to you and me. When the government gives it back to us, it comes not with strings attached, but with chains.

Chapter 6

———— 🏛 ————

MISMANAGEMENT AND CORRUPTION

Unprecedented budget cuts at hundreds of colleges and universities, "front-loading," "forward funding," massive deficits in federal grant and loan programs—these are a few of the warning signs that indicate the ivory tower is falling apart. And there are many more, including a national epidemic of cheating, "bait and switch" admissions tactics, test score and grade inflation, and race-norming (see Chapter 8). Indeed, mismanagement and corruption appear to go hand in hand in modern higher education, as the following examples amply demonstrate.

————— BIG ATHLETICS —————

Athletic scandals in colleges and universities have become so well known that Americans have actually come to *expect* this kind of corruption in academe, especially at big universities. The number of institutions charged with major National College Athletic Association (NCAA) violations in a single two-year period—1992 through 1993—is overwhelming, including: Adelphi University, Auburn University, Austin Peay State University, Ball

State University, Chicago State University, Clemson University, Colorado State University, Florida State University, Hampton University, Howard University, Jackson State University, the University of Kentucky, Lamar University, Lock Haven University, Memphis State University, Miami University, Middle Tennessee State University, Northwestern State University, Oklahoma State University, Southeastern Louisiana University, Syracuse University, Texas A & M University, Tulane University, the University of Arkansas-Fayetteville, the University of the District of Columbia, the University of Florida, the University of Illinois-Urbana, the University of Lowell, the University of Maryland-College Park, the University of Michigan, the University of Minnesota-Twin Cities, the University of Missouri-Columbia, the University of Nebraska, the University of Nevada-Las Vegas, the University of New Mexico, the University of New Orleans, the University of Pittsburgh, the University of Oklahoma, the University of the Pacific, the University of Tennessee, the University of Texas-El Paso, the University of Texas-Pan American, the University of Tulsa, the University of Washington, Upsala College, and Vanderbilt University.[1] Remember—these schools have been charged with major violations that go well beyond ignoring fine print regulations and in some cases include criminal as well as deceitful practices.

Deceit, says Murray Sperber, author of *College Sports, Inc.,* is evident in other areas besides rules violations. In reporting athlete graduation rates, the NCAA and the College Football Association (CFA) do not count all student athletes who begin as freshmen. Those who transfer or drop out in "good academic standing" (that is, with a "D" or better average) are simply omitted, and this inflates graduation rates significantly. Colleges and universities that make individual reports to donors, parents, and students often are even more flagrantly deceptive when they count only senior athletes who graduate, omitting those who dropped out in their freshman through junior years. In true terms, many schools are graduating a fraction of their student athletes. Minorities suffer most of all. At nearly half of 248 Division I colleges and universities recently surveyed by the *Chronicle of Higher Education*, fewer than one-third of their black athletes graduated within six years. At Texas A & M University, only about 7 percent of black athletes manage to earn a diploma. At the University of Houston, there have been years when not a single black football player graduated. At Memphis State University not long ago, there was a ten-year period in which no black varsity basketball player graduated. The implicit promise schools once made—that every scholarship would lead to a degree—is, as *USA Today* editorializes, long dead and forgotten.[2]

Excessive emphasis on sports also cheats student-athletes in other ways. Cash "awards" and under-the-table bribes, all-expense-paid vacations, sports cars, no-show jobs, free tuition coupled with princely allotments for "living expenses," signing bonuses, game bonuses, tourney bonuses, liquor, drugs (from "recreational" substances to steroids), parties, and female "escorts"—name any kind of corruption, and it has been practiced by some of our nation's "best" colleges and universities in order to convince eighteen-year-old youngsters with physical talent to step onto the playing fields of big-time intercollegiate athletics.

But once there, student athletes are not always pampered or even well treated. They are expected to spend twenty grueling hours per week on conditioning, practice, and watching game films, and another ten or more hours a week on travel and games. The latter are often played hundreds of miles from home or in some cases in the middle of the night to gain national television coverage. Players are expected to complete their homework and attend class the next day, although, of course, many do not, and their professors are encouraged to turn a blind eye.

During the season, these athletes are forced on average to miss classes two days a week.[3] They also are encouraged to isolate themselves from extracurricular activities and "normal" campus life and relationships, and as long as their grades meet the minimal requirements for athletic eligibility, they are not expected to display any significant academic progress or even to learn basic skills. (There have been, of course, a number of varsity athletes who were discovered to be nearly illiterate *after* they received their diplomas.) Hoover Institution Senior Fellow Thomas Sowell says, "If General Motors or Exxon formed a cartel to treat their workers even half as badly as college athletes are treated, there would be antitrust suits in courts across the country and whole armies of executives would be led away in handcuffs to the federal penitentiary."[4]

And if that were all to the story of mismanagement and corruption in intercollegiate athletics, it would be enough to condemn it. But there is much more. Despite the huge gross revenues colleges and universities generate (through bowl games and other tournaments, regular game ticket sales, and television coverage), almost all of the 2,300 intercollegiate sports programs in the country are money-losers. Only about forty or fifty break even or make a net profit in any given year. This is all the more astonishing considering that each Division I-A school rakes in an average of nearly $10 million a year, and that a five-year contract between the CFA and Capital Cities/ABC Television is worth $300 million, and that a single bowl game can mean as much as $6 million for each of the participating teams.[5]

This record of poor financial performance isn't widely known because, as a report prepared by the American Council on Education called "The Money Game" admits, "Intercollegiate athletics is an area of university operations that tends to be shrouded in secrecy."[6] Murray Sperber agrees: "Athletic departments are often autonomous units, not directly supervised by a dean or other university official," and, he adds, "They like to erect 'Iron Curtains' around their operations, particularly their finances. Even at public universities they are unwilling to open their books. In addition, because they frequently use 'creative accounting' and try to remove as many expenses as possible from their financial statements, they are adept at concealing their real losses."[7] Here are some of the deficits we *do* know about. Each figure represents a deficit for a single year of operations in the late 1980s: the

University of Michigan, $2.5 million; the University of Houston, $3.4 million; the University of Wisconsin-Madison, $5.9 million; the University of Illinois, $1.45 million; the University of Central Florida, $1.1 million; Florida A & M University, $700,000; the University of South Florida, $655,000; and all Arkansas public colleges and universities, $6.3 million.[8]

Most athletic departments spend hundreds of thousands and, in some cases, millions of dollars each year. One big-ticket item is salaries. Most Division I men's basketball and football coaches have annual incomes in the $100,000 range; more than fifty earn over $250,000.[9] For other sports like soccer, baseball, track, and swimming, many earn more than $75,000 a year.[10] While the University of Alabama athletic department was accumulating a $39 million debt in the late 1980s, its director, Ray Perkins, was raking in salary and perks worth $220,000. But this was really small potatoes; here is what some of his peers were earning in salaries, benefits, and commercial deals (which don't come out of the university's pocket, but which are the direct result of their university position): University of Michigan basketball coach Bill Frieder, $400,000; University of Kentucky basketball coach Rick Pitino, $800,000–900,000; University of Louisville basketball coach Dennie Crum, $600,000; Georgetown University basketball coach John Thompson, $600,000; University of Notre Dame football coach Lou Holtz, $500,000-$700,000; Florida State University football coach Bobby Bowden, $400,000; University of Miami football coach Dennis Erickson, $400,000; University of Louisville football coach Howard Schnellenberger, $400,000; and University of Florida football coach Steve Spurrier, $400,000.[11]

Booster clubs also regularly kick in "supplemental pay" for coaches; while at the University of Nevada-Las Vegas, basketball coach Jerry Tarkanian, for example, was receiving a reported $80,000 a year in booster funds on top of more than a half million dollars in other income.[12] And then there is the slick trick practiced by some coaches who wait to pay the dorm fees incurred during summer camps (for-profit businesses that universities generally allow them to operate for only nominal cost) until the end of the fiscal year. They thus have as much as $100,000 accumulating interest in their personal bank accounts for twelve months.[13]

Endorsements provide coaches with opportunities to cash in on their special status in higher education and make it difficult to tell sometimes, says the *Chronicle of Higher Education,* for whom they work. In mid-1993, shortly before the expiration of his lucrative team shoe contract with Adidas, it was reported by various sources that Duke University basketball coach Mike Krzyewski had been approached by Nike with the following offer: annual salary, $375,000–750,000; $1 million signing bonus; and a $75,000 annuity after his retirement.[14] A Duke spokesman admitted that the coach and the university president were jointly involved in the negotiations.

Athletic directors and coaches often live, says the *Chicago Sun-Times,* like maharajahs or at least like *Fortune* 500 CEOs.[15] They have luxurious offices, scores of highly paid staff, and unlimited expense accounts for recruiting, "entertainment" and other vague purposes. Their travel budgets, if made known, would be the envy even of the Clinton White House. But apparently they do not feel the burden of responsibility that comes with such benefits. When Neal Stoner left the athletic director's position at the University of Illinois in 1988, after an audit revealed what was characterized as "massive misuse of funds," he claimed self-righteously that he was only doing what was "long-standing practice" for others in his profession.[16] He was right on that score: For decades, many athletic directors have had *carte blanche* when it comes to determining how money is spent in their departments. Only in the last few years, as college and university finances have been scrutinized more closely, have thorough investigations really begun. But there were a few well-publicized cases as early as the mid-1980s. At the University of Louisville, it was discovered that, among other irregularities, athletic director Bill Olsen had arranged for $62,000 in "excess" tournament revenues to be paid to twenty-one employees and four merchants (one of whom was a car dealer who accepted about $4,000 out of the $7,500 sent to him as a down payment on a car for Olsen's wife).[17] He, like Stoner, claimed that this was an accepted custom in the world of intercollegiate athletics. At the University of New Mexico-Lobo, hardly an athletic powerhouse, athletic director John Koenig was indicted by a grand jury on forty-seven counts, including "embezzlement, conspiracy, receiving kickbacks, and receiving a bribe from a public official."[18] Since his predecessor, Jim Bridgers, had managed to rack up over $800,000 in athletic department debts in a single year, there was widespread speculation that Koenig had not been an aberration.

Coaches at many colleges and universities can also sell complimentary tickets (legally) for retail prices and trade them (illegally) for goods and services, from haircuts and house repairs to first-class airfare and deluxe family vacations. The sums involved are not trifling. During the University of Illinois scandal involving Stoner, tickets were exchanged for over $10,000 in free dry cleaning for athletic staff members and their families.[19] A state audit at the University of Missouri revealed that $125,000 worth of complimentary tickets were distributed in one year, and at Louisiana State University, the figure for one year was said to be as high as $450,000. (In neither case was there any mention of how many tickets were given away or sold, but their sheer value is suggestive.) And players have learned to imitate their coaches. The NCAA estimates that there are about eight thousand cases of illegal football ticket sales by players every season.[20]

The public has every right to feel outraged about these abuses; it is directly and indirectly footing the bill for them. Students pay activity fees to colleges and universities which then hand over a good portion—an average of $1.2 million at Division I football schools—to the athletic department.[21] At the College of William and Mary, for example, each student "tithes" $500 to support sports.[22] In 1989, the University of Wisconsin-Madison's athletic department was $2 million in the red, prompting administrators to raise individual student fees by an arbitrary amount of $10 specifically to eliminate the deficit. But three years later, it still stood at $1.9 million.[23] At the University of Nevada-Reno, the student union fund was raided for a total of $175,000 in one year to help reduce the athletic department deficit, and at the University of Houston, student fees devoted to athletics quadrupled between 1985 and 1988.[24]

In the mid-1980s, athletic departments at Division I football schools also received an average of $736,000 in federal, state, and local support.[25] Sperber points out that this total is probably less than 50 percent of the public monies actually spent, since it only reflects direct support. He cites some schools that did far better in soaking taxpayers: Illinois public colleges and universities, $7 million; California State University-Fullerton, $2.5 million; the University of Alaska-Anchorage, $1.2 million; the University of Montana, $961,000; Montana State University, $1.34 million; and the University of North Carolina, $2.3 million.[26] The most common ploys to divert additional tax money to athletics, he explains, are: (1) to classify coaches and other athletic staff as faculty; (2) to record athletic program expenditures as "student services"; and (3) to waive tuition for athletes or pay their tuition out of the academic budget. Colleges and universities also put tax dollars into the general operating fund only to assign them to the athletic department at a later date. Sperber comments wryly, "Some people call this money laundering."

Given the severity of higher education's current financial crisis, athletic departments will be forced to cut back like every other division on campus, but if past experience is any guide, their suffering will be delayed as long as possible, and when it does happen, it will be comparatively minor. In the 1980s, for example, the state of Washington was pouring direct subsidies of more than $2 million and even more indirect support into athletics even as public colleges and universities were slashing academic expenditures.[27] Utah State University cut $500,000 from its academic departments while allowing the football program to expand and the athletic department to run up $800,000 in debts.[28] And in 1992, the University of Massachusetts-Amherst was still spending money on a number of questionable expenses, including dozens of trips to resorts for athletic staff, at a time when the school was cutting its general operating budget and when at least four sports programs had been dropped for lack of funds.[29]

In summary, Hoover Institution Senior Fellow Martin Anderson says: "Everyone knows how admission, eligibility, and graduation rules have been bent and twisted to accommodate athletes. But for a long time it was pretty much nickel-and-dime corruption, done as much to boost the spirit of the school's alumni and students as it was to raise money. Like prostitution and gambling, it was always with us, but it was controlled, mostly out of sight."[30] All that has changed. A private commission sponsored by the Knight Foundation declared in 1991 that intercollegiate athletic corruption had become so widespread that it could "no longer be swept under the rug or kept under control by tinkering at the edges."[31] Not long after, the Federal Trade Commission subpoenaed the financial records of over one hundred colleges and universities to investigate the charge that their sports programs are commercial rather than educational, and the IRS ruled that at least one school, Ohio University, as well as any schools playing in the Cotton Bowl and the John Hancock Bowl, must pay taxes on their advertising revenues.[32]

Since colleges and universities have failed to conduct their own housecleaning, it looks as if the government will try to do it for them. I use the word "try," since it probably will only make things worse. Yet sports are potentially one of the best elements of the undergraduate experience. All the clichés about character building, about teamwork, about discipline, and about school spirit are true. That is why the corruption that exists in modern intercollegiate athletics is so troubling, and why it should be eradicated by administrators and coaches rather than politicians and bureaucrats.

———————— BIG SCIENCE ————————

Many colleges and universities are also establishing an unenviable reputation for greed and corruption in the field of "big science." Since the beginning of World War II, the federal government has spent more—vastly more—on science than has private industry, and, typical of a huge bureaucracy, it has favored those institutions that most closely resemble its own image. Some twenty "mega-universities," for example, received 40 percent of all federal research funds in the mid-1970s. In 1990, more than $1.5 billion went to just five.[33] But that still leaves plenty for the second string, meaning the merely large and middle-sized research schools. Today, dozens of these receive $100 million or more a year.[34] The characteristic all share is that their federal research revenues are many times greater than their tuition revenues.

Plain old-fashioned pork-barrel politics also determine where much of the taxpayers' money ends up. In recent years, the State University of New York's Buffalo campus called upon its allies in Albany and Washington, D.C., to beat out several California schools for a $25 million earthquake study center.[35] (New York has had fifteen seismic disturbances in the last century compared to nearly 4,500 in California; this is comparable to funding an institute for the study of snowstorms in Hawaii.) In another case, through an adroit combination of lobbying and political pressure, Florida State University, despite being far down on the list of qualified candidates, walked away with $120 million for a state-of-the-art magnet laboratory.[36]

No fewer than twenty-five states engaged in a bitter contest in the 1980s over which would be the home of the Superconducting Supercollider. Texas finally succeeded in winning over the Department of Energy with a carefully orchestrated P.R. campaign and help from prominent politicians like then-Speaker of the House James Wright. Thousands of university scientists and researchers were put to work constructing the world's largest subatomic particle instrument near Dallas. But, by the time the federal government had sunk $1 billion into what was supposed to be a $4.4 billion project, mismanagement and overspending had caused estimates to rise to $8.25 billion and then $11.8 billion. Feeling (rightly) that it had been hoodwinked, Congress voted to kill funding in mid-1992, but soon was pressured into restoring it. A year later, funding was killed again.[37] Similar although less dramatic examples of waste, mismanagement, and political wrangling over the $1.5 billion Hubble Space Telescope and the multimillion-dollar Human Genome Project also provide evidence of how "big science" is increasingly bureaucratized and politicized, no matter how sound or well-intentioned the original idea.[38]

On the subject of corruption, here are some well-known individual cases, most of which are summarized in Robert Bell's recent book, *Impure Science*:[39]

• At Harvard Medical School, three co-workers witnessed a fourth, Dr. John Darsee, fake data in an experiment. Since he had published an unusual number of papers—nearly one hundred in a two-year period—it was suspected that he had faked other data as well. His departmental superior and co-author of many of those same papers, Dr. Eugene Braunwald, delayed a full investigation, and Darsee was allowed to continue working in the lab, although not in his former position, since he readily admitted to the incident in which he had been caught red-handed. Eventually, a sympathetic internal review board found him innocent of further charges and declared the case closed, but when the National Institutes of Health (NIH) convened its own independent board, it found, says Bell, that "nearly every paper Darsee produced was fabricated."

• At the University of Pittsburgh, Dr. Stephen Breuning pleaded guilty before a federal judge to charges of faking data on all his government-funded research projects. As the author of twenty-four of the seventy major papers published between 1979 and 1983 on severe mental retardation in children, he advocated the use of stimulants, which since has turned out to have disastrous medical results.

• At the University of Michigan's Institute of Gerontology, nationally renowned researcher Marion Perlmutter was found guilty of taking credit for another's work. In a legal suit that cost U of M nearly $1 million in damages, the jury found that administrators "grossly mishandled" the case and that Director Richard Adelman illegally threatened to fire the researcher whose work had been stolen if she dared to file charges. Significantly, it was noted during the trial that Adelman was worried about jeopardizing the institute's $6.1 million in federal funding.

• David Baltimore, the Nobel Prize-winning president of Rockefeller University, resigned over the furor caused by his indirect involvement in a case of fraudulent genetic research. He insisted, long after what many called "compelling evidence" to the contrary had come to light, that co-author Thereza Imanishi-Kari had not faked the experiments described in a paper on immunology they published with four others. This case, which still sharply divides the scientific community, was not just an academic dispute—a half-dozen congressional committees and federal agencies, including the CIA, intervened in what quickly degenerated into a politicized investigation with reckless charges on all sides.

Lately, there have been a number of other cases of faculty misconduct at the nation's leading research schools and a number of other published papers on everything from the wrinkle-reducing properties of Retin-A to cold fusion theories that have turned out to be unsubstantiated. But do they constitute a nationwide "crisis of scientific integrity"? Those who believe that corruption goes far deeper than what has been acknowledged publicly certainly have considerable circumstantial evidence in the form of certain disturbing new trends in big science.

First among these trends is that blind peer review and replication of experiments—essential safeguards of scientific integrity—are no longer strictly followed and are sometimes altogether bypassed.[40] As federal funding has allowed them to establish their own quasi-independent centers of research, many scientists deliberately have distanced themselves from the universities with which they are associated and, indeed, from *any* external authority. It is perhaps only natural that, over time, some also have become less and less accountable to the demanding procedures and ethical standards within their own disciplines.

Second, scientists have become reluctant to second-guess one another's research. This is not just a matter of professional courtesy or fear that someone's reputation may be damaged by false allegations; to challenge a colleague's findings these days jeopardizes federal funding for everyone working on the same project or at the same institution.

Third, whistleblowers are considered at best troublemakers and at worst Judases. Despite recently enacted federal protections, their careers are still at risk when they report scientific misconduct. This is especially true for graduate students and untenured, junior-level professors who, since they spend most of their time in the lab assisting in experiments, are in the best position to observe any transgressions.

Fourth, since it is routine for scientists to "co-sign" experiments they did not conduct and "co-author" papers they did not write, they often have very obvious reasons for turning a blind eye to possible misconduct. While they may not necessarily fear being named as an "accessory," they want at all costs to avoid being linked even indirectly to any "crime." If that means that the perpetrator goes undetected and false data go unchallenged, it's just too bad.

Fifth, in case after case, authorities have dragged their feet when it comes to examining possible misconduct. An allegation is first investigated in a closed-door session by an internal review board. (Precious few allegations ever make it to the second stage, which is an independent investigation.) Most members of internal review boards strive to be as objective as possible, but they are still very uncomfortable with their task. Others secretly wish they could sweep everything under the rug and get back to their own pursuits. Still others harbor resentments related to departmental feuds or personal jealousies or hold sharp differences of opinion about theories and procedures involved in the case. Whatever the disposition of internal review boards, there is great potential for conflicts of interest. (This is not a warning against internal review boards or self-regulation, but against the ineffectual methods scientists and college and universities have chosen to practice.)

Sixth, there is a growing tendency in such cases to rely more on the "intent" of the researcher being investigated than on his actions. This allows review boards to exonerate almost any defendant, no matter how damning the evidence, if he can convince them that what he did was merely "an error in judgment" or the result of sloppy record-keeping.

Finally, there are just too many inconsistent standards of what constitutes proof of misconduct. The eleven different federal agencies that supply the grants that are the mainstay of the research done by colleges and universities have been unable to agree on a single, uniform set of rules. While various scientific commissions and academic organizations have had more success in adopting some general theoretical guidelines, many members of the scientific community regularly disregard them when faced with an actual case in which popular Professor X, a "giant" in his field and the university's "biggest grant-getter," is accused of misconduct.[41]

There is a great deal of further evidence suggesting that many scientists are deeply worried about the health of their profession. A majority of the respondents to a recent poll conducted by the American Association for the Advancement of Science believes that colleges and universities are lax in investigating misconduct. And in another major university poll, 32 percent of the scientists who responded said that they suspected a colleague of faking data. (More than half of them also admitted that they did not report it or even attempt to verify their suspicions.)[42]

Still, circumstantial evidence is just that—circumstantial. Harvard microbiologist and best-selling textbook author Bernard Davis is skeptical of the claim that there is a widespread crisis in academic science. He argues that it has largely been manufactured by politicians like Rep. John Dingell (D-MI), who has used his powerful position as chairman of the House Subcommittee on Oversight and Investigations to extend his own personal ambitions as well as the scope of government control. (Dingell shoots back that he thinks the crisis is real and spreading, that federal supervision of academic science has been grossly inadequate, and that it is high time that somebody—namely he and others in government—step in.) Somewhere in between are individuals like *Christian Science Monitor* science editor Robert C. Cowen, who reflects that science is a "very human, very career-oriented, temptation-ridden pursuit" just like any other, and, though it may not be afflicted by crisis or require a new cadre of "science police," it has some very real ethical problems that must be addressed by scientists themselves.[43]

Scientists are under enormous pressure to publish new research in order to gain tenure, professional acclaim, and, even more important, federal grants. They cannot otherwise justify their flight from undergraduate teaching, or conduct costly high tech research, or pay for their multimillion-dollar labs and facilities. The incentives to "cut corners" are strong, as are the incentives to let politics determine the content and outcome of their research.

Numerous cases in the last fifty years have demonstrated that many politicians and bureaucrats are only willing to pay for research if they can dictate the results. And if the "big money" is currently in AIDS, global warming, and acid rain, then those are the issues on which many scientists will concentrate. If sensational findings are required in order to revive waning public interest or to ensure that next year's budget is secure, then many scientists will supply them, even if premature or misleading. If specific conclusions are needed to suit whoever is in charge at the Department of Health and Human Services or the National Science Foundation or some other agency, then many scientists will cooperate, even if data must be doctored or rewritten. If Congress is willing to sign off on more mammoth pork barrel projects like the Supercollider, the Hubble Telescope, and the Human Genome Project, many scientists will be willing to endorse them and work on them, even if those projects are wasteful, or soon will become obsolete, or will divert badly needed funds from more useful but less politically attractive kinds of research.

University of Dayton Professor Joseph P. Martino argues as much in *Science Funding: Politics and the Pork Barrel*. Scientists, he maintains, refuse to admit that more money for big science invariably squeezes out small-scale and risky research and breeds favoritism, red tape, and high overhead costs. Martino insists, moreover, that the problems in big science are inherent in government funding and that "they cannot be overcome by 'vigilance' or 'congressional oversight'. . . . Nor will they be corrected by 'turning the rascals out.' " They will endure "so long as government supports research as a mission," rather than as a needed service for which it contracts.[44]

Meanwhile, two totally new kinds of pressures are bearing down upon all science. The first is financial: The decades of massive federal funding are over. The end of the Cold War and domestic budget cuts have left the federal agencies that support research and development with far less money to give away to far fewer schools. Nearly $200 million in congressional earmarks for science research was awarded in 1992-93, but the $4 trillion–plus federal debt began forcing Congress to cut them in 1993-94. These earmarks are likely to rise again, but they can't be counted on as a steady source of income. And within their own financially strapped institutions, college and university scientists are facing new challenges to their highly prized autonomy as well as "mounting pressures to justify every dollar spent on research and squeeze every research nickel for its full value."[45]

The second new pressure is increasing government intervention. Many Washington politicians and bureaucrats advocate federal control not only over cases of scientific misconduct but over the way all academic science is conducted. Several federal agencies have established "watchdog" groups like the National Institutes of Health's Office of Scientific Integrity, which has a large full-time staff of investigators and broad powers to conduct all sorts of fishing expeditions into college and university affairs. Representative Dingell is also pressing for more intense congressional scrutiny of how federal funds are awarded, spent, and accounted for and for new restrictions on the relationship between industry and science. Since a considerable number of college and university research faculty have major and sometimes clandestine financial relationships with commercial firms marketing products they have patented, produced, or endorsed, he is likely to gain a great deal of support for those restrictions. But Bernard Davis warns that micromanaging the laboratory and hounding scientists will not cure what ails science; it only will lead to a new-style Inquisition.

OVERHEAD

Then there is the overhead corruption in higher education. Several years ago Paul Biddle, a navy auditor, stumbled across the fact that Stanford University was overcharging the government for research that did not cost as much as was reported, for dubious costs of administering that research, and for costs that had nothing at all to do with research. His own department and the university fought long and hard to suppress his report, but eventually it was made public, and the sensation-hungry media pounced on it as a "new and startling discovery." But it was not new at all; almost any junior-level college or university administrator could have told you about this "con" years ago, for it has hardly been a secret, and it has hardly been limited to Stanford.

Hundreds of colleges and universities have taken full advantage of the fact that, until recently, the government did not set a strict limit on overhead charges or require standardized accounting procedures or regular reports on how research funds were spent. Martin Anderson explains: "Essentially the government accepted whatever amount the universities claimed as research overhead charges. The feeling seemed to be that if you can't trust Yale and Berkeley and MIT, whom can you trust?"[46] (Since it was awarding $9-$11 billion a year on university research in the early 1990s, more than $2.5 billion of which was for overhead, this amounted to *a lot* of trust.)[47]

What are overhead costs? They are anything that a school claims is indirectly connected to research: salaries of nonresearch "support staff," from the secretary who types purchase orders and the janitor who cleans the offices to the maintenance man who mows the lawn and the head mechanic at the motor pool; physical facilities, including staff residences; depreciation on facilities and equipment; interest on construction or other loans; heat, water, electricity, and other utilities; office equipment like furniture, artwork, telephones, copy and fax machines; newsletters, brochures, and books; postage; liability and malpractice insurance; conference fees and travel; consulting fees; meals and "entertainment," and more. Dwight Purdy, a professor of English at the University of Minnesota-Morris, explains how overhead commonly can take precedence over academic concerns:

> For the three years in which I served on the All-University Committee on Research, the dominant issue was indirect cost recovery—who should get how much back from funding agencies for the cost of electricity, office space, etc. incurred in doing a research project. Would the department get the money? The researcher? Or would it go to the president to distribute throughout the institution? . . . The sum could amount in any given year to well over a million dollars. The issue consumed the medical and scientific researchers who dominated the committee.[48]

How are overhead costs billed? In an article in *The New Republic* called "Schools for Scandal," Brian Hecht notes that until recently a college or university actually "negotiated" its overhead rate with federal agencies: "If a university receives, say, $11 million in direct research grants, it will first subtract a standard amount (say $1 million) for certain equipment and subcontracts to obtain the 'modified direct costs.' If the school then determines that $5 million is needed for overhead costs, its indirect cost rate will be 50 percent. That percentage is then tacked on to all federal grants for the negotiated amount of time. . . ."[49] Thus, for every dollar spent on federally funded university research, says the General Accounting Office (GAO), the government has been paying an average of about 50 cents more to cover its share of overhead.

Let's indulge in another theoretical example to illustrate how overhead billing works: Suppose a college receives a four-year, $4 million grant for chemistry lab research. For the first three years, the grant pays for research as well as the costs of administration and the depreciation of facilities. But, quite typically, the college will claim so many overhead costs that during the fourth year all remaining funds will be redirected to administration, and the chemistry department will get none. The purpose for which the grant exists is what is deemed expendable.

At Stanford University, the second richest school in America, the overhead rate for federal grants in the early 1990s was 74 *percent,* which meant that for every $100,000 taxpayers were paying to support research, they were shelling out an additional $74,000 to cover overhead costs.[50] Stanford became so expert at this game that it even held seminars for administrators from other universities to teach them "how to get the very last dollar in their indirect costs."[51] It billed the government for a whopping $550 million in overhead costs in the 1980s, some $231 million of which auditors now suspect was overcharged.[52]

On what kind of indirect "research expenses" did it spend much of this money? Among other items, there was $184,000 toward the depreciation of a 72-foot yacht and athletic equipment, $186,000 to operate the Stanford Shopping Center, $6,000 for the renovation of President Donald Kennedy's closets, a $4,000 wedding reception, $2,000 a month for flowers, $7,000 for bed linens, $1,000 a month for charges at a French laundry, and various sums for an antique fruitwood commode, a brass bed, refinishing a piano, "edible art," and for maintaining two other administrators' residences.[53] When challenged about these expenses, the university argued that they were always allowed in the past, and it wasn't fair for the government to "change the rules." When told that it must reduce its overall overhead rate, it agreed to go as low as 72 percent, but no more; after all, Harvard Medical School was charging the federal government *88–96 percent* and was angling for an increase to *104 percent!*[54]

Stanford, Harvard Medical School, MIT, and the University of California-Berkeley were the subject of one General Accounting Office report in the early 1990s that found definite proof of $29 million in excess overhead charges.[55] Another inquiry by the Defense Contract Audit Agency turned up $390 million in ineligible claims by twenty-two colleges and universities.[56] Some of the indirect "research expenses" recently ruled ineligible, or that various institutions have volunteered to retract, presumably in order to avoid full-scale investigations, include:[57]

- $20,000 at the California Institute of Technology for a trustee meeting at a Palm Springs resort (about $8,500 for a dinner party including meals, cigars, parking, musicians, and dancing);
- $746,031 at Dartmouth College (including $20,490 for President James Freedman's chauffeur, $46,500 for his parties, $60,393 for expenses "connected to laying off employees," and thousands of dollars in legal fees in a case against the *Dartmouth Review*);
- $2,628 at the University of California for an employee wedding reception (until challenged by auditors, UC also

was spending thousands of taxpayer dollars on first-class airfare, luxury hotels in close proximity to campus, and other "perks" for administrators);

- $4,894,845 at Rutgers University for a wide variety of ineligible expenses;
- $3,112,150 at the University of Southern California;
- $160,000 at Carnegie Mellon University for commencement and $7,000 for a ski trip;
- $25,000 at Cornell University in chartered plane flights for President Frank Rhodes, $6,000 in wine, $1,000 in Steuben wine glasses, and dinner at Mad Marvin's Seafood;
- $32,537 at the University of Texas, including the cost of a dozen engraved crystal decanters from Nieman Marcus;
- thousands of dollars at the University of Pittsburgh, including the cost of former President Wesley Posvar's golf club membership, opera tickets, liquor supplies, mobile phone, Christmas cards, and trips abroad (to Tokyo, Grand Cayman Island, and Dublin);
- $7,406 at Johns Hopkins University for a farewell dinner for the outgoing president, Steven Muller, and $23,480 for thirty other catered affairs;
- $731,000 at MIT (including $2,301 spent at a jewelry store, a $4,655 contribution to the Museum of Fine Arts, $951.46 for the deputy treasurer's trip to Barbados, the president's dues at the Cosmos Club and his personal chef's salary, and an even bigger item—49 percent of the university's library costs);
- $6 million at the University of Michigan in ineligible "research" expenses (the university contested the total, but did admit applying for reimbursement for, among other items, a Christmas tree for President James Duderstadt, schoolwide Martin Luther King Day festivities, and Rose Bowl travel expenses for a university administrator and his wife).

The chronicle of extravagance and impropriety goes on and on; there have been, for example, similar cases at the University of Chicago ($348,000), Duke University ($906,245), Emory University ($672,557), the University of Hawaii ($500,000), and Washington University ($985,000).[58] Ironically, while chancellor of the University of Wisconsin, Health and Human Services Secretary Donna Shalala attempted to bill HHS and other agencies for nearly $11 million in overhead charges that ended up being disallowed or withdrawn.[59] Another new federal agency head, National Endowment for the Humanities Chairman Sheldon Hackney, managed, as president of the University of Pennsylvania, to rack up thousands of dollars in ineligible expenditures for personal household expenses, alumni mailings, hotel rooms for football games, and videos defending rising tuitions. He even billed the government for "research expenses" of $137,980 that in reality turned out to be for salaries and fringe benefits of employees working in alumni relations.[60]

Since scandals like these have become public, the government has decided to adopt an arbitrary overhead rate for administrative costs of no more than 26 percent. It has yet to implement this policy fully, and, as it only applies to administrative costs (which cover only four of seven overhead categories), it will not completely address the problem of abuse. It will, however, mean a devastating loss of revenue for big research universities that for years have been negotiating highly inflated overhead rates instead of billing for reimbursement of actual expenses.[61] States will lose, too, for they often commandeer "excess" overhead generated by colleges and universities for their own uses. In 1992, North Carolina Governor James G. Martin proposed keeping a record sum—$16.8 million—rather than let it go to the schools themselves or back to the federal government. Traditionally, reports the *Chronicle of Higher Education,* his state had retained about *30 percent* of all research overhead revenues, but tough economic times led him to call that year for a "50-50 split."[62]

And colleges and universities must now look forward to another consequence far worse than the loss of revenue; they have virtually guaranteed more federal intervention in higher education. Again, Representative Dingell is leading the bureaucratic charge. He has pledged to instigate blanket investigations and audits of all nonprofit organizations, but especially of all colleges and universities, and he warns that stiff penalties will be levied for any refusal to cooperate. The new cost accounting procedures and regulations Dingell has in mind will be extremely expensive and restrictive, but in all likelihood will be imposed anyway because past abuse has left Congress in a vengeful mood.

There is an important postscript to this story of corruption. Many student government leaders have followed educators' lead by misspending the student fees placed in their trust in precisely the same way that educators have misspent research and overhead funds on limousine rentals, trips abroad, lavish parties, huge restaurant bills, unspecified "entertainment," and other dubious expenses. They have a lot of money to play with, too; annual revenues from student fees at large schools like the University of Florida, for example, total $4 million.[63] At a single City University of New York campus in 1991, the student government managed to squander its budget of $345,000 in just six months. The annual salaries the officers voted to pay each other were incredible. One part-time executive assistant, the twin sister of the student senate chairman, received $26,000. But even after this news was made public, the popular, free-spending chairman, Jean La Marre, was reelected while the university stood idly by.[64] Until recently, when certain minimal reforms were passed as the result of prior abuse, the University of Iowa student government could spend $800,000 a year in student fees without any supervision by school authorities. But this was not an unusual case. Student governments on the overwhelming majority of campuses have free rein to spend funds on whatever they see fit.

OTHER FINANCIAL
———— CORRUPTION ————

In 1989, the U.S. Department of Justice began an investigation of twenty-three schools—Brown University, Bryn Mawr College, Dartmouth College, Columbia University, Harvard University, the University of Massachusetts-Amherst, Princeton University, Wellesley College, Yale University, and the University of Pennsylvania among them—on charges of illegal price-fixing and collusion. MIT was found guilty, and eight others were compelled to sign pledges to halt their "overlap" activities regarding financial aid and admissions. A federal judge recently ordered a new trial (a move in MIT's favor), so the Justice Department, under a new administration, dropped the case. Yet these institutions had been meeting regularly for over three decades to compare notes on aid packages offered to specific students. Says Thomas Sowell in *Inside American Education:*

> The lists of students [were] compiled before the annual meetings and officials from various colleges [had] decided how much money could be extracted from each individual, given parental income, bank account balance, home equity, and other financial factors. Where their estimates differed, these differences were reconciled in the meetings and the student then received so-called "financial aid" offers so coordinated that the net cost of going to one college in the cartel would be the same as the net cost of going to another.[65]

Sowell notes critically that most cartels and monopolies set artificially high list prices and then offer varying "discounts"—in academe, "this list price is called 'tuition' and the discount is called 'financial aid' "—but colleges and universities "carry this to the ultimate extreme of charging each individual customer what the traffic will bear."[66] The *Wall Street Journal* concludes that this amounted to a "price-fixing system that OPEC might envy."[67]

Some miscellaneous reports of other administrative corruption during the early 1990s are as follows:[68]

- Four Ohio community college presidents were indicted for "using public money for political and personal gain." Fourteen others waived their right to a trial and accepted the finding of the state prosecutor on charges of theft, records tampering, and concealing political contributions. The state claimed that a total of thirty-four presidents should be made to pay restitution.
- After several years of allegations of misconduct and a grand jury investigation, Wesley C. McClure resigned as president of Virginia State University in 1992. (The board of trustees had already voted to cancel his contract.) He is now president of Lane College in Tennessee.
- John Merritt resigned as president of the New Mexico Educational Assistance Foundation after an audit revealed $40,000 in misspent funds.
- The University of Texas was found guilty of using more than $11 million in student fees to pay for the construction of an off-campus microelectronics facility.
- Oklahoma State University President John R. Campbell resigned after it was discovered that he had diverted $35,000 to a prolottery political campaign.
- Former University of Colorado Chancellor Glendon F. Drake was pressured to quit because of numerous allegations of abusing university funds. (He left with $232,000 in severance pay.)
- Former Stanford University President Donald Kennedy resigned after the overhead scandal at his institution became public.
- The Stanford University bookstore also has been investigated for possible misuse of $300,000 in university funds.

(The same operation lost $2 million in the stock market in 1991 while its managers received $100,000 salaries.)

- A former Eastern Kentucky University administrator embezzled $170,000 between 1987 and 1992.
- Former University of South Carolina President James B. Holderman admitted accepting $25,000 illegally through the school's privately run foundation.
- Michigan Technological University's $40 million-plus investment company was revealed by a state audit to be rife with all kinds of corruption, from embezzlement to tax fraud.
- Mississippi College brought suit against its former president, W. Lewis Nobles, Jr., in 1993 for allegedly embezzling $3 million.
- Employees at Johnson C. Smith University were charged with stealing over a half million dollars in student aid funds between 1989 and 1991.
- A former New York University financial aid officer embezzled $1 million over the course of ten years by filling out financial aid forms for students who did not exist.
- Paul Quinn College in Texas was discovered to be secretly transferring endowment funds to general operating accounts. Its president was forced to resign.
- Central Michigan University made an illegal profit selling educational materials that, according to the terms of the federal grant involved, were intended to be distributed free.

"Double-dipping" is another increasingly common form of corruption on campus. One New York University professor kept her teaching position while taking on a $66,000-a-year, full-time job at the Department of Education in the 1980s. Unbeknownst to her government bosses, they were even picking up the tab for her travel expenses back and forth between Washington, D.C., and New York. Another jet-setting professor made over $146,000 a year teaching one course on Mondays and Wednesdays at the University of North Carolina–Charlotte and two courses on Thursdays at the University of Minnesota–Twin Cities. He was even tenured—at both schools![69]

Some educators also abuse "matching gift" programs. These were established years ago by the private sector in order to make the charity of individual donors go further. The employer agrees to match every dollar an employee donates, up to a certain annual maximum. In a recent sample year at one major U.S. corporation, there were about eleven thousand matching gifts to over eight hundred colleges and universities. The employees' $2.2 million was matched by the corporation's $2.2 million. But now this corporation and others have discovered that they have been "ripped off." For years, they simply trusted the word of colleges and universities about the total number and dollar amount of matching gifts, requiring no proof of signed employee checks or stock transfers. That trust turned out to have been misplaced. A corporation executive, speaking on the condition of anonymity, reports that over an extended period of years one Ivy League university put in ineligible claims worth $300 million. (It did refund the total amount, but only after the discovery had come to light.)

An even more common scam is "fudging" the numbers in fund- raising campaigns:[70]

- During its nine-year, $300 million campaign, Wichita State University fund raisers were caught inflating totals and counting gifts improperly. The university subsequently abandoned the campaign in the early 1990s, even though it was not due to conclude until 1996, which meant that it also abandoned its commitment to donors who had already supported the campaign.
- During its $120 million campaign, Virginia Military Institute was found guilty of engaging in some of the same practices. In one instance, it counted at face value a $100,000 life insurance policy that named VMI as beneficiary, even though the alumnus who took out the policy

was in his twenties. It also counted at face value many similiar bequests from younger alumni.

- During its on-going $1.5 billion campaign, Yale University has been called to account for including four separate gifts of $20 million in its totals, since each was made prior to and was unconnected with the campaign.
- During its current $1.1 billion campaign, Stanford University has made a number of questionable decisions, including one to count at face value a charitable trust of a ten-year-old, despite the fact that the trust will not be realized until his death.
- During its $100 million campaign, the University of Vermont has even been counting state and federal grants as "donations."

It comes as no surprise that the IRS has recently audited about a dozen colleges and universities, including Michigan State University, Princeton University, the University of Michigan, the University of Nebraska, and Vanderbilt University. Improprieties are easy to commit because for years there have been no uniform accounting standards for colleges and universities, and they have had considerable leeway in portraying their financial conditions.[71] Schools also have been lax in requiring proof from donors about the actual value of noncash gifts and bequests involving fine art and real estate, and many routinely count gifts that come in before or after a campaign to help boost overall totals. Since the expenses are usually split between the general operating budget, the endowment, and restricted accounts, they can even camouflage what it truly costs them to conduct a major campaign. Some go one step further, hiding the fact from donors that they have hired professional fund raisers and giving the impression that they are raising funds on their own. As for the fund raisers, whether "hired guns" or school employees, they are under such tremendous pressure to raise enormous sums that they are often tempted to violate the spirit if not the letter of the law when it comes to reporting on their progress.

Regarding the fiscal health of colleges and universities, Gordon C. Winston, a professor of economics and former provost at Williams College in Massachusetts, comments that there is no end to the sleight-of-hand tricks that they will employ: "The 'budget deficits' we tell our communities and our alumni and the press about—the deficits that are assumed to show how hard times are getting to be, even for elite colleges and universities— are not at all what they seem to be." Though, as the first chapter in this volume suggests, there is evidence that the current crisis is real enough, he explains why we must still be wary about reported deficits:

> They *seem*, reasonably, to describe the economic fortunes of a college for the year: A deficit seems to show that the college spent more than it took in, and a surplus seems to show the opposite. That's what you, I, and the press are led to believe. That's the way our family budgets and our checkbooks work. But, in fact, the "budget" for a college includes only a certain part—about two-thirds—of the total economic activity of a school. So whether that part shows a deficit or a surplus is arbitrary: Money is regularly "transferred"—moved in or out of the budget, making it show red ink or black ink—at will, with no relation to how the college actually performed economically.
>
> A college can, and often does, show a big budget deficit at the same time that a whole lot of savings are being generated to increase its wealth (or vice versa). Some colleges (like Swarthmore and Kalamazoo, and Harvard and MIT for awhile) routinely move dollars around after the fact so they'll always show they've operated with a balanced budget.[72]

The same applies, says Professor Winston, to potentially embarrassing surpluses. He recalls the scandal in 1973 when research done by two Cornell University accounting professors led to a CBS report and a *Wall Street Journal* feature on page one headlined: "Ten Eastern Colleges Accused of Crying Wolf in Reporting Deficits." Incredibly, MIT had a $100 million surplus, but reported a deficit of $5 million; Princeton University saved $151 million instead of losing $1.5 million; and Harvard University claimed it lost $1.4 million when it had gained $314 million.[73] The universities complained that these totals weren't adjusted for inflation, but they did not deny them.

Professor Winston also notes that the public would be angry to learn about the common practice of "interest arbitrage":

> It works like this: state and federal legislators, who apparently want to support elite higher education with taxpayers' dollars without making that fact too apparent to their constituents, have made it possible for colleges like ours to sell tax-exempt bonds, just as if we were the government. Because the people buying our bonds don't have to pay tax on the interest they earn, they're willing to let us pay them a lower interest rate. So the college pays less to borrow money. But the flip side of that arrangement is that the state takes in less taxes. Or putting it the right way around, the taxpayers are paying part of our interest bill on the money we borrow. . . . We borrow, say, at a 5 percent interest rate when the market rate is 10 percent, and the taxpayer and the Commonwealth pay the rest.[74]

But that is not all arbitrage means. Winston continues:

> It describes making money on price differences— simultaneously buying and selling the same thing and doing nothing else in the process. What makes us guilty of interest arbitrage is that wealthy colleges simultaneously loan money . . . to some people and borrow from others, dollar for dollar. But—and here's the magic of arbitrage—each dollar we lend pays us more interest than we pay out on the dollar we borrow. If we earn 10 percent on our assets and pay 5 percent on our borrowing, each dollar of simul-

taneous lending-and-borrowing earns us a nickel a year of arbitrage profits; $20 million of lending-and-borrowing earns us $1 million in arbitrage income each year. And that $1 million of profit is paid for by the taxpayers, available to us because we're allowed to borrow tax-free.[75]

All told, colleges and universities are issuing over *$7 billion* a year in tax-free bonds. As the old saying goes, "What a racket!"[76]

FINANCIAL STEWARDSHIP

Most people share a mental picture of colleges and universities as dedicated to "the life of the mind," dwelling in an idealistic realm far removed from the venal world of commerce. They probably would be stunned to discover that many colleges and universities not only are big businesses in themselves but that they are such wealthy, powerful investors that, in another age, they would have been referred to as "robber barons." They are not passive investors either; they take an active role in the market. One college fund to which Clarkson University, Stanford University, and Emory University belong owns a string of industrial parks and luxury apartment complexes, a Saks Fifth Avenue store in downtown San Francisco, and an office building in Washington, D.C.[77] Others buy shopping malls and factories and speculate in the bond market. None of these examples of ownership is unethical—colleges and universities should have the the right to invest their funds just as other businesses. But how good are they at acting like other businesses?

For the last thirty years, it is true that many colleges and universities have been investing their own wealth for a "total return."[78] After all, although nonprofit institutions, they do have resources running into the millions and even billions of dollars. When it comes to financial management, however, they are among the worst-run institutions in the country. Often, this is the result of federal and state aid, a disproportionate amount of many institutions' budgets that leads to bureaucratization and to all kinds of faculty, staff, and facility expansion that can't be reversed once the original funds are reduced or exhausted.

As of 1990, Harvard University had assets valued at $5.9 billion. Stanford University, the University of Michigan, and Yale University had assets ranging from $3.5 billion to $3.8 billion. Princeton University and Columbia University were worth $2.7 billion each.[79] Yet lately, nearly every one has over-spent (or at least claimed to have overspent) its budget by millions of dollars, deferred millions of dollars more in maintenance, and mismanaged its huge portfolio. Harvard University, which pays at least one of its many money managers a cool $1 million a year, only made a 1.1 percent return on its investments in 1991.[80] It attributed this, of course, to lingering consequences of the stock market crash and bad real estate investments in the 1980s, but this excuse is not altogether convincing. Imagine a *multibillion-dollar* corporation that made only a *1.1 percent* return—stockholders would be pounding down the door demanding an explanation and/or dumping their stock as fast as they could. But Harvard is brazenly asking its loyal patrons in government as well as the private sector to give it billions more dollars. Its mediocre finan-cial stewardship is considered irrelevant to its pressing future needs. Harvard fund raisers typically make the pitch to donors: "Your money is needed to ensure that we offer the best education to deserving students." They do not want to tell them what a miserable job they've done with the $5.9 billion in assets they already have.

But Harvard isn't the only big institution guilty of mediocre financial stewardship; others have earned low returns year after year. Aetna Capital Management Company's recent report on small colleges noted that their record has been unimpressive, too. The average endowment earnings for all of higher education stood at 7.2 percent in 1991, two points below Standard and Poor's average index of stocks.[81] Even more revealing is the case of Ohio State University, which in 1990 gave $5 million of its $400 million endowment to a group of business students to invest and manage as a two-year class project; the students grossed a 50 percent return.[82] Looking at their annual record of performance, these "kids" outperformed all six of their university's professional money managers, and, overall, they did three-and-a-half times better than the average college or university and twenty-three times better than Harvard.

"Thirty years ago," admits S. Frederick Starr, president of Oberlin College, "nearly all of the top 20 or 30 private institutions covered a third of their budgets from the return on their endowments. After a generation of unrestrained growth in programs scarcely one can cover more than a fifth of its budget from this source today. Fifteen percent is more typical, whether at Harvard University or Oberlin College."[83] As of 1992, Aetna also reported that at least 40 percent of small colleges were spending *all* of their investment income every year without putting any back into the endowment, and of these some still were operating in the red. John Synodinos, president of Lebanon Valley College, says, "Faced with growing deficits, some institutions are spending at a rate they clearly can't sustain."[84] The vast majority don't have the luxury of squandering even small sums, for, as he points out, fewer than one in ten have endowments of as much as $25 million. (This may sound like a lot of money, but it takes roughly $16 million to accumulate enough interest just to pay for the annual utilities bill at a small campus.) For these institutions, the situation is desperate. They have negligible reserves and are perpetually in debt. They also face increasing competition for students and donors as well as for a dwindling pool of federal and state aid. If they have courageous leaders, astute money managers, a coherent and feasible plan for cost reduction, and a strong sense of direction . . . well, if they had these things, they would not be so desperate.

The truth is that most colleges and universities, whether heavily or modestly endowed, whether public or private, have responded to the current financial crisis mainly by pleading for more money from the government—indulging the very addiction that has gotten them into so much trouble in the first place.

Only reluctantly have they chosen to retrench, and invariably they have taken the easiest ways out with hiring freezes, layoffs of staff and untenured professors, early retirement bonuses, fewer courses and services, and deferred maintenance.

They have also tried to attract students using every device from huge tuition increases to huge tuition discounts and a whole truckload of trendy new programs and gimmicks. The effect has been, claims Arthur Levine, executive editor of *Change* magazine, "to randomize mediocrity. By the luck of the draw, and without planning, excellent programs were robbed of the resources they needed to maintain quality, and weak programs were supported at higher levels than they deserved." He goes on to argue that retaining quality too often has been "defined as synonymous with keeping all existing programs and staff," while preserving access has "remained a rhetorical goal—a cause for handwringing and lofty words. . . . Maintaining morale has been a higher priority. It has generally meant inconveniencing faculty, and often staff, as little as possible. Students have seldom been part of the equation, unless major demonstrations were antici- pated."[85] Levine concludes with this excellent analogy:

> Imagine if this same approach were taken with a foundering ship. The captain would announce the highest priority as saving the crew, though caring statements would be made about the passengers as the staff boarded the lifeboats. The captain would state that the next goal would be to maintain all services—bingo through the midnight buffet—on schedule and uninterrupted. The following priority would be to repair the ship. And finally, if time and resources permitted, every human effort would then be made to rescue the passengers![86]

Chapter 7

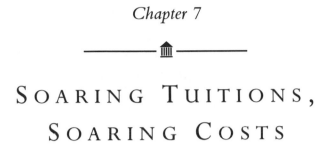

SOARING TUITIONS,
SOARING COSTS

—————CRISIS AND PROTEST—————

At Brown University, a normally placid Ivy League campus, things were getting tense for the administration. Hundreds of students occupied a campus building and were not about to move until their demands were met. This was not a scene from the sixties with students angrily protesting the draft, U.S. involvement in Vietnam, nuclear power, or some other Cause with a capital "C." It was 1992, and the students were up in arms over rising college costs—$23,000 at Brown that year.[1] They insisted that the university (1) abandon all considerations of students' ability to pay in awarding financial aid and (2) provide millions of dollars more in additional aid.

From coast to coast, thousands of students have staged protests with exactly the same demands. Nervous educators (who, for once, are not in a position to cave in and grant concessions, because of declining government aid and their own fiscal mismanagement) are predicting worse to come. Already, half of all college students are not completing their degrees—and, since one of the most common reasons cited for

165

dropping out is high college costs, "worse" means disaster for higher education.

During the 1970s, tuitions and fees began to rise steadily, but in the 1980s, increases consistently were in double digits—every single year.[2] From 1980 to 1990, they rose, on average, *141 percent*.[3] As of 1992–93, average public tuitions and fees were $2,315, and total costs of attendance (including room, board, and a few incidentals) amounted to $8,000 a year. Average private tuitions stood at $10,500 and total costs at $17,000 a year. More than one hundred schools were charging over $15,000 just in tuition and fees. The top contestants for the 1992–93 Most Exorbitant Tuition and Fees Award were: Bennington College (VT), $19,780; Tufts University (MA), $18,344; Reed College (OR), $18,190; and Tulane University (LA), $18,185.[4] The disturbing fact is that in recent years tuition, in addition to other college costs, has grown nearly three times as fast as inflation and twice as fast as the general economy. *Harvard Magazine* laments that unless the states and the federal government (i.e., the taxpayers) shell out more financial aid "many deserving students" will be robbed of the opportunity to receive a college education.[5] (This is more than a little hard to swallow coming from Harvard, where the total cost of attending for four years is pushing $100,000.)

Some like Robert D. Peck, president of Phillips University, claim that parents and students actually welcome high tuition and fees; if they are too low, he says, "they'll think you are a low-quality institution and they won't come." Common among educators, this elitist presumption explains why so many parents and students have lost confidence in academe. It is true that when Mount Holyoke College lowered its tuitions recently, enrollments declined sharply, and when Swarthmore College rather arbitrarily decided to leap into the Ivy League price range, enrollments went up 35 percent in one year.[6] But the crucial factor that remains undiscussed is financial aid—when it fails to keep up with or at least cushion the blow of tuition increases, enrollments are adversely affected. Huston-Tillotson College in

Texas, for example, recently tried economizing on financial aid and lost 22 percent of its enrollment. Even schools like Cornell University admit that their need–blind admissions policy is necessary to keep applications rolling in.[7]

The Economist says of rising tuitions that hundreds of nonelite as well as elite institutions have degenerated "into finishing schools for the rich."[8] A student who does not qualify as rich can still attend, of course, but, unless he is lucky enough to receive a "full ride," his diploma will plunge him deeply into debt before he even has had a chance to land a job or earn his first paycheck. For him, says Aims McGuiness of the Education Commission of the States, "College education is no longer a four-year expense, but a lifetime mortgage."[9]

————— LESS FOR MORE —————

Despite spending vastly more, students are not getting more for their money. When it comes to classroom instruction, they are increasingly processed in a kind of cattle car approach. The University of Colorado, for example, conducts a marketing class with over six hundred students; the University of Illinois has a political science class crammed with over one thousand students.[10] Michigan State University teaches one required course for thousands of students with a videotape instead of live professors (see Chapter 8).

Hundreds of schools have slashed the number of courses they offer, creating another impossible situation; the University of Wisconsin, for example, has been known to close courses in the *first hour of registration*—even for seniors in their field of concentration.[11] Recently at the University of Texas, nearly *one thousand* students were turned away from a required English course.[12] At Harvard University, says Charles J. Sykes in *Profscam*, the course catalogue lists courses not being offered in a given year in brackets. So many courses in history were bracketed recently that students began wearing T-shirts that read simply: "[History]."

He adds that it takes five-and-a-half years for the average student to get a bachelor's degree at many schools these days.[13] In the 1980s, the state of Colorado conducted an investigation which revealed that only 19 percent of all college students within the state were graduating within four years. After a hugely expensive five-year reform effort, the rate now has been raised to about 44 percent—which legislators feel is high enough to brag about.[14] A recent study tracking the education of over half a million students at three hundred institutions documented that only about 50 percent earned a bachelor's degree within six years. Reginald Wilson, a senior scholar at the American Council on Education, bluntly says that this "is a condemnation of higher education. If we were running an automobile plant, we would be out of business."[15]

WHO PAYS?

No one would deny that rising tuition and fees are becoming a huge financial burden, or that delays lead students to become, as the *Chronicle of Higher Education* puts it, "increasingly frustrated because every additional year they spend in college increases the amount of debt they incur."[16] But the truth is that what students and their parents pay doesn't begin to cover the true costs of a college education. Even after a 40 percent tuition increase, in the early 1990s, an in-state resident could attend California State University full-time for a year for $1,308 or, roughly, the cost of a high-end stereo system. (This same university, incidentally, claims it needs at least a $1 billion budget boost by the year 2001, mainly to help students afford the "skyrocketing costs of higher education." Obviously, this call for new aid is meant to help replace lost revenues, not just to assist individual students.)[17]

Claims vary about how much of the total institutional cost tuition and fees *do* cover, and, given the way colleges and universities keep juggling their accounts, it is no wonder. But most experts tend to agree that at private institutions they only cover one-half to two-thirds of actual costs and that at public institutions they cover far less—only about one-quarter to one-third.[18] In some cases, the figures are drastically lower; at the University of North Carolina, for example, state auditors have determined that in-state students pay as little as 11 percent of the total cost of their education.[19] Whatever the degree of subsidization, as Kent Halstead, director of Research Associates, notes, this is a phenomenal deal. "Where else," he says, "can you buy anything that provides such immediate direct benefits to you as an individual and pay less than [a fraction] of the cost?"[20]

The trouble is, as with all "phenomenal deals," you usually end up paying more than you think. In this case, the hidden costs are passed along to you as a taxpayer. The federal government and the states use public money—billions of dollars—to subsidize many private colleges and universities directly. By broadening financial need standards (and, in the case of Stafford Loans, abandoning them altogether) for federal student assistance, they have also freed up private institutions' own funds for financial aid, tuition discounts, and rebates. At Columbia University in the 1980s, less than half of the students were charged up front for full tuition; at Harvard University, the figure was less than one-third.[21] This is, to put it loosely, welfare for the wealthy.

At public colleges and universities, which roughly 80 percent of all students choose to attend, taxpayers also subsidize artificially low tuitions available to anyone, regardless of financial need. At Illinois State University during the early 1990s, students' average annual family income was $60,000, and 11 percent had incomes exceeding $100,000, but tuition and fees were only about $2,500.[22] At the University of California during the same period, more than 40 percent of all students had annual family incomes over $60,000, and 23 percent had incomes over $84,000, but tuition and fees were under $1,000 on all campuses. Daniel Ritchie, chancellor of the University of Denver, estimates that at least one-third of all students attending the nation's public colleges and universities have annual family incomes over $60,000. The *Chronicle of Higher Education*'s estimate is even higher; it claims that a more accurate figure is over 50 percent.[23] Ritchie also adds:

> The upper middle class and the wealthy benefit in two ways at public colleges. First, they pay the same tuition as their poorer classmates. Second, they benefit from an average state appropriation of $5,500 to cover the difference between their tuition payments and the true cost of their educations. The $5,500 is a taxpayer's "scholarship donation," sent in the form of a state appropriation directly to the college. In many states, a disproportionate share of this donation is collected from lower-income and minority citizens through regressive taxes.[24]

This is income redistribution on a scale that would have been appreciated in the Soviet Union. Nonetheless, many educators are ardent fans. W. Ann Reynolds, chancellor of the City University of New York, says, "I must disagree that the best way to finance public higher education is a 'high-tuition' policy," and she further argues that convincing legislators of the need to raise financial aid for all students is among her top goals.[25] (Ironically, she is under strong attack by her own faculty for not opposing recent tuition increases forced on CUNY by state budget cuts.) Darryl G. Greer, executive director of the New Jersey State College Governing Boards Association, says, "In my view, to finance institutions based on students' ability to pay will, in the long term, undercut the common good that distinguishes American public higher education."[26] Theirs is the prevailing attitude in higher education—that we should adopt a sort of "Robin Hood" policy in reverse: Rob the poor to subsidize the rich.

PRICE-FIXING, GOVERNMENT SUBSIDIZATION

Justifiably, parents and students are angry about rising college costs, but they often are all too ready to blame inflation, or the recession of the early 1990s, or other impersonal economic factors instead of the real culprits. Two of the worst are price-fixing and government subsidization. Regarding the first: The MIT court case that created so much notoriety in the early 1990s (see Chapter 6) made it obvious to many that dozens of the nation's most prestigious schools have been guilty of collusion when it comes to offering financial aid packages to specific students, but for years, says the *Wall Street Journal,* college and university leaders have been doing what "few businessmen would be bold or foolhardy enough to try"—divulging to each other sensitive information on tuition. For example, "Months before telling students or the public, Harvard told other Ivy League schools that its tuition would rise 5.8 percent in 1987-88. Princeton said 6.5 percent. With one exception, each school was planning tuition increases in a tight range between 5.8 and 7.5 percent." The one exception was Dartmouth College. One of its spokesmen boasted that it did not need to fall in line with the others: "We get eight applications for every one seat here. The demand is such that we could charge whatever we want."[27] But, of course, in these days of multiple applications, an eight-to-one ratio is nothing to brag about. Dartmouth's leaders may not admit it, but they know it is true; immediately after they got wind of their competitors' tuition increases, they revised their own to match. This is price-fixing, plain and simple, but the "Ivy cartel" as well as many other colleges and universities continue to get away with it by communicating through unofficial channels.

Many private colleges and universities also routinely "discount" full tuition by as much as $7,000 a year.[28] As noted earlier, in business these are called "kickbacks" because they make advertised prices meaningless. Meanwhile, inconsistent application of aid formulas can be just as harmful as consistent collusion. One student was told by Dartmouth College that her Pell Grant award would be $1,350, while Wesleyan University claimed it would be $2,200. Another student accepted by Boston University in 1993 was told she would have to pay $21,000 as her share of college costs, but Union College wanted to *give* her $21,000. "As never before," says the *Wall Street Journal,* "wide variations in financial aid awards are roiling the admissions process, leading to confused parents, anxious students and more haggling and negotiations with schools over terms and final prices."[29]

As for government subsidization, here is an impressive number: *$24 billion.* That's roughly how much federal and state student assistance was available in 1992. Of all available student assistance, the federal government provided 74 percent, the states 6 percent, and institutional and other sources 20 percent, for a grand total of $30.8 billion. At least 65 percent of all private college students and 38 percent of all public college students depend on it to pay for their schooling and living expenses.[30] The ostensible purpose of government subsidization has always been to make college affordable for all. It is a noble goal, but one fact remains indisputable: As state and federal awards increase, so do tuitions.

Former Secretary of Education William Bennett was one of the first to make this case, pointing out that the supposed beneficiaries of increased aid—low and middle income students—gain nothing as a result. In a recent Brookings Institution study, *Keeping College Affordable: Government and Educational Opportunity,* Michael S. McPherson and Morton Owen Shapiro attempted to argue that, to the contrary, federal aid causes more students to enroll and makes the "distribution of educational opportunity broader across colleges and the pattern of burden sharing fairer." They claim to find no evidence of the perverse effects of aid on college pricing, but they do not appear wholly convinced by their own arguments. On the subject of health care, for example, they concede that there *is* a direct connection between government subsidies and increasing fees. They also admit that it would be "remarkable if schools' decisions about pricing and the allocation of their own aid funds were entirely independent of federal student aid policy."[31] Alexander Astin, director of UCLA's Higher Education Research Institute, also opposes the Bennett thesis. His fifteen-year analysis, he says, shows that college costs have gone up because government aid has not kept pace with inflation. According to him, only more federal and state dollars will drive tuition down.[32]

But college costs have gone up because colleges have *chosen* to spend more in many areas than they did fifteen years ago, not because they are getting less money from the government—in fact, in most areas they are getting more than ever before, even after inflation. Higher education is one of the most generously subsidized enterprises in history, and yet tuitions have never once gone down as a result. Obviously, generous subsidies can result in lower increases in the short run, but they raise them in the long run. Speaking before Congress in 1979, Allan W. Ostar, executive director of the American Association of State Colleges and Universities, noted:

> The United States has had extensive experience with what amounted to an open-ended student assistance system. The post–World War II G.I. Bill paid for tuition and fees of up to $500 a year—higher than the tuition then charged at any college. As a result, many public, private, and profit-making institutions were able to increase their charges very substantially, with the federal taxpayer picking up the entire cost for millions of veterans.[33]

Veterans, of course, were not to blame for these increases; it was higher education that seized the opportunity to enrich itself at public expense.[34] In his testimony, Ostar also quoted a revealing statement from Kenneth Reeher, executive director of the Higher Education Assistance Agency of Pennsylvania:

> There are 25,000 BEOG [Basic Educational Opportunity Grant] recipients in our state-owned colleges, where costs are less than $2,800. So we have room to raise tuition and thus to capture more BEOG dollars. For every $100 that we raise tuition, Pennsylvania would capture an additional $1.25 million in BEOG. Currently, costs at the state-owned institutions are about $2,200; with the BEOG half-cost provision, we could raise tuition by $600, going up to

$2,800. So Pennsylvania has the potential of capturing $7.5 million more in BEOG funds.[35]

Ostar noted that officials from the State University of New York, the Vermont State Colleges Board of Trustees, and the Rhode Island Department of Education had on numerous occasions freely acknowledged that government aid influenced their schools' tuition charges and, furthermore, that these were always "sold" to students and parents with the understanding that government funding would "make up the difference."

Former Assistant Secretary of Education Chester E. Finn, Jr., summarized the whole issue of government subsidization's effect on tuitions when he wrote some years ago:

> . . . if Washington holds out the promise of large enough subsidies to a large enough group of students, colleges and universities will raise their prices to take maximum advantage of their consumers' enhanced ability to pay, and the federal government will shoulder the burden of some educational costs that would have been borne by others or perhaps not incurred at all. . . . The temptation to transfer educational costs to Washington would prove irresistible to many.[36]

——————OUT-OF-CONTROL SPENDING——————

A third culprit behind soaring tuitions—out-of-control spending—deserves special emphasis. Although it is a $170-billion-plus-a-year industry and serves more than 12 million "customers," higher education refuses to act as a responsible business or to live within its budget. According to James Buchanan and Nicos E. Devletoglou in *Academia in Anarchy: An Economic Diagnosis*, this is because: "(1) those who consume its product do not purchase it; (2) those who produce it do not sell it; and (3) those who finance it do not control it."[37]

Higher education is also nearly impossible to audit or evaluate.

Take a simple question like: "How much is the net revenue from college tuitions?" *Business Officer* magazine explains that there is no accurate answer to this question because financial aid is not deducted from tuition revenues, and there is no indicator of the real net revenue an institution is earning. Tuition and fees can increase dramatically, but because of discounting, scholarships, and other forms of aid a school offers, they may have little or no impact on revenues.[38] Nor is it possible to state, in conventional accounting terms, what constitutes a "cost" in the world of higher education. Thomas Sowell notes:

> Whatever colleges and universities choose to spend their money on is called a "cost." If they hire more administrators, or build more buildings to house them, or send the college president on more junkets, these are all additional costs. If they hire more research assistants for the faculty or more secretaries for the administrators, these are all costs. . . . When a college expands its range of expensive activities first, and then calls it "increased costs" later, when seeking more money from various sources, this tends not only to confuse the issue but to erode the concept of living within one's means.[39]

If a university executive starts to spend, say, as much as $879 a night for hotel rooms or $7,000 a year on limousines (as the president of the University of South Carolina did recently), these are categorized as increased costs—the implication is that they are a necessary part of continuing to do business in the same old way rather than a new, questionable extravagance. If a university chooses to allot $350,000 in travel and salary to a single professor (as, again, the University of South Carolina did, paying the widow of Egyptian President Anwar Sadat for teaching one class a week for three semesters) that figure, too, is merely an increased cost.[40] Imagine if a corporation ran up these types of expenditures and tried to pass them off as ordinary costs—would anyone, from the lowliest stockholder to the chairman of the board, buy it? Probably not. Yet, says one observer, higher education persists in utilizing a cost-plus pricing strategy: "Here's how much we would like to spend; let's set prices accordingly."

There are also many miscellaneous "cost factors" that can be cited for out-of-control spending. Here are some:

Cost Factor #1—Faculty and Administration. While complaining for decades about rising costs, educators certainly have not responded by scrimping and saving. Indeed, there has been plenty of money for their ranks. When Tulane University President Eamon Kelly explained in a recent letter to parents and students justifying a 12 percent tuition hike that higher education is a "labor intensive enterprise," he certainly wasn't kidding.[41] There is one faculty member for every sixteen college students in the United States.[42] While they generally do more than Mrs. Sadat, many professors have comparatively light workloads and paid teaching assistants to handle the drudgery of teaching and grading. Robert Iosue, former president of York College, says that what professors need is a "work audit." Three University of Georgia professors agree: "The faculty are teaching too little, devoting too much time to research, and earning salaries disproportionately high for their hours in the classroom." Although there is a lot of talk about potential reform, the cost of maintaining a faculty these days is steep, no matter how much its members teach. Hoover Institution Senior Fellow Martin Anderson estimates that "a full professor can easily cost a college or university $70,000 a year—at elite institutions more than $100,000."[43]

And the amount higher education spends on faculty is a drop in the bucket compared to what it spends on what William Bennett refers to as "the Blob," meaning the educational bureaucracy. Its numbers expand even when enrollment contracts. For example, while the student population in the state of Washington declined significantly during the 1980s, the size of each public university's administration more than doubled and, according to one critic, actually quadrupled in the case of the University of Washington.[44] Nationwide, between 1975 and 1985, full-time faculty grew 6 percent and student enrollment grew 10 percent, but nonteaching staff grew 60 percent.[45] Today, there is one nonteaching staff member for every eight college students, which means that they outnumber faculty two to one.[46]

At larger colleges and universities, executive administrators are paid an average of $153,400. Chief administrators in the health professions average $195,000 a year, and deans in the same department average between $131,000 and $133,000. Deans in other divisions, from agriculture and architecture to home economics and political science, average $83,000–$105,000. Affirmative action directors average $52,000; library directors, $49,000–$84,000; government relations directors, $68,000–$71,000. Even "campus recreation" directors pull down $34,000–$48,000 a year.[47] And that doesn't begin to cover all the nonteaching staff colleges and universities boast: senior vice presidents, junior vice presidents, student affairs deans, academic deans, assistant deans, executive assistants, senior development (i.e., fund-raising) officers, junior development officers, comptrollers, accountants, data analysts, research analysts, systems programmers, payroll managers, budget managers, business office assistants, endowment and investment directors, pension fund directors, insurance and risk management officers, conference managers, faculty relations staffers, community relations staffers, alumni relations staffers, public relations staffers, admissions counselors, registrar's office personnel, student services directors, clinic doctors, nurses, physical plant managers, expediters, security patrolmen, bookstore staffers, food service workers, house directors, secretaries, clerks, receptionists, garage mechanics, indoor and outdoor maintenance and repair staffers, janitors. . . . The list goes on and on, and there are also legions of expensive off-campus personnel, from high-priced lawyers and investment counselors to fund-raising consultants and P.R. men.

Cost Factor #2—Benefits. Personnel costs can be as high as 60–70 percent of the operating budget at some institutions, and they don't include just salaries; in addition, there is a burgeoning category called "employee benefits."[48] This refers to paid sick days, vacations, sabbaticals, bonuses, free and subsidized housing, college automobiles for business and personal use, "entertainment," travel, free tuition for family members, and more. On top of that, to remain competitive, colleges and universities must offer full-time employees full health care coverage.

For every payroll dollar, they must pay an additional 30 cents to cover the usual array of financial benefits—retirement, health insurance, life insurance, short- and long-term disability, and so on. Health care costs alone have risen as much *100–400 percent* in recent years. For an administrative employee who made $40,000 in 1993, the college or university's annual payroll "contribution" was: retirement, $4,000; Social Security/Medicare, $3,060; health insurance/medical benefits, $2,400; short-term disability, $172; long-term disability, $148; life insurance, $200. Some colleges and universities also pay federal and state unemployment taxes; others are self-insured and pay as individuals collect. Student health care benefits, which more and more schools are offering in the effort to keep up with their competitors, also can be expensive. Title IX of the 1972 Education Amendments requires that all plans be "equitable," meaning that they must offer features like pregnancy benefits, which increase premiums for everyone. At large schools, such "extras" in student health insurance can cost colleges and universities up to $500,000 a year.[49]

Cost Factor #3—Government Regulations. These cost American businesses somewhere between *$600 billion* and *$1.6 trillion* a year, and hundreds of thousands of them directly affect colleges and universities.[50] They are like quicksand: always unpredictable and always shifting, since federal bureaucrats are constantly rewriting and reinterpreting them. Most campuses have to hire a full-time staff of attorneys and "compliance officers" whose only job is keeping up with the latest edicts from Washington, D.C., and the mountain of paperwork that accompanies them.

One of the big "growth" areas for regulation is health and safety; as one wag put it, "If you think OSHA is a small town in Wisconsin, you're in deep trouble." In the mid-1970s, implementing the first tidal wave of federal employee health and safety standards cost higher education $3 billion.[51] Successive waves have cost billions of dollars more, especially since "environmental impact" has become a major health-related issue. The Americans with Disabilities Act of 1990 is also raising costs. For example, new buildings and renovated buildings now cost at least 10 percent more because of revised regulations regarding mandatory handicapped access, even when such access is not warranted.[52] Only after a huge uproar did the Federal Communications Commission suspend its new disability rule that colleges and universities must make all phones in areas with twenty or more employees accessible to hearing aids—even if the users had no hearing problems.[53] The *Chronicle of Higher Education* also reports that at least one school, Broward Community College, has a unique problem created by "disability" regulation: it is compelled to deal with a growing homeless population, including mentally unstable and violent individuals, since a 1992 Florida law waived tuition for them.[54]

These are not, however, the only areas where regulations are imposing huge costs on campus. For example, the Student Right to Know and Campus Security Act of 1990 requires schools to implement costly new data systems and conduct exhaustive research on campus crime, graduation, and placement rates. And for the last twenty years, Title IX "affirmative action" regulations and other laws on employee hiring and student admissions have cost millions of dollars more (see Chapter 5).

The rules on state and federal student financial assistance also necessitate a small army of staff in campus aid offices. The 1992 reauthorization of the Higher Education Act requires them to take on additional responsibilities, including providing the Department of Education with frequent updates on student and parent borrowers and grant and loan disbursement schedules. The catch is that the DOE has yet to release its official version of the regulations interpreting those new responsibilities as well as most of the other provisions in the reauthorization that affect colleges and universities. Schools are left, says the *Chronicle of Higher Education,* "with the choice of trying to guess what the legal requirements will be, or doing nothing and facing the risk of being held liable by department auditors."[55]

This is not a new problem; there always is a huge gap between the passage of federal legislation and the issuance of actual agency regulations. It reveals what one observer has called "Washington's other face, the bureaucratic behemoth," and it reacts with glacial slowness. Many education regulations are years out of date, and a number of the "new" ones (mandated by education amendments passed in 1978, for example) have yet to be written! Be that as it may, the 1992 reauthorization requires colleges and universities to supply more information to the DOE than ever before. Karen L. Fooks, director of financial affairs at the University of Florida, says, "There is no conceivable way that we can do what we are being held responsible for doing. Our computers can't do it, which puts this university back in a manual operation when we have 27,000 applications each year."[56]

The pilot program of direct student loans initiated by the Clinton administration in 1993 is expected to become the main form of federal student financial assistance in the near future, so the burden on schools will become even greater. The DOE assures that a $10 loan origination fee will cover all additional financial costs, but at least one educational association claims that the true costs to schools for participating will be closer to $50 per loan.[57] Schools will also have to assume financial liability for failure to perform their "designated" functions under this program.

Cost Factor #4—Programs/Facilities/Services. For decades, there has been fierce competition among colleges and universities to operate their own world-class graduate programs, law schools, medical schools, dental schools, veterinary schools, and so on. In some cases, this is because specialty programs and schools have proved to be what the *Wall Street Journal* calls "milkable cash cows," but mostly because there has been plenty of state and federal money to subsidize them—that is, until now. Higher education has also spent vast sums on a miscellaneous collection of expensive budget items. Among them:

- Computer systems: These are for the use of students, faculty, and administrators and for institutional record-keeping, data retrieval, and analysis. Even on a small campus the expense of maintaining and upgrading (let alone purchasing and installing) computer systems can run into millions of dollars.
- Libraries: A typical large research library spends $5-$30 million a year just on new books and periodicals. Harvard University, which has over 12 million volumes, spends anywhere between $54 million and $77 million a year.[58]
- Science laboratories and medical facilities: The National Science Foundation estimated that, adjusting for inflation, the cost of equipping a full-time researcher in the physical or natural sciences had risen from $85,000 in 1958 to $225,000 in 1989. Costs of research facilities have also grown uncontrollably; in the 1960s, it cost $75 million to build a medical facility; now it takes $170 million a year just to keep it up to date.[59]
- Campus security: Johns Hopkins University, as one example, spends $7 million a year on security.[60] Schools in high crime or urban areas obviously have to spend more on this budget responsibility, but the cost at small and rural institutions is still considerable.
- Utilities bills: The cost of heat, water, electricity, and telephone service at a small school of one thousand or so students costs a staggering $1 million per year. For a school with tens of thousands of students, the cost for these necessities runs into the tens of millions of dollars.

- Student services: These include career and placement centers, legal clinics, banking, postal and packaging services, quick-printing, day care centers, preschools, medical clinics and dispensaries, "sex education" and "sensitivity training" workshops, plus personal and group counseling for everything from drug abuse, sexual abuse, and physical abuse to pregnancy, dysfunctional family relationships, stress, eating disorders, and mental instability.
- Curricular revisions: Adding a single course to the college catalogue is a bit like ordering *à la carte* in a fancy restaurant: It is scandalously expensive, running into the thousands or even tens of thousands of dollars. Whole new departments cost hundreds of thousands and even millions of dollars. But in order to be "politically correct," most schools have added women's studies, black studies, Hispanic studies, Native American studies, and Third World studies, and are contemplating full-fledged departments of gay and lesbian studies.
- Athletics: This area deserves special mention since the amount of money spent on "bigger and better" programs and facilities actually amounts to tens and hundreds of millions of dollars. Between 1981 and 1985, NCAA colleges and universities increased their football and basketball budgets an average *55–60 percent*. One reported that its football team had a surplus of $1.37 million. However, after an audit, the "surplus" was reduced to $13,000; the excess revenue had been overstated by 105 times.[61] All but a handful of athletic programs actually *lose money* (see Chapter 6). But, between 1985 and 1989, the expenses of athletic programs at NCAA colleges and universities rose by at least double the cost of living in all divisions—in two divisions, it tripled.[62] And a College Football Association study examining college athletic department budgets between 1986 and 1990 found that while revenues were up 21 percent, operating costs were up 35 percent.[63]

In the same period, big spending on sports complexes was nothing short of astonishing: Boston College, $25 million; Cleveland State University, $47 million; Illinois State University-Normal, $17.4 million; Kansas State University, $17.5 million; Michigan State University, $45 million; North Carolina State University, $40 million; Saginaw Valley State University, $18.7 million; San Diego State University, $30 million; the University of Alabama-Birmingham, $12 million; the University of Connecticut-Storrs, $24.5 million; the University of Hartford, $9.8 million; the University of North Carolina, $35 million; the University of Tennessee-Knoxville, $43 million; Wake Forest University, $20.2 million; and Wright State University, $20 million.[64]

Cost Factor #5—Admissions/Student Assistance. Hundreds of millions of dollars more are spent on recruiting students, especially minorities, athletes, and high academic achievers, in the all-out bidding war known as college admissions. Thomas Sowell recalls that just after World War II, the admissions staff at Harvard University consisted of a single administrator and his assistant. Now it boasts a staff of dozens and costs nearly half a million dollars a year. Even small colleges have admissions staffs of fifteen or more. They have their work cut out for them, because the number of high school graduates has been declining since 1978, and many schools are unable or are struggling to fill their freshman classes.

As a result, says the *Chronicle of Higher Education,* the function of college admissions offices has shifted from selection of qualified students to marketing and sales. Their budgets have undergone a transformation, too, rising *64 percent* between 1980 and 1986.[65] In a *Money* magazine article entitled "The Agony of College Admissions," Eric Schurenberg comments, "Most admissions departments spend the bulk of their energies not trying to identify students who could benefit from studying there but rather in deploying commercial marketing techniques to lure new applicants." S. Frederick Starr, president of Oberlin College, confirms this: "Far too many colleges measure their success by the number of applications they receive. It's like the stock price to a corporation." One school recently spent $700 per student on admissions information material alone, and another paid $100,000 for full-page ads in *Time* and *Sports Illustrated*. Not counting what they spend on financial aid, tuition discounts, and rebates, a typical institution spends an average of $1,700 to bring in each new student, and quite a few are spending as much as $2,400-$2,800.[66]

Colleges and universities also vie with each other to retain students once they have been admitted, and this has given rise to a thriving cottage industry of outside consultants as well as new services, new programs, and, above all, fancy new campus facilities. Richard Pierson, dean of admissions at Clark University, compares this aspect of the frenzied recruitment drive to the arms race, with schools trying to outdo each other with everything from Ritz-quality hotel/conference centers to Olympic-quality sports complexes. One Georgetown University administrator speaks for many of his peers when he says that his school's emblem ought to be changed to a building crane.[67]

Colleges and universities are also now spending more than ever before on financial aid. The *Chronicle of Higher Education* reports that this is, in fact, one of the fastest-growing budget items of all. At Wesleyan University, where President William M. Chace has likened financial aid to an "open spigot" in the budget, it was eating up *20 percent* of all general revenues in 1993. Earlier it was noted that one of the most common reasons students cited for dropping out of college was lack of sufficient financial aid, but institutional financial aid increased by *130 percent* in the 1980s and continues to rise in the 1990s. Need-based financial aid at the University of California, for example, grew 88 percent—from $49 million to $92 million a year—between 1990 and 1993.[68]

Cost Factor #6—Deferred Maintenance. Quite literally, the "ivory tower" is falling apart. The total amount of deferred maintenance on college and university campuses is estimated at

$60 billion. In "The Decaying American Campus: A Ticking Time Bomb," two national associations of college physical plant managers and business officers reported that $20 billion is required urgently, but that most schools are unwilling or unable to devote the necessary resources to meeting the need. For the first time, Harvard recently included on its balance sheet the amount it *should* spend each year to keep facilities in good condition: $76.5 million.[69] But "Harvard now looks decidedly seedy compared with Oxford or Cambridge," writes *The Economist*, and Yale University, which has been putting off a desperately needed *$1 billion* overhaul, is rapidly deteriorating from "neo-Gothic into neo-slum."[70] California's public universities need nearly $6.5 billion for maintenance and seismic upgrading in the next ten years.[71] Minimum overdue repairs at fourteen Michigan public colleges and universities total $492 million. A good portion of that could be applied at the University of Michigan; it has 65 miles of crumbling sidewalks in addition to scores of aging buildings (the average is over sixty years old), each with its own usually decrepit electrical, heating, ventilation, plumbing, and water systems as well as sagging roofs, moldy plaster, rotting walls, and unreliable elevators.[72]

When referring to "prewar infrastructure" on such campuses, educators mean pre-World War I, or, often as not, pre-Spanish American War. Naturally, they are lobbying the federal government for billions of dollars to pay for repairs that they themselves have failed to make because they have preferred to spend their money on faculty, administration, program expansion, and new construction.

Cost Factor #7—Overexpansion. Some recent figures tell the story of overexpansion in higher education, although "explosion" might be a more apt description:[73]

- Between 1950 and the early 1990s, total college and university enrollment grew nearly *400 percent*, from 2.7 million to over 12.5 million students.

- The total number of institutions grew *83 percent*, from 1,800 to 3,300.
- Campus facility space grew by more than *500 percent*, from about 500 million to about 3 billion square feet.
- During the 1980s, costs of operations rose, in constant dollars, *27–30 percent* at public four-year colleges and universities and *45–54 percent* at private four-year colleges and universities.
- Between 1982 and 1992, total college and university budgets soared from $84 billion to *$171.6 billion* a year.

Heavily financed by taxpayers, colleges and universities have indulged in a spending spree in the last half-century that has no equal in American history. As education consultant Sean C. Rush notes, in an era when quality was defined as "more-is-better," and when there seemed to be an endless amount of government funding to pay for it, colleges and universities grew without a thought for the ordinary laws of supply and demand. Budgeting was right at the margin. The only important question seemed to be: "How much more can we offer/do next year?" How much money already had been spent and what results had been achieved were, in the words of another observer, secondary concerns. Now, says Rush, colleges and universities are faced with an altogether different task—salvaging core programs, cutting costs, and retrenching—and the new question they are asking themselves is: "How can we fund the institutions we have become?"[74]

Chapter 8

THE COLLEGE
CURRICULUM AND
POLITICAL CORRECTNESS

In 1992, Secretary of Education Lamar Alexander issued a report stating that during the previous ten years spending on education, including higher education, had *doubled* and that even after inflation the total was up 40 percent. He noted, however, that college enrollment had risen only slightly and that the results of efforts to improve educational quality and access were disappointing.[1] His proposed solution? It was identical to that of his Democratic successor, Secretary of Education William Riley: Spend more money on "changing schools." Is more money the answer? Let us look briefly at what we have paid for so far with billions of state, federal, and private dollars spent on higher education.

THE CORE CURRICULUM

For much of American history, the heart of undergraduate education was what was known as the "core curriculum." It consisted of a deliberately sequenced set of rigorous courses in

mathematics, science, philosophy, history, languages, and literature that all students must master in order to receive a bachelor's
degree. Though not every college or university taught these
courses in precisely the same fashion, they were in unquestioned
agreement about the nature of what undergraduates should
learn. As early as the 1890s, however, a few individual educators
began to express doubt about the "relevance" and "efficacy" of
the core curriculum. Their main spokesman was university scientist and educational philosopher John Dewey, who viewed
higher education's main task not as leading students toward the
pursuit of truth, which he saw as a shifting construct rather than
as a permanent reality, but toward "socialization" in order that
they might be recruited into the intellectual movement to
"change the world."

Once challenged, the curriculum was not transformed overnight, but gradually it did change. During the decades of Progressivism, the New Deal, and World War II, Dewey and his
disciples on the Left gained influence and power in the academy,
and new, rival disciplines like sociology and psychology, once
reserved for graduate study, began to intrude upon the core. It
was not long before they were joined by "practical" instruction
in everything from accounting to shorthand. With so many new
majors and courses available, colleges and universities increasingly began to rely on the "elective system" rather than the core
because it allowed students to design their own patterns of study
after taking a minimal number of required courses. The core was
reduced to something to be gotten over or gotten through.

As a kind of smorgasbord approach, the elective system really
came into its own during the 1960s under the banner of the
student's "right to choose." The net result was not more freedom
but the trivialization of learning, says George H. Douglas, professor of English at the University of Illinois and author of
Education Without Impact. Everything was "pummeled, shrunk,
detoothed," as "faculties discovered ways to defreight the traditional curriculum so that students could be bused along to law or
professional school or to the job market painlessly and without

complaint."[2] Although still considered a useful vehicle for "so-cialization" and, increasingly for political and ideological trans-formation, now *all* undergraduate education, not just the core curriculum, became something to be gotten over or gotten through, and a bachelor's degree became a mere useful credential rather than a mark of special academic achievement.

Also in the 1960s, Brown University introduced the "New Curriculum." This quickly became the hottest fad in the nation with countless imitations. As Charles J. Sykes, author of *Pro-fscam,* has pointed out, it was in reality more like a noncur-riculum. Students were free to take whatever courses appealed to them, often on a pass/fail basis. At Brown "D"'s were also abolished and "F"'s were not recorded on transcripts. A Brown dean justified the policy by saying, "I regard recording [failures] for the external world both superfluous and intimidating, or punishing."[3] The courses themselves were specifically designed to cater to adolescent tastes and centered on fashionable intel-lectual trends rather than time-tested academic subjects. Any-thing that smacked of the traditional was *boring.* It was also *Establishment,* so it had to be carted off to Madame Guillotine while the liberated citizens of the First Republic On Campus cheered and congratulated themselves on having thrown off the yoke of academic oppression. With a few minor changes, the noncurriculum still dominates higher education, but many of its features seem to have been dreamed up not by the New Jacobins but by Ripley's Believe It or Not. Here are some examples from the early 1990s:[4]

- At San Francisco State University, the humanities re-quirement could be fulfilled by taking a course in interior design.
- At American University, a course called "Lifetime Fit-ness" met the social studies distribution requirement.
- At Pennsylvania State University, it was possible to earn a Leisure Studies degree in golf management. Students christened it a "Fore-Year Degree."

- At Michigan State University, one could earn a master's degree in "packaging."
- The University of Pennsylvania granted a Ph.D. for a dissertation on the New England clambake, and the State University of New York granted one for "Women's Shopping: A Sociological Approach."
- At Lehigh University, marketing students could earn class credit for going on a date.
- At Stanford University, an upper division course was called "Black Hair as Culture and History."
- Middlebury College in Vermont had a class devoted, among other things, to the "eroticism, esthetics, voyeurism, and misogyny" of the films of Brigitte Bardot.
- Auburn University had a course called "Recreation Interpretive Services."
- Kent State offered "Camp Leadership," "Socio-Pyschological Aspects of Clothing," "Basic Roller Skating," and "Dance Roller Skating."
- The University of Illinois offered "Pocket Billiards" and "The Anthropology of Play."
- The University of Massachusetts–Amherst offered "Ultimate Frisbee."
- At Harvard University, students received class credit for "evaluating the nutritional content of their own diets" and for "studying the Harvard football team's offense under the tutelage of the quarterback." One of Harvard's more serious academic courses called, impressively enough, "The Concept of the Hero in Hellenic Civilization," was so undemanding that students regularly referred to it as "Heroes for Zeroes."
- Rutgers University devoted a course for German majors to "The Seduced Maiden Motif in German Literature."
- At Johns Hopkins University, a course on biomedical research was taught using the format of "The Tonight Show."
- Kenyon College's "Biology of Female Sexuality" class

used as one of its course texts *Witches Heal,* which asserts, "As lesbians, we . . . must question male medical authority, dare to hear and follow the witches, uncover the old wyve's tales, and heal ourselves."

- Brown University, the pioneer of the noncurriculum and an early proponent of such new, noncore disciplines as women's studies in the 1970s and 1980s, offered in this field: "Seminar on Sexuality," "Feminist Film Criticism," "Writing and Sexual Difference," "Feminism and Drama," "Tough Women and Tender Men in Modern Fiction," "Black Women: Psychological Perspectives," "Social Inequality," "Cold War: Language, Gender, and Representation in the 1950's America," "Behind the Lavender Curtains: Problems in 20th-Century Lesbian and Gay American Drama," "The Social Construction of Sexuality and the Making of the Modern Lesbian/Gay Community," "Comparative Sex Roles," "Psychology of Gender," "The Biology of Gender," and "Society and Behavioral Sciences Selective: Gender and the Health Care Delivery System."

In its 1985 report "Integrity in the College Curriculum," the Association of American Colleges lamented that "almost anything goes" in what passes as a college curriculum and expressed serious reservations about the content and purpose of many courses being taught today.[5] In the late 1980s (and still today, I suspect), it was possible to graduate from *78 percent* of the nation's colleges and universities without taking a course in the history of Western civilization; *38 percent* without taking any history course; *45 percent* without taking an American or English literature course; *77 percent* without taking a foreign language course; *41 percent* without taking a mathematics course; and *33 percent* without studying the natural or physical sciences.[6] Requirements for majors have also been eviscerated. At Duke University, for example, students are not required to read Homer, Dante, Donne, Milton, Eliot, or even Shakespeare in order to graduate with a B.A. in English.[7] And requirements also vary widely from department to department, creating at best a problem in "quality control" and at worst a kind of academic schizophrenia. No single campus authority seems to be able to offer a rationale for it, let alone control it and, as a result, course catalogues have exploded. Many list anywhere between five hundred and nine hundred offerings.

But, as George Douglas earlier pointed out, freedom of choice has hurt, not helped. A 1993 Rand Corporation study reports: "Over one-half of a national sample of college upper class students were unable to perform cognitive tasks at a high school level; three-quarters of the faculty surveyed in a recent poll felt that their students did not meet minimum preparation standards."[8] Thousands of students are graduating from college without acquiring critical thinking skills, let alone such basic skills as reading, writing, and arithmetic. Some are actually illiterate; they cannot read their own diplomas. Rightly, much of the blame has been directed toward the K–12 system, but higher education is also culpable. It has lowered standards and expectations to such an extent that it has given up on helping those who are hard to teach or who are ill-prepared for college.

Even though 30 percent of all college freshmen take at least one remedial course, many public and private campuses are dropping them since, says the *Chronicle of Higher Education,* neither tuition-paying parents nor state legislators like paying twice for students to take high school subjects.[9] But a 1987 Gallup poll of more than seven hundred *college seniors* indicates that perhaps more rather than less remedial education is desperately needed: 24 percent thought Columbus had landed in the New World after 1500; 42 percent could not place the Civil War in the correct half-century; 58 percent did not know that Harry Truman was president when the Korean War began; 55 percent could not identify the Magna Carta; and 23 percent identified Karl Marx's dictum, "From each according to his ability, to each according to his need," as a part of the U.S. Constitution. Fifty-five percent were given the theoretical grade of "F," since they missed more than 60 percent of the correct answers on the test of rudimentary knowledge the pollsters devised.[10] (Many of them, by the way, attended "prestige schools" where their parents assumed they were getting what they were paying for.)

Average SAT scores have declined about 75 *points* since the 1960s, but the response of colleges and universities has been to cover up rather than address the problem. When reporting scores for their institutions, they commonly cite the figures on students accepted rather than actually enrolled. This means, as Thomas Sowell points out, that if a student with combined math and verbal skills of, say, 1,400, applies to five schools, all five will count his scores in their official reports. As many as one-quarter of all students also are categorized as "special" or "provisional," and their scores do not need to be counted at all. Naturally, students with the poorest scores are always put in this category.[11]

Colleges and universities have also responded by making entrance exams less of a factor in the admissions process; a *USA Today* survey of nearly five hundred four-year institutions reveals that only 7 percent now rank them as most important. Fifty-eight percent depend on high school grades even while acknowledging that they are highly inflated.[12] Grade inflation is not limited to high schools; colleges and universities award passing and even high marks to thousands of students for substandard and minimal achievement. Charles J. Sykes reports that at the University of Michigan in 1975, the freshman class had the weakest SAT scores in decades but was given the highest grade point average ever. In the same year, 70 percent of all grades at Princeton were "A"s or "B"s, and at Stanford University, the average grade was "A-."[13] Sowell adds that at Harvard University in 1978, 78 percent of the student body made it onto the dean's list, compared with 20 percent in the 1920s and 26 percent in the 1930s. At Yale University, the proportion of "A"s awarded to students in the 1980s never fell below 40 percent.[14] And Douglas notes that at the University of Illinois in the late 1980s, 80 percent of all students enrolled in "Freshman Rhetoric" received "A"s and "B"s, and in some sections 100 percent received "A"s.[15]

Former journalism professor David Berkman gives one reason why this particular brand of academic corruption is so common: "If two-thirds of the students do not possess the skills necessary for professional success, there is no way you can flunk out a number anywhere near that percentage. There is simply too much intimidation in the academic environment. This is especially true for junior—meaning untenured—faculty members. . . . No junior professor who wishes to gain tenure will flunk out 67 percent in an introductory course."[16] But there is another, even more important reason for grade inflation: Professors have lost faith—faith in their students, that is. They simply don't expect more than a handful to excel or to be interested in what goes on in the classroom.

There is, of course, considerable cause for their defeatist attitude. Sowell reports in *Inside American Education* that less than a quarter of all college students put in sixteen or more hours of study per week, and only about 27 percent check at least one book out of the library during the year.[17] And Jacques Barzun relates a story in *Begin Here* that is becoming all too common in academe:

> The screening committee had to interview 150 young people—the three top students from each state—and award ten of them full scholarships, each worth $60,000. One member of the committee asked every candidate this question: "Did you, during the past year, read a book that was not assigned? If so, please tell us a little about that book." Only one student out of 150 was able to comply.[18]

Professors are also under enormous pressure to practice "affirmative grading," i.e., race-norming for minorities, which further lowers expectations and casts even more doubt on student abilities.[19] Defended by many groups, including the National Education Association, the American Bar Association, and the U.S. Departments of Labor and Education, as well as by many prominent college and university leaders, this form of grade inflation is based on the premise that "academically challenged individuals" (a code term for minority students) should not be "discriminated against" in the testing and grading process. University of Texas Professor Emeritus of English James Sledd contends in defense of affirmative grading: "A person (need one say it?) can learn a huge amount without being able to read or write at all. . . . Quite simply, it is a gross injustice to demand a mastery of standard English from students who through no fault of their own have had no chance to master it."[20] Anne Green, an associate professor of English and director of the writing program at Wesleyan University, concurs that too much emphasis is placed on spelling, punctuation, grammar, and "surface features of writing."[21]

But in truth there is nothing that justifies cheating students out of a good education. Chronic writing and mechanical errors by white as well as minority students are only the "tip of an iceberg of ignorance."[22] There are plenty of professors who feel this way and are opposed to the noncurriculum, lowered standards, and affirmative grading. But since they are afraid of creating controversy and jeopardizing their jobs, they remain, for the most part, silent critics. Perhaps they would be tempted to speak up if they recalled the lesson of the miserly farmer, who decided to save money by mixing sawdust with the grain he fed his horse. Gradually he added more and more sawdust, until there was so little grain in the feed that the horse died from starvation.

——————POLITICAL CORRECTNESS——————

While they are at it, today's educators must also decide what is the aim of undergraduate education. Once, they shared a clear consensus (just as they did about the core curriculum and about what should be expected of students) that it was to share with succeeding generations the inherited wisdom of mankind and the historical and moral traditions of their own culture. But for some years many of them have been trying to substitute a new aim known as "relevance" in the 1960s-1970s and "political correctness" in the 1980s-1990s.

Political correctness has three main doctrines. The first: *There are certain ideas, issues, and actions that simply are unacceptable within the academic community, and it is educators' prime responsibility to "reeducate" students so that they will automatically eschew the "incorrect."*

Thus more than two hundred colleges and universities have attempted to enforce speech codes or revised codes of conduct in the last several years. These have been struck down as unconstitutional once at the University of Wisconsin and twice at the University of Michigan, but de facto codes have taken their place and have been given added support by a 1992 Supreme Court decision that makes it legal for administrators to invoke tough penalties for supposedly "bias-motivated" crimes.[23]

Duke University Professor of English Stanley Fish, widely acknowledged as the "high priest" of political correctness, defends outright as well as de facto speech codes by arguing (reminiscent of John Dewey) that free speech is only a "political construct," and that "the First Amendment is the first refuge of scoundrels."[24] But the most common "PC" argument is that the unrestricted right to freedom of speech belongs only to victims of discrimination. Liberal Harvard University law professor Alan Dershowitz, by no means the stereotypical opponent of PC, objects that this line of reasoning has led to an intolerable situation in which women and minorities are entirely free to attack white men "in the most offensive of terms." He continues, "Radical feminists can accuse all men of being rapists, and radical African-Americans can accuse all whites of being racists, without fear of discipline or rebuke. But even an unintentionally offensive parody of women or blacks provides the occasion for demanding the resignation of deans, the disciplining of students, and an atmosphere reminiscent of McCarthyism."[25] Unabashed, however, many colleges and universities have embraced PC fully. In the early

1990s, they went so far as to publish and distribute warnings against certain forms of "politically incorrect" language and behavior:[26]

- The University of Missouri's school of journalism handbook outlawed " 'burly' (too often associated with black men, implying ignorance), 'glamorous' (sexist), 'white' (refers to a racist power structure), 'banana' (offensive to Asian-Americans), 'gyp' (offensive to Gypsies), 'mafia' (offensive to Italian-Americans), 'Dutch treat' (offensive to those of Dutch extraction), 'community' (implies a monolithic culture in which people think, act, and vote in the same way), and 'Ugh!' (offensive to Native Americans)."
- Nebraska Wesleyan University, like many schools, forbad "freshman" and "chairman" as sexist.
- Michigan State University's "Fact Sheet on Bias-Free Communications" warned against "culturally deprived," "black mood," "yellow coward," and "he."
- The College of William and Mary disapproved of "kingpin," and suggests substituting "key person."
- The University of Arizona outlawed "nerd."
- Several campuses also included "child-free" instead of "childless" in their PC lexicon.
- At the University of Michigan even "minority" was out; "multicultural," however, was definitely in. The school also dictated use of "sexual orientation" over "sexual preference," "life partner" over "spouse," and (my personal favorite) "personhole" over "manhole."
- Smith College had penalties for "lookism," i.e., discrimination on the basis of physical appearance.
- Duke University prohibited "disrespectful facial expressions or body language."
- Until compelled to reverse its policies, the University of Connecticut banned "inappropriate laughter."

Another popular PC device introduced in the early 1990s was "sensitivity training" on race, gender, and "sexual orientation." Today, many colleges and universities are forcing students and faculty to undergo this particular form of reeducation. Here are just a few recent examples:[27]

- At the University of Tennessee's required sensitivity workshops, trainers betrayed their own lack of sensitivity by publicly berating and humiliating several staff employees for their reluctance to participate.
- A Stanford University neurosurgeon was forced to resign his department chairmanship and undergo a year of "sensitivity training" after being accused of sexism by a colleague.
- At the University of Arizona, the creative writing faculty was ordered to undergo reeducation as the result of unsubstantiated campus rumors that they might be "insensitive."
- At the University of Minnesota, the faculty was informed by the dean of liberal arts that they not only must attend "Mandatory Sexual Harassment Training" but also sign certificates of attendance.
- At the University of Florida, a new policy forced sororities and fraternities to send all new members to a month-long series of sensitivity seminars.
- At Emory University, the entire faculty was told to attend sensitivity workshops after an instructor was accused but found innocent of sexually harassing a student. The Atlanta branch of the Department of Education's Office of Civil Rights insisted on the workshops and warned that less than full cooperation would put the university *in danger of losing all federal funding.* (Look for much more of this kind of federal intimidation in the future.)

The price of being sensitive, as we all know from personal experience, is dear, but perhaps not so dear as it is in higher education. "Sensitivity trainers," though they possess no real credentials, charge as much as $2,500 for a half-day workshop and up to $16,000 for follow-up sessions. Colleges and universities scrambling to show their own high degree of institutional sensitivity are also hiring full-time "diversity directors" and "deans of multicultural affairs," with starting salaries of $35,000-$60,000.[28] (Of course, they must also pay for all the expensive new programs, newsletters, brochures, secretarial help, office space, and equipment that go along with these positions, but they have become ingenious at finding ways to make taxpayers pick up the tab for such things.)

Colleges and universities also mete out stern punishment to the "politically incorrect," which is what occurred at Stanford University in the 1980s when a graduate student was expelled for documenting the government policy of coerced abortions in communist China and at Dartmouth College where conservative student newspaper editors were expelled for confronting a black music professor whose lectures routinely featured obscenities and racial and sexual epithets. Dartmouth also suspended two students who dared appear dressed as Indians at a hockey game after displays of the traditional school symbol had been banned as offensive to Native Americans. (It was a week before the end of the term; the students received no class credit and no tuition refund.)[29]

Yet, in a clear case of double standards, those who persecute the politically incorrect go unpunished. At the University of Pennsylvania in 1993 a group called "Concerned Black and Latino Students" stole fourteen thousand copies of the *Daily Pennsylvanian*. Even though the group readily admitted responsibility, administrators ignored the theft, just as it had largely ignored all verbal threats, physical harassment, and vandalism directed against the conservative student newspaper. Administrations at Massachusetts' College of the Holy Cross, North Carolina State University, Pennsylvania State University, Dartmouth University, the University of California-Berkeley, the University of North Carolina, and the University of Michigan have behaved similarly.[30]

Even classroom debate has been curtailed by PC, as Thomas Sowell documents. At Humboldt State College, a student who disagreed with a professor's antinuclear views was barred from returning to class, and, at the University of Michigan, a student who dared question his professor's statements about Central American politics (made in biology class) was told by the professor that he should go to El Salvador and get blown up. At the State University of New York-Farmingdale, an enraged professor called in security guards to escort a student out of class because he criticized the professor's parodies of Ronald Reagan and the Bible. At the University of Washington, a male student was physically barred from attending the women's studies course in which he had enrolled.[31] But controversial ideas are fine in the classroom as long as they are approved by the campus thought police:[32]

- At the University of Massachusetts-Amherst, one American history professor began the first day of class by announcing, "This class will be consistently anti-American."
- At St. Cloud State University in Minnesota, one course included class credit for protest marching.
- At the University of Texas-Austin, a Marxist economics course syllabus announced that the class "provides you with an opportunity to learn how to view the world from a new point of view and the tests are aimed at evaluating whether and to what degree you have learned to do this."
- At the University of Wisconsin, a course called "Curriculum and Instruction" was taught as a how-to lesson in political protesting and in "interrupting business as usual (that is, social relations of racism, sexism, classism, Eurocentrism as usual) in the public spaces of the library mall and administrative offices."

PC also extends to other issues of "social relevance." A number of schools are now considering imitating the University of

Georgia, which requires every student to demonstrate "environmental literacy" before graduation. Haverford College in Pennsylania has a "social justice" requirement for undergraduates.[33] At the University of Alabama-Birmingham, the art department recently chose to elevate the cultural consciousness of its student body by raising $4,200 to buy a photograph of Andres Serrano's "Piss Christ." (It reveals a plastic statue of Jesus submerged in a jar of urine and cow's blood.) The student government voted ten-to-two to condemn the purchase while the faculty senate voted unanimously in favor of it. President Charles A. McCallum admitted he found the work personally offensive, but that it had "significant artistic and educational merit."[34] An exhibit at Harvard Divinity School in 1992 featured condoms in rainbow colors, covered with beads, fur, yarn, leather, feathers, bracelet charms, filled with honey, alphabet soup, a baby's sneaker, globes, and sunflower seeds. Defenders of the show said this was "serious art," and the acting director of the school opened the exhibit with a dedication ceremony devoted to the cause of AIDS victims.[35]

It is a political rather than an educational agenda that now rules the campus. And the deliberate intention of the politically correct professor is no longer to be neutral but to propagandize and indoctrinate. Andrew Ross, a Princeton University professor, admits freely, "I teach in the Ivy League in order to have direct access to the minds of the children of the ruling classes."[36] Sam Abel, a gay activist and assistant professor of drama at Dartmouth College, says, "Teaching is a form of political action," and adds, "Deconstructing *Moby Dick* can't change the world, but the student who learns to think deconstructively can."[37] Charles Paine, a Duke University teaching assistant, writes in a similar vein in an article in *College English* that students must be taught about "radical visions of the world," and that "the teacher must recognize that he or she must influence (perhaps manipulate is the more accurate word) students' values through charisma or power."[38]

In class, the primary objective is to preach the second doctrine of political correctness: *All differences in ideas, values, and lifestyles are equally valid, and any attempt to prefer one over the other or to devote more attention to one than to the other is an act of prejudice. Moreover, the differences between people—between blacks and whites, men and women, rich and poor, Westerners and non-Westerners—are more important than the qualities they share in common. For that reason, questions of race, gender, class, and power are the real issues that govern human events.*

Because Western culture rejects this doctrine, it is racist, sexist, and oppressive, and the curriculum as it has been taught for the last two hundred or more years is also racist, sexist, and oppressive. History, philosophy, science, the arts—all are invalid because they have not given equal time to nonwhite, nonmale, non–Westerners. But it is literature that comes in for the worst censure. The traditional canon, comprised of the "Great Books" of the Western world, is nothing more than the imposed intellectual domination of dead white males. A representative sample of this view may be found in an anthology used in many introductory freshman composition classes entitled *Racism and Sexism.* Former National Endowment for the Humanities Chairman Lynne Cheney summarizes it:

> This book begins by defining racism as something only white people can be guilty of and sexism as unique to men. It goes on to portray the United States as a country in which racism and sexism pervade every aspect of life. The book offers no comparison with other cultures, no context to show how American ideals and practices measure up against those of the rest of the world or the rest of history. Instead, it paints a picture of unremitting oppression and suggests that any solution will require "fundamental changes in the ways that wealth is produced and distributed"—that is, the abandonment of capitalism.[39]

Rereading America is another popular anthology assigned to college freshmen. It offers essays that argue that "the American dream . . . is governed not by education, opportunity and hard work, but by power and fear," and that "class standing and consequently life chances are largely determined at birth."[40]

Why do college and university leaders tolerate this kind of vicious, ideological axe-grinding, particularly when it is passed off as educational material? Generally it is because they, too, worship at the altar of political correctness. Donna Shalala, for example, the former chancellor of the University of Wisconsin and current secretary of the Department of Health and Human Services, has commented repeatedly: "American society is racist and sexist."[41] There have been other administrators, of course, who object to political correctness. Former Yale University President Benno Schmidt has decried the fact that "universities have become saturated with politics, often of a fiercely partisan kind," and former Harvard University President Derek Bok has warned, "What universities can and must resist are deliberate, overt attempts to impose orthodoxy and suppress dissent."[42] But they have done little or nothing to stop political correctness; indeed, while in office, they presided over its growth.

To cite just one example of capitulation, they, like other college and university leaders, allowed freshman orientation to become "a crash course in the strange new world of university politics" where students are urged to identify themselves as the oppressors or the oppressed. "Within days of arrival on campus," says Heather MacDonald in the *Wall Street Journal*, students "learn the paramount role of gender, race, ethnicity, class, and sexual orientation in determining their own and others' identity." They are told, furthermore, that "bias lurks around every corner," and to suspect all persons and ideas that they will encounter during the next four years.[43]

Specifically, she notes:

- At the University of California-Berkeley, they are informed that the American system perpetuates racism, homophobia, ableism, ageism, sexism, and statusism.

- At Dartmouth College, they are presented with a mandatory program called "Social Issues," which features skits on politically correct responses.
- At Columbia University, they listen to other students read essays on what it is like to be gay or some other kind of "victim of society."
- At Stanford University, they learn about the "Faces of Community" and how previous generations ruthlessly discriminated against them.
- At Bowdoin College, they are hit with the less felicitously titled program, "Defining Diversity: Your Role in Racial-Consciousness-Raising, Cultural Differences and Cross-Cultural Social Enhancers."
- At Oberlin College, they are segregated into different groups to watch performance theatre on race and gender issues—blacks are grouped with blacks, whites with whites, Asian-Americans with Asian-Americans, gays with gays, and so on.

College and university leaders have also allowed political correctness to enter the classroom under the guise of "multiculturalism." Supposedly broadening the curriculum by introducing minority and Third World perspectives, this new fad has gained the support of many who are not in the PC camp but who are generally in favor of vague concepts of "diversity" and "pluralism."

But multiculturalism, as *The New Republic* points out, is "neither multi nor cultural," and it is part of an effort to impose "unanimity of thought on campus."[44] Dinesh D'Souza agrees that multiculturalism "does not present the historical realities of other cultures but instead advocates modern Western political ideologies, using other cultures as no more than masks, distorted and misrepresented to provide as much evidence as is needed for present political purposes."[45] Still, multiculturalism is immensely popular in academe. In 1988, Stanford University's faculty voted to drop its traditional "Western Civilization" course and replace it with "Culture, Ideas, and Values," which is specifically designed to focus on race, ethnicity, gender, and class issues. In the years since, hundreds of schools have followed Stanford's lead and junked their old courses for "new and improved" multicultural ones.

Most of these have a Marxist emphasis. Though largely an extinct intellectual doctrine in other nations, Marxism flourishes in the modern American university. Nearly half of all recent Ph.D.s in literature, for example, say that Marxist approaches to literature influence their teaching of undergraduates.[46] Even *Newsweek* has concluded that the new politically correct/multicultural tilt in the college curriculum is "Marxist in origin in the broad sense of attempting to redistribute power from the privileged class (white males) to the oppressed masses."[47] And those who pooh-pooh the idea that Marxism is a dominant force still admit that "there will always be a little room for a brand of academic theorizing that includes the notions that what we already have is rotten, that old values must be thrown overboard, that tradition should be undermined, that the smug and comfortable world of parents, or of corporate executives, or of liberal education, should be trashed if at all possible."[48]

Even more troubling, however, than all these features of political correctness—its restrictive limits on speech and behavior, its counterfeit multiculturalism, its Marxist, anti-establishment origins—is its third doctrine: *"Truth" does not exist, and it cannot be taught. What has been passed off as "truth" are merely the collective prejudices of the dominant ruling class and culture. Students must be shown how to "deconstruct" what they think is "true."*

If you ask, "How, if truth does not exist, can anyone believe in political correctness?" you have caught on to the contradiction in this doctrine; but academics thrive on contradiction. The politically correct professor freely admits that what he teaches is dogma, like everything else, but he argues that *his* dogma is more compelling, more socially and ideologically acceptable. His first announcement to new students on the first day of the semester invariably is: "This class will challenge everything you always took for granted to be true. It will strip away all your myths and preconceived notions. . . ." To impressionable, young under-graduates who have always suspected that they were "missing the real story" in those boring high school classes where they were expected to memorize dates and facts, this sounds bold, innova-tive, and "fun," but what they are being offering is a more rigid bunch of stereotypes than any they have encountered before, as in "All white males are. . . . All women are. . . . All blacks are. . . ."

In literature, there is supposedly no truth in language; words are subjective and the real meaning of a text rests in each reader's response, not in the words themselves or in the author's intent. Since different readers will have different responses, no one meaning can be true, and the accumulated insights of previous generations are not to be trusted. The same goes for insights in history, psychology, biology, sociology, religion, political science, economics, and the law: One person's reality is another person's hallucination.

The only "truth" political correctess *will* admit is that everything—every poem, every book, every historical event or person, every emotion, attitude, or belief, every action—must be viewed in a political context as an instrument of exclusion, oppression, or liberation. This ties in nicely with the first and second doctrines of political correctness, but, as Lynne Cheney warns, it also brings us "perilously close to the world of George Orwell's *1984,* the world where two and two make five, if it's politically useful."[49]

THE NEW SEGREGATION

Jacques Barzun has noted that political correctness does not legislate tolerance; it only organizes hatred.[50] Nowhere can this be seen more clearly than in the "new segregation" on campus. It began as intellectual segregation in the doctrine that white males are oppressors. There are no exceptions; every white male is an oppressor and a racist, "with the only distinction being between those who are overt and those who engage in psychological 'denial.' "[51] For centuries, white males have persecuted their permanent victims—women and minorities—and, according to new "evidence" in politically correct books like *Stolen Legacy* and *Black Athena*, they have even robbed them of credit for the most important developments of civilization. Women and minorities are told, says San Jose State University Professor Shelby Steele, that their real identity lies in their particular *grievance* against white males. And, accordingly, they are encouraged to demand special entitlements: "No longer is it enough just to have the right to attend a college or a university on an equal basis with others or to be treated like anyone else." Schools must set aside special money and special academic departments just for them, based on their grievance, says Steele.[52]

Intellectual segregation has led to physical segregation. A number of colleges and universities now offer with pride separate dorms, homecomings, yearbooks, and graduations for black students. Separate departments for black studies, Hispanic studies, and women's studies have also become the rule, and they are generally well funded, even when budget cuts are imposed on other departments. (When in rare circumstances they, too, have to absorb cuts, this is regarded as further "proof" of discrimination. As Sykes has pointed out, it is always "easier to blame 'racism' than to allocate scarce resources.")[53]

Three-fourths of all student newspaper editors responding to a *U.S. News & World Report* survey reported that segregation between races is common at their school. Seventy percent of all black undergraduates at the University of Michigan admitted recently that they lived such a segregated existence on campus that they had no close white acquaintance.[54] Higher education has resurrected, say numerous observers, the "separate but equal" world of *Plessy v. Ferguson*. It also has resurrected racial tension and violence:[55]

- At Oberlin College, Missouri Valley College, and North Carolina State University, there have been racial protests involving anywhere from a few hundred to a thousand students.
- At the University of Massachusetts, the Rodney King trial led to protests and violence and what was described as a "dorm rampage."
- At the University of Rhode Island, hundreds of black students staged a sit-in protest because a Malcolm X quotation newly inscribed on the campus library building omitted the words "fighting the white man."
- At UCLA, two hundred black students marched, protesting alleged racism of fraternities.
- At the University of Oregon, students tore down a banner with the message, "You meet the most interesting people in summer school," and painted the word "racism" over the faces of Michelangelo, Plato, Jane Austen, and a number of other well-known historical figures.
- At Georgia State University, a large demonstration was sparked by racist graffiti on a trash can.
- At Iowa State University, a brawl between black and white students required the police to use tear gas.
- At Southern Illinois University, mace was used to halt another race-related fight between students.
- At Harvard University, law school students disrupted commencement exercises to demand more hiring of women and minorities and the resignation of the dean.
- At Olivet College in Michigan, a single alleged racial incident was so sensationalized by the media and political activists that the campus was plunged into a state of emergency and the president eventually resigned.

One of the campuses worst hit by the new segregation is the University of North Carolina-Chapel Hill. John Moody, student body president in 1992, remarked: "Our campus is already largely two separate campuses through all-black or all-white fraternities and sororities; black business, law and pre-professional organizations; self-segregated living arrangements; and extracurricular activities."[56] UNC's Black Student Movement has demonstrated repeatedly, demanding a new multimillion-dollar cultural center exclusively for their use and threatening black faculty members who do not lend complete support to their cause. On his visit to the troubled school, film director Spike Lee suggested to an audience of five thousand students that black athletes should boycott all athletic events, saying, "There wouldn't be no Final Four, no Rose Bowl. . . ." At the same rally, a representative of Louis Farrakhan called Socrates a "faggot," and added, "We are tired of a blond-haired, pale-skinned, blue-eyed, buttermilk complexioned cracker Christ or peckerwood Jesus." A National Public Radio reporter on the scene could not find any campus official or faculty member willing to go on record protesting these remarks.[57]

Students have been cowed into silence, too. Blacks, for example, who have criticized minority vandalism and harassment directed against whites have been physically threatened by other blacks. Thomas Sowell notes that this also is common at other institutions: "Campus political activists in various groups attempt to stigmatize those students of their own race who do not join their political constituency and share its group think."[58] *Washington Post* columnist William Raspberry adds that it has come down to a stark choice for students bullied by their peers: "Are you gonna hang with us or are you gonna hang with them?"[59] Inevitably, there will be more racial tension and violence on campus in the future—on the part of nonminority students who are resentful of the preferential treatment minorities receive and of the PC attitude that brands them as oppressors—and on the part of minorities, who are taught to resent both real and imagined injustices and to use them as justification for retaliation.

Chapter 9

THE FACULTY AND THE COLLEGE COMMUNITY

FACULTY: PRIORITIES AND REWARDS

"The story of the collapse of American higher education is the story of the rise of the professoriate," Charles J. Sykes alleged in his damning indictment of the teaching profession entitled *Profscam*. Richard M. Huber, former Princeton professor and author of *How Professors Play the Cat Guarding the Cream,* agrees and says, ". . . University teaching is the only profession in which you can become a success without satisfying the client."[1]

They and other critics have produced volumes of evidence to prove that teachers are being paid more and more to teach less and less. By any objective standard of productivity, our educators' record has been abysmal. A recent House Select Committee on Children, Youth, and Families investigation reported that "parents are paying ever-increasing tuition to have students teach students," and that since teaching loads are half of what they were a generation ago, twice as many professors now are needed to teach the same number of courses.[2]

The average professor is in class only six to nine hours a week.

But, says Sykes, even that is questionable: "After two decades of The Historic Escape from Teaching (which has the fitting acronym of THEFT), university administrators have grown remarkably imaginative in concealing the reality of the academic workload."[3]

Often they put sabbatical research, administrative duties, and committee service in the category of "teaching," and they base their overall numbers on the fall semester, because at larger schools, it is customary for a professor to teach two courses in the fall and only one in the spring. Some even cheat by counting "student contact hours," Sykes says, so that classes taught by teaching assistants can be credited to professors.[4] (Boston Herald columnist Don Feder calls this "grand theft pedagogy.") In 1986, state auditors found at the University of Wisconsin that fewer than two-thirds of the faculty on the payroll were doing any real teaching at all and that state funding increases had been used to reduce teaching loads rather than increase the number of classes.[5] At the University of Illinois at about the same time, only slightly over 50 percent of the economics faculty taught as many as two classes in the fall semester; in the political science department not even one-third taught that many. And at the University of Michigan, some professors taught so little that it was estimated that they were making nearly $1,000 an hour for their actual contact with students.[6]

In a Wall Street Journal article wryly called, "What Me Teach? I'm a Professor," another strong critic, Martin Anderson, charged that "too often, teaching is of a scandalously substandard kind," and that too many unqualified, inexperienced graduate students were carrying the burden of real teaching by preparing and giving lectures, leading class discussions, making up and grading exams, and handling student counseling, all the while trying to complete their own education.[7] He openly condemned schools like the University of California-Berkeley, which boasts in its catalogue that its faculty, which "is made up of some of the most distinguished teachers and scholars in the world," is in close, constant contact with undergraduates. Berkeley repeats this claim to gullible parents not just once but many times throughout the catalogue: "Students who attend Berkeley have the benefit of learning from world-renowned theorists and researchers who are often distinguished teachers," and "Every year, departments nominate many of their faculty as distinguished teachers. You will encounter excellent teachers in all departments, all disciplines." But, as Anderson revealed, in the mid-1980s, three out of five freshman and sophomore classes were taught by graduate students acting as teaching assistants, and by 1992, the ratio was *three out of four.*

He is not the first to point out that this is a "bait and switch" game. For years, every educator in the country, down to the last junior professor, has known what has been going on, but most have remained mum. As of the 1980s, teaching assistants made up an average *53.5 percent* of university faculties. Harvard University, Yale University, Princeton University, and Columbia University have hundreds of teaching assistants; the University of California-Berkeley, the University of Massachusetts, and Ohio State University, to name a few, have several thousand.[8] In the last few years, teaching assistants have taught:[9]

- 50 percent of all undergraduate courses at Princeton University;
- approximately 50 percent of all freshman courses at the University of North Carolina;
- 75 percent of all freshman composition courses at Brigham Young University;
- 39 percent of all introductory courses at Ohio State University;
- 100 percent of all freshman composition courses and 25-75 percent of other introductory courses at Stanford University;
- and 45 percent of the teaching load in college and university math departments across the country.

Under the circumstances, it seems plausible that there are many students who could echo the recent complaint of a senior economics major at the University of Minnesota: "I am graduating from one of the best economics departments in the country, and I have never had a professor."[10]

Undergraduates are not the only ones who have been cheated. Teaching assistants, comments Sykes, are "paid wages that most businesses would be embarrassed to pay their parking lot attendants," and yet they are saddled with almost complete responsibility for teaching and counseling hundreds of undergraduates.[11] On a number of campuses, they have gone on strike for better pay and benefits and have demanded to be included in collective bargaining agreements between the faculty and the administration, but their position has not improved much.

To make matters worse, many teaching assistants—sometimes more than half of all those in a given department—are foreign, with little command of English. This can lead to disastrous results in the classroom. English-speaking or not, at least one-third of all teaching assistants receive no formal training, and where it is offered it is totally unstructured, "leaving T.A.s to ferret information on their own."[12] Additional "slave labor" is provided by thousands of part-time faculty with full Ph.D.s, who work for low salaries and benefits and are treated with scant respect. By late 1980s, *38 percent*, or more than *one-third* of all faculty members, were part-time.[13] They and many nontenured professors with temporary one-year appointments wander like gypsies from campus to campus, teaching survey courses that the regular faculty won't touch.

With budget cuts looming, colleges and universities are bound to resort to using even more teaching assistants, part-timers, and temporary appointments in order to save costs. But economizing is not the real explanation for their proliferation. In the 1960s and 1970s, their main function was to free "star professors" to pursue their own research interests, but since then they also have been exploited in order to free rank-and-file faculty from the "drudgery" of teaching; it simply isn't the faculty's main job anymore. Several observers have explained how an "academic ratchet" effect developed over time. As elite groups of professors on larger campuses began to receive lighter teaching loads twenty to thirty years ago, other faculty became envious and demanded the same treatment. Under ordinary circumstances, their demands would have gotten nowhere, but the sudden influx of billions of dollars in state and federal funding for higher education in this period meant that it would cost little or nothing for administrators to give in. Smaller campuses that received little or no government funding eventually were forced to give in, too, or risk losing their best faculty.

And lighter loads are not the only new benefit senior professors have acquired. Today, they automatically have the option to teach less demanding upper division and graduate classes with small numbers of students whom they only have to meet a few times during the semester. Often, they require students to write only one paper or exam, and class preparation is minimal since the courses often are more like "bull sessions" than a series of lectures.

Each college and university states that teaching undergraduates is its highest prerogative, but precious few require faculty members to spend any significant amount of time in the classroom or invoke penalties for bad teaching. They have also allowed tenure to evolve from a conditional contract into a guarantee of lifetime employment. Tenure as well as hiring and salary committees look almost solely at candidates' publication and research credits rather than at their actual teaching contact hours or their performance in the classroom. Accreditation, admissions, academic reputation, and other institutional issues also have become linked to professors' research and publishing activity. It is no wonder then, as a recent Carnegie Foundation for the Advancement of Teaching poll indicates, that only 35 percent of all full-time college and university professors consider teaching their "chief interest."[14] Of course, professors can be prevailed upon to put their research aside if the proper incentives are provided. One says the attitude among his colleagues is: "We'll prepare new courses *if* we get extra money over the summer; we'll take on these students *if* we get partial course credit; we'll avoid committees because they take too much time from research, whence come our grants, mobility, and professional respect."[15]

There are no regular rewards, apart from these kinds of bribes, for close contact with students or for good teaching. "Mere teachers" are not even eligible for tenure; at the very least, they must have published essays and reviews in the "right," though often obscure, journals. Jacques Barzun quips: "Neglect your teaching and you will rise; attend to it and you will be fired."[16] Bryan Barnett, a former Rutgers University administrator, is more prosaic: "The present requirements for high quality undergraduate education ultimately are incompatible with the sort of research programs now required to secure tenure, promotion, external support, and scholarly reputation and status."[17] A science professor at the University of Michigan says even more bluntly, "Every hour I spend in a classroom is costing me money and prestige."[18] (Arrogance like this makes me feel that of all the educational models we adopted from nineteenth-century Germany it is too bad we didn't adopt the one in which college professors were paid directly by their students.)

Speaking of making money and being a professor in the same breath may have seemed absurd in the days when taking a job in academe was akin to taking a vow of poverty, but that is no longer the case. College professors now earn enough to belong in tax brackets reserved for the "upper middle class" and the "rich." And these days, as Rep. Patricia Schroeder (D-CO) observes, a professor's salary seems to be inversely related to the number of hours he or she works.[19] Barzun notes that huge salaries have become the norm for "star professors" because they are the ones who bring to campus lucrative research projects, and he characterizes them as "valuable properties like top baseball players."[20] (I would add that they have about the same degree of allegiance, frequently "changing teams" by moving from one university to another, always negotiating a more lucrative contract in exchange for fewer responsibilities.)

In 1990–91, Cornell University provided one of its medical professors with a package worth $1.7 million. It paid another medical professor $1.3 million and three others between $777,000 and $885,000. The same year, Stanford University, Columbia University, and the University of Pennsylvania all paid medical professors more than $1 million.[21] In fact, Columbia University, Cornell University, Georgetown University, George Washington University, Johns Hopkins University, Stanford University, Tulane University, the University of Chicago, the University of Miami, the University of Pennsylvania, Vanderbilt University, Washington University, and Yale University each had half a dozen or more employees in various departments making between $335,000 and $1.7 million that year.[22] (More institutions undoubtedly belong on this list, but not all release salary information.)

The average "star professors" in liberal arts disciplines like English and history and in nontraditional disciplines like African-American studies and women's studies make as much as $150,000–$200,000 a year, but the nonstars make out pretty well, too. On average, academic salaries rose faster than the rate of inflation every year during the 1980s.[23] A full professor at a top university made over $80,000 a year in the early 1990s; an assistant professor was making well over $40,000. The average salary for full professors at all public and private four-year universities was over $56,000. Even at community colleges, where pay scales are the lowest, a full professor made over $45,000—all for a few hours of work each week, nine months out of the year.[24] Sykes notes that "the upward pressure of smaller schools struggling toward the light of academic prestige" means that even in second- and third-ranked institutions big salaries are paid to attract prestigious, although not necessarily "star professors." In one semester at the University of Wisconsin-Milwaukee in the 1980s, for example, a business school professor taught only four hours a week on Mondays for a salary of $66,300. Another faculty member in the English department on the same campus was pulling down more than $70,000 for teaching two and-a-half hours a week.[25]

As Martin Anderson reminds us, professors do not punch time clocks and are rarely under any direct supervision. They often enjoy a wide range of benefits, ranging from comprehensive health insurance and housing subsidies to free college tuition for their spouses and children. Their pension plan is more generous than the federal government's. Every six or seven years, many are awarded a year's leave with half-pay called a "sabbatical." He concludes that in the multibillion-dollar industry that is higher education, college and university professors always go first class.[26]

FACULTY: RESEARCH AND ——— PUBLICATION ———

As Charles Sykes points out, the debate over research versus teaching "presupposes that professors really do as much research as they claim and that the research they do actually has merit."[27] But former Department of Education Assistant Secretary Chester E. Finn, Jr., has alleged that after eliminating "the horde of papers, articles, and books whose publication or presentation accomplished nothing save, perhaps, for the authors' curricula vitae," only one research project in ten is worthwhile.[28] Sykes says that even this may be too generous: "Although the assumption that professors are busily at work on the frontiers of knowledge is the justification for their featherweight teaching loads, 60 percent of all college faculty members have never written or edited a book and one-third have never even published a single journal article."[29]

One Princeton professor's main "research interests" are Batman comics, computer hackers, New Age channeling, the "semiotics" of the Weather Channel, Mapplethorpe's homo-erotic photography, and the rap music of 2 Live Crew.[30] Another professor is busy promoting the "Evolution of the Potholder: From Technology to Popular Art."[31] And one researcher has won a fellowship to pursue "Linguistic and Pedagogic Exegeses of Some (Jieng) Dinka Tongue Twisters, Riddles and Song and Dance Games."[32] Here, too, for the record are samples of papers presented at several past conventions of the Modern Language Association, one of the largest and supposedly most "mainstream" academic bodies in the nation:[33]

- "The Sodomitical Tourist";
- "Victorian Underwear and Representations of the Female Body";
- "Jane Austen and the Masturbating Girl";
- "Is Alice Still in Phallus Land?";
- "The Detective as Pervert";
- "Strategies for Teaching a Feminist Political Latin American Culture Course";
- "The Lesbian Phallus: Or, Does Heterosexuality Exist?";
- "Self-Consuming Fictions: The Dialectics of Cannibalism in Recent Caribbean Narratives";
- "Assume the Position: Pluralist Ideology and Gynocriticism";
- "Personal Experience Stories of Amazonian Enchanted Beings";
- "Gender and Sexual Relationships in the Great Beyond."

And lest it be assumed that I am merely picking on the humanities, here are some faculty papers presented at past academic conventions for various other disciplines:[34]

- "Submerged Sensuality: Technology and Perceptions of Bathing";
- "A Functional Approach to Interruptions in Conversation: A Mathematical Analysis";
- "The Influence of Contextual Variables on Interpersonal Spacing";

- "Does Foraging Success Determine the Mating Success of Male Tungara Frogs?";
- "Using Television to Alleviate Boredom and Stress: Selective Exposure as a Function of Induced Excitational States";
- "Effects of a Signal of Timeout from One Reinforcer on Human Operant Behavior Maintained by Another Reinforcer";
- "The Facilitation of Preschoolers' Verbal Responding by Attachment Objects: The Influence of Mothers, Fathers, and Security Blankets Upon Projective Testing";
- "The Effects of Operant Control on Disruptive Behavior During Swimming Instruction";
- "Evaluating Judgments of Aspects of Like as a Function of Vicarious Exposure to the Hedonically Negative."

It should be noted that politically correct topics are most likely to receive acclaim. In 1991, for example, the *Journal of American History* awarded its top prize for the best essay by a graduate student for a submission called, "America's Boyfriend Who Can't Get a Date?: Gender, Race, and the Cultural Work of the Jack Benny Program, 1932–1946." The same year, JAH gave its top faculty prize to "The Leo Frank Case Reconsidered: Gender and Sexual Politics in the Making of Reactionary Politics."[35]

New "scholarly books" also range from the sublimely ridiculous to the sublimely obscure. This is just a small taste of what's currently in print:

- *Girls Lean Back Everywhere: The Law of Obscenity and the Assault on Genius* (Random House);
- *Talk on the Wild Side: Toward a Genealogy of a Discourse on Male Sexualities* (Routledge);
- *The First Sexual Revolution: The Emergence of Male Heterosexuality in Modern America* (New York University Press);

- *The Sexual Politics of Meat: Critical Feminist-Vegetarian Theory* (Continuum);
- *Enlightened Racism: "The Cosby Show," Audiences and the Myth of the American Dream* (Westview Press);
- *Language Shift and Cultural Reproduction: Socialization, Self, and Syncretism in a Papua New Guinea Village* (Cambridge University Press);
- *Droppin' Science: Critical Essays on Rap and Hip Hop Culture* (Temple University Press);
- *Hitchcock and Homosexuality: His 50-Year Obsession with Jack the Ripper and the Super-Bitch Prostitute—A Psychoanalytic View* (Scarecrow Press);
- *Discrimination by Design: A Feminist Critique of the Man-Made Environment* (University of Illinois Press);
- *Changing Channels: America in* TV Guide (University of Illinois Press);
- *Gender on the Line: Women, the Telephone, and Community Life* (University of Illinois Press);
- *(Sem)Erotics: Theorizing Lesbian Writing* (New York University Press);
- *Earth Follies: Coming to Feminist Terms with the Global Environmental Crisis* (Routledge);
- *Not Just for Children: The Mexican Comic Book in the Late 1960s and 1970s* (Greenwood Press);
- *Gay Catholics Down Under: The Journeys in Sexuality and Spirituality of Gay Men in Australia and New Zealand* (Prager Press);
- *The Search for a Woman-Centered Spirituality* (New York University);
- *Mama Lola: A Vodou [Voodoo] Priestess in Brooklyn* (University of California Press);
- *The Homoerotic Photograph: Male Images from Durieu/Delacroix to Mapplethorpe* (University of California Press);
- *New Lesbian Criticism: Literary and Cultural Readings* (Columbia University Press);

- *Boots of Leather, Slippers of Gold: The History of a Lesbian Community* (Routledge);
- *Staying Tuned: Contemporary Soap Opera Criticism* (Bowling Green State University Press);
- *The Politics of Popular Representation: Reagan, Thatcher, AIDS, and the Movies* (Fairleigh Dickinson University Press);
- *Acting Gay: Male Homosexuality in Modern Drama* (Cornell University Press);
- *Sadomasochism in Everyday Life: The Dynamics of Power and Powerlessness* (Rutgers University Press);
- *Men, Women, and Chainsaws: Gender in the Modern Horror Film* (Princeton University Press);
- *Clowning as Critical Practice: Performance Humor in the South Pacific* (University of Pittsburgh Press);
- *African American Gardens and Yards in the Rural South* (University of Tennessee Press);
- *Feminist Fabulation: Space/Postmodern Fiction* (University of Iowa Press);
- *Vested Interests: Cross Dressing and Cultural Anxiety* (HarperCollins);
- *A Carnival of Parting: The Tales of King Bharthari and King Gopi Chan as Sung and Told by Madhu Natisar Nath of Ghatiyali Rajasthan* (University of California Press);
- *Window Shopping: Cinema and Postmodern* (University of California Press);
- *The Saga of Gunnlaugur Snake's Tongue: With an Essay on the Structure and Translation of the Saga* (Fairleigh Dickinson University Press);
- *Development and Disenchantment in Rural Tunisia: The Bourguiba Years* (Westview Press);
- *Masculine Landscape: Walt Whitman and the Homoerotic Text* (Southern Illinois University Press);
- *Young, White, and Miserable: Growing Up Female in the 1950s* (Beacon Press);

- *The Way We Never Were: American Families and the Nostalgia Trap* (Basic Books);
- *This World, Other Worlds: Sickness, Suicide, Death, and the Afterlife Among the Vaquieros of de Alzada of Spain* (University of Chicago Press);
- *Redesigning the American Lawn: A Search for Environmental Harmony* (Yale University Press);
- *Same Sex Unions in Pre-Modern Europe* (Random House);
- *Androgynous Objects: String Bags and Gender in Central New Guinea* (Harwood Academic Publishers);
- *Brooklyn Is Not Enough: Expanding Woody Allen's Comic Universe* (Fairleigh Dickinson Press);
- *The Gendering of Melancholia: Feminism, Psychoanalysis, and the Symbolics of Loss in Renaissance Literature* (Cornell University Press);
- *Fish and Chips and the British Working Class, 1870–1940* (St. Martin's Press).

Gay and lesbian studies in particular, says the *Chronicle of Higher Education,* have moved from the sidelines to the center of academic publishing.[36] There are special gay and lesbian book series at Duke University Press, New York University Press, Oxford University Press, and the University of Chicago Press, and many more universities publish individual books in this burgeoning new field.

On academic research and publishing in general, Charles Sykes rather mildly concludes, "It is not necessary to insist that no worthwhile or valuable research is being done at the universities to recognize that much of what passes for knowledge creation makes only the most piddling contribution to the pool of human wisdom." Much may even represent a massive subtraction. But, he continues, "The research culture is founded on an almost religious faith in the search for new knowledge, and professors have a marked tendency to drift toward pietistic unctuousness in describing the importance of their work."[37]

———————— ACADEMIC QUALITY ————————

To review, then: (1) The curriculum is a shambles; (2) professors are grossly overpaid and underworked, and the teaching of undergraduate courses is left up to a sundry collection of teaching assistants, part-timers, and temporary, untenured instructors; (3) much of the research being done and published is worth little or nothing.

But these are not the only reasons why academic quality in higher education has hit rock bottom. Another factor, George Douglas says, is that among faculty and administrators there is a widely shared belief in the unimportance of undergraduate education. Most courses are considered merely as "something to be endured by those who teach them and those who are obliged to take them."[38] Jacques Barzun agrees, saying that introductory instruction has been reduced to a rote exercise in boredom, good only for winnowing out recruits for graduate school.[39]

Yet the leaders of higher education are adamant that they need more financial support in order to pay top dollar for the "best" faculties money can buy. In its current campaign, for example, Cornell University is asking alumni and other donors for more than $400 million to endow professorships that will in all likelihood have zero effect on the quality of the school's undergraduate program.[40] Michigan State University, which receives more than $230 million a year from the state treasury, says it needs millions more in state aid to "face the teaching challenges of the future." This is hard to swallow from a school that, as noted earlier, uses a video to teach about six thousand students each year in a required history course called "The United States and the World." Its professors, among the most well paid in the nation, are just too busy to perform "live." Martin Anderson notes that this is "just the logical extension of what's already in place at many elite and not-so-elite universities these days: classes in which engaged teachers and aggressive, expert teaching are considered expendable resources." Author and education critic

Midge Decter adds that this is why undergraduate education is "the biggest consumer fraud in America."[41]

Academic quality reform is desperately needed, but don't look for it to come from within. As George Douglas points out:

> Every once in a while, when universities are under particularly heated attack for their handling of undergraduate instruction, fumbling attempts are made to show that things aren't really all that bad, although usually not much is done to make drastic changes in the system. Administrators pretend to take teaching abuses seriously and call for committees to study them. A few senior professors are asked to offer a beginning course for a semester or two. The administration puts out guidebooks or white papers on teaching. Teaching assistants are monitored and checked up on. . . . The main problems, of course, are in the total system itself—its sickly and moribund courses, its gutted liberal arts tradition that is being kept on display in mummified form.[42]

And don't look for reform to come from government either. A few states have passed and many more are considering legislation stipulating minimum teaching and advising loads for public college and university faculty. They are spending about $40 billion a year on higher education and they want to know if they are getting what they are paying for, but they can't legislate academic quality anymore than they can legislate fair weather. Forcing faculty back into the classroom doesn't force them to engage students' imaginations. Real learning requires a voluntary commitment as well as "strong interaction between teacher and student, something that has long disappeared from the modern university."[43]

And reform will not come from throwing more money at colleges and universities. Academic quality, in fact, has declined as aid to higher education has soared. In the 1950s through the 1980s, state and federal subsidies led to exploding enrollments and programs. There was no time for planned and controlled growth. The flight from teaching was also made inevitable by massive infusions of "easy money." Says Sykes: "The new cash meant laboratories, assistants, sabbaticals, research grants, leaves of absence. Compared with this jackpot, traditional academia seemed hopelessly dreary."[44] Look, he continues, at what more money did to undergraduate education at Harvard University between the 1950s and the 1970s. Despite dramatic increases in the number of departments (up by one-third), faculty (up nearly 100 percent), and graduate students (up 45 percent), the undergraduate population only grew by 14 percent and the number of courses available to them actually fell by 28 percent.[45] He also cites the fact that "while the top schools spent three times more per student than their less selective counterparts, their research budgets were 50 times greater." More money, therefore, has a negative rather than a positive impact because, in the minds of administrators and faculty, undergraduate education just doesn't "count."

—————— MORALITY ON CAMPUS ——————

In the same heedless "out with the old, in with the new" campaign against the core curriculum, traditional standards, academic freedom, an actively involved teaching faculty, and academic quality in undergraduate education, there also has been a concerted effort to destroy colleges and universities' *in loco parentis* role. Ask almost any educator today, and he will tell you that students' morals and personal conduct are no longer his rightful concern. There are even legal precedents to back up this disclaimer, as evidenced by a 1991 Delaware Supreme Court decision on hazing, which decreed that the college or university is not "a policeman of student morality." Its only job is to prevent illegal, dangerous activities on its property.[46]

And one needn't look too deep to discover that the campus of the 1950s is no more. Old-fashioned "housemothers" have gone the way of the dinosaur. So have check-in times, visitation rules, single sex dormitories, quiet hours, dress codes, honor codes, and mandatory class attendance. Parents are not encouraged—in fact, they are discouraged—to influence students' choice of college, choice of major, choice of friends, choice of living arrangements, and, even more ominously, choice of "lifestyle." Often, they also are kept in the dark about their child's academic, personal, or medical problems. The message Cornell University President Frank Rhodes sends to parents is: "stand back; don't push."[47] Admissions directors at the College of William and Mary and the New College of the University of South Florida add: "overcome the protective urge," and "stop meddling."[48]

But it is perfectly alright for educators to meddle as much as they want when it comes to introducing students to the sexual revolution on campus. Duke University runs as many as twenty student seminars a year explaining sexual techniques and contraception devices. One program is called, "Was It Good for You? Eroticizing Safer Sex."[49] Dartmouth College's pamphlet on "Birth Control Facts" mentions nine methods, none of which includes abstinence.[50] There are "Condom Weeks" at a number of colleges, including Stanford University, the University of California-Berkeley, San Jose State University, Virginia Tech, the University of Iowa, and the University of North Carolina, complete with free samples and "taste tests."[51] And to show how concerned they are about "education," nearly every college and university in the country hands out free "safe sex kits" to its students. In the 1980s, Thomas Sowell described Stanford's, which included *THE SAFE SEX EXPLORER'S* ACTION-PACKED *STARTER KIT HANDBOOK*. It began: "*Welcome Explorers!* This is the safe sex universe where you will find many new galaxies of hot and healthy risk reduction, pleasure *and* peace of mind!" and went on to advise "MUTUAL MASTUR-BATION IS GREAT—but watch out for cuts on hands or raw genitals. . . . Use condoms for f-----g: with several partners, ALWAYS CLEAN UP AND CHANGE RUBBERS BEFORE GOING FROM ONE PARTNER TO ANOTHER!"[52]

At the University of Puget Sound, the school newspaper is allowed to run full-page ads like this one:

When it came to safe sex, I thought he'd be like all the rest . . . quick, boring and then long gone. How could I have *known* he had been to the workshop? How could I have *known* he was about to give me the most searingly romantic night of my life? And how could I have *known* he would want to *stay?* He gave me . . . a dozen red condoms."[53]

At Williams College, Mills College, Randolph Macon College, and the Florida Institute of Technology, to name just a few examples, male and female students can spend the night in each other's rooms. According to Sowell, this policy is called "24-hour visitation" or "unlimited visitation." Beloit College, Princeton University, and other institutions also offer co-ed bathrooms and showers. But the biggest push today is for freedom of "sexual orientation." Thus an ad in Dartmouth's main student newspaper reads: "IF YOU'VE NEVER SLEPT WITH A PERSON OF THE SAME SEX, IS IT POSSIBLE THAT ALL YOU NEED IS A GOOD GAY LOVER?"[54]

At many schools, like Pennsylvania State University, the official policy is that students may not be granted a room change request on the grounds that their roommate is homosexual.[55] And at one school where a freshman requested reassignment because her roommate habitually invited men to their room for sexual relations (starting with the first night of the term), officials gave a similar sort of answer; her roommate's "sexual orientation" was not a justification for "discrimination." When the student kept making an issue of it, she was called in for "counseling."

According to the National Gay and Lesbian Task Force, over 150 colleges and universities have policies prohibiting discrimination on the basis of "sexual orientation," but this is not enough; there must also be special programs, benefits, and protections for this new "minority":[56]

- In 1992, Emory University joined a growing group of "forward-looking" colleges and universities by establishing its Office of Lesbian, Gay, and Bisexual Life, which not only counsels but recruits students. Bobbi Patterson, Emory's associate college chaplain, explained that this new office is meant "to enhance dialogue and offer a clear affirmation on the university's part that our lesbian, gay, and bisexual students, staff, and faculty are valued by the community."

- Michigan State University's three-volume report, "Moving Forward: Lesbians and Gay Men at Michigan State University," discusses the "rich heritage" of gays and lesbians on campus and recommends affirmative action-style admissions and hiring programs for them as well as a complete revision of the school's curriculum, budget priorities, and campus policies to include special treatment for gays and lesbians.

- In 1991, the University of Iowa openly recruited a lesbian couple to join its law school faculty.

- Columbia University, Harvard University, Middlebury College, MIT, Stanford University, the University of Chicago, the University of Iowa, the University of Minnesota, the University of Vermont, and Yale University already have "domestic partner" provisions that allow gay and lesbian couples to receive insurance and other spousal benefits. (Not every school volunteered, however, says the *Chronicle of Higher Education*; the University of Vermont was ordered by the state labor relations board to offer such benefits.)

- The University of Massachusetts-Amherst has defined pedophiles (persons who have sex with children) as a protected minority in its nondiscrimination code.

- Auburn University's student senate has been threatened with a lawsuit for refusing to charter a gay and lesbian group.

- The Association of American Law Schools now prohibits

members from offering placement services to employers that discriminate against homosexuals.

- In 1992, the American Association for the Advancement of Science canceled its planned educational programs with the Boy Scouts of America because the Scouts do not accept homosexuals. (Other education associations that promote gay rights include the American Council on Education, the American Association of College and University Housing Officers, the American Association of College Registrars and Admissions Officers, and the American Association of University Professors.)
- At Cornell University, resident advisor job applicants have been forced to watch movies of men engaged in sex in order to be evaluated for "homophobic" tendencies.
- Stanford University has advertised in the *Stanford Daily* for homosexual resident advisors in student dormitories.

The curriculum and campus life are being "broadened," too:

- The University of Minnesota–Twin Cities (one of many schools) is developing a department of gay studies.
- The University of Michigan held a student-sponsored conference in 1992 on prostitution, complete with photographs and videos.
- At San Francisco State University, films are shown in class of humans having sex with animals.
- Harvard University's African Studies Chairman Henry Louis Gates (one of the highest paid "star professors" in the nation) teaches his students that the "exuberant use of hyperbole" and "so-called obscenity" of the rap group 2 Live Crew's lyrics are meant only to express frustration in an unjust world. (Some of those lyrics are: "suck my d--k, b---h, and make it puke," and "Evil 'E' was out coolin' with a freak one night/F----d the b---h with a flashlight/ Pulled it out and left the batteries in/So he could get a charge when he begin.")

- At the University of Wisconsin-Madison, eighty men were arrested in campus restrooms for "lewd and improper" behavior in June and July of 1992. They got off with fines from the local police; the school issued no punishment.
- College and university restrooms have become such popular trysting places for homosexuals that a book has been published listing all the best locations.
- "Glory holes" (holes drilled between stalls "for the performance of anonymous sexual acts") are commonplace at the University of Florida, Dartmouth College, Georgetown University, and the University of California-San Diego.

Another by-product of the abandonment of morality on campus is the soaring crime rate. Some of the crimes that are classed as "minor" (dumped garbage, graffiti,and malicious destruction of property) cost colleges and universities tens of thousands of dollars every year. Violent crimes were up nearly 18 percent between 1989 and 1991, and these were only crimes committed on college and university property, not in surrounding neighborhoods. On 580 campuses between 1990 and 1992, there were 2,528 assaults, 15,313 burglaries, 5,081 car thefts, 928 robberies, 493 rapes, and 16 murders.[57] Says one campus security consultant: "Some of the best academic institutions have had horrible crimes." In a single sample year (1991–92), there were murders at Jacksonville State University, Bakersfield College, University of California-Berkeley, Athens Area Technical College, the University of Chicago, Indiana University-Bloomington, Purdue University, the University of Iowa, Wichita State University, Highland Park Community College, the University of Southern Mississippi, the University of Missouri-Kansas City, the University of Nevada-Reno, Herbert H. Lehman College, Lenoir Community College, Central State University, Kent State University, Prairie View A & M University, Hampton University, Clinch Valley College, and Marquette

University.[58] Colleges and universities have become, it seems, literal battlefields in the "war of ideas."

Plagiarism and other forms of cheating are also on the rise. Despite the dumbing down of the curriculum, pass/fail courses, and grade inflation, it is estimated that *at least half of all college students cheat.* Some experts say the figure is much higher; in a 1991 survey, for example, 67 percent of the six thousand respondents from thirty-one of the nation's most exclusive colleges and universities admitted cheating.[59] One in five in another national survey of thousands of college students said they would falsify a report in order to keep a job.[60] A Rutgers University student has sold over one thousand copies of his new book, *Cheating 101: The Benefits and Fundamentals of Earning the Easy A.*[61] His publisher is confident that he will sell millions of copies in the next several years. Notices are routinely posted on dormitory bulletin boards and printed in student newspapers and such national publications as *Rolling Stone* advertising term papers for sale.[62] One professor of English at California State University notes, "Many faculty members know not to put students' graded papers outside their offices for the students to pick up, because papers are now valuable commodities that will disappear to surface later for sale," and he recounts the story of a colleague who discovered that a female student in his class had submitted a paper *he* had written as an undergraduate.[63]

Cheating, as some defenders of the status quo would have it, is an old story; but between 1966 and 1988 another national survey reports that the number of students cheating increased *78 percent.*[64] Professors, as pointed out, to some extent are to blame for not bothering to teach their students about proper use of sources or how to write and research using their own words instead of others'. Yet the real problem is that higher education is no longer willing to respond to cheating on a moral level. Says one observer: "Even though the mission statements of most institutions still include the development of students' ethical standards as an educational goal many colleges and universities have taken a neutral position concerning traditional values in recent years, including a laissez-faire attitude toward students' moral development."[65] "Political correctness" may also be to blame. If we do not ask students to study virtue in the classroom, why should we expect it of them in their personal lives? If we do not admit to the existence of truth, why should we expect students to be truthful?

————A Loss of Community————

Even though virtually all big colleges and universities claim that within departments there is a "small college atmosphere" and that they treat students as if they were "family," the reality is that from the day the typical freshman arrives on campus to the day he graduates, he remains a stranger. To all but a few individuals with whom he comes into frequent contact, he is just a name and a number in the main computer banks, along with thousands or even tens of thousands of others like him. He finds freshman orientation an impersonal affair, convenient mostly for picking up his safe sex kit. He stands in line for hours to register for classes (many of which are closed within the first hour or two) without anyone to advise him on what he should register for.

He is given a "Where's Waldo?"-style map to find how to get from his dorm (which bears a striking resemblance to a Soviet housing project) to class and to the bookstore and cafeteria, where he must stand in line for service with hundreds of other students. If he is homesick, lonely, or confused, or has any perfectly ordinary problem, there is no official to help him, unless he belongs to an acknowledged, politically correct minority, or he is suicidal, or he seeks drug rehabilitation. He will try to join a little island of community within his dorm or Greek house, but he certainly won't rub shoulders with the faculty; to most members of this elite class he is just one of the nameless, faceless students who come and go every four years and, because of his probable lack of academic skills, he is also a disappointment rather than a challenge.

He will attend classes, sometimes in groups of five hundred to one thousand in large amphitheaters, or, since many of them seem boring and pointless, he will stay in his room and watch soap operas instead. Later, he will borrow someone else's notes or purchase a term paper or exam in order to earn a passing grade. He will not join clubs or honoraries, and he will never attend any campus events except rock concerts, protest rallies, and varsity athletic games. Like over three-fourths of all college and university students, his most common extracurricular activity will be drinking.

This is the "undergraduate experience" on many campuses today. Fueled by federal and state aid, college and university enrollments have soared to astronomical levels, changing once-small campuses into huge hives of impersonal activity and destroying any sense of community or institutional identity. After World War II, says George Douglas:

> American society wanted our universities to be big, to serve "everybody," whether they had a genuine interest in higher learning or not. It was therefore inevitable that the handling of these multitudes would take on the character of the mechanical and the perfunctory. If society tells universities "process 'em, put 'em on a conveyer belt and we'll send you big money," then universities will process them and put them on a conveyer belt.[66]

But, by and large, he says, this tremendous loss to the students has gone unnoticed since the "megauniversity" or "university emporium" has found ways to make mass education appear easy and appealing. On big campuses, not only are expectations of performance and achievement considerably lower, but students are offered freedom with few corresponding obligations.[67] Administrators and faculty members say in their own defense that they are treating students like adults, but Douglas calls their answer a petty excuse for neglect and isolation. Claire L. Gaudiani, president of Connecticut College, sums it up when she says that if they don't receive direction from the adults nominally in charge—faculty and administrators—"chaos, under the guise of 'freedom,' " is all that will reign in the lives of many students.[68]

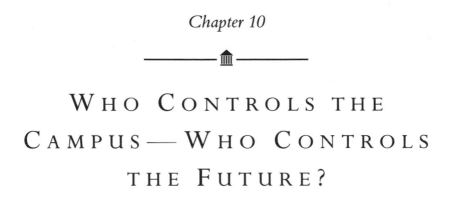

Chapter 10

WHO CONTROLS THE CAMPUS—WHO CONTROLS THE FUTURE?

————— LEADERSHIP VALUES —————

In *Impostors in the Temple,* Martin Anderson comments on a paradox that has been explored throughout this book: Although today's colleges and universities look much like large business corporations with thousands of employees (faculty and staff) and customers (students and parents), they are not organized or run like them. "There is nothing comparable," Anderson says, for example, "to stockholders to whom corporate boards and executives must ultimately answer. No one 'owns' a university. Virtually all the major universities and colleges in America are mini-socialist states in which trustees, administrators and faculty answer only to themselves."[1]

I would go even further than this to state that modern higher education not only has pursued an intellectual love affair with socialism but has adopted its basic principles of internal management. Since the 1960s, much of the control of institutional as well as academic affairs has shifted from the "bourgeoisie" (administrators) to the "proletariat" (faculty members). Federal funding has financed this shift every step of the way by directing billions of dollars to professors and their research. Faculty senates and committees now typically exert a major influence on admissions, scholarships, financial aid, hiring, firing, tenure, promotion, research, facility use, construction, pay and benefits, investment policies, student conduct, course and department expansion, curriculum revision, graduation requirements, and last, but certainly not least, budgets. In *Profscam,* Charles J. Sykes says:

> Depending on your point of view, the university is either like a vast medieval-style corporation or . . . Woodstock. On paper, its lines of authority seem clear enough. The university is gilded with the full panoply of power associated with the more traditional organizations: On top sits a president, with a salary and perquisites that normally accompany great power; below the president are chancellors, vice chancellors, a pride of vice presidents of various denominations and suitably vague responsibilities, a whole assortment of provosts, deans, and department chairs, and at the very bottom, a fractious and improvident faculty.
>
> But despite the elaborate pyramid, universities are notoriously unruly. The organizational charts are for outside consumption only. Internally, the real distribution of power is an inverted pyramid, with all the most important powers concentrated not at the top, but at the bottom, tightly held and jealously guarded by the professors themselves.[2]

Advocates of this system never call it by its true name, which is socialism; they prefer "shared governance." Shared governance sounds wonderful; theoretically, it is meant to give faculty members a greater voice in campus concerns and prevent the often all too real abuse of authority by administrators. In practice, however, it creates worse abuse by leading to the breakdown of effective decision making, the tyranny of the majority, and control without accountability for *both* groups. It pits them against one another as bitter rivals, and consequently all decisions become politicized.

Shared governance also allows both groups to avoid difficult situations, to skew institutional and academic priorities, to postpone needed reforms, and to rely on convenient, stop-gap strategies instead of prudent plans for the future. Look, for example, at the current financial crisis in American higher education. It did not spring up overnight; the warning signs were clear for years. Yet administrators and faculty members were so busy fighting over control of the campus that they ignored them. More than a decade ago, reliable demographic studies revealed that there would be a dwindling pool of traditional college-age students in the 1990s and that most would be unable to pay even a fraction of the real cost of their education. It was equally well known that institutional operating costs were rising far faster than ever before and that, in fact, they were spiraling out of control. In the mid-1980s, a number of state governments gradually but consistently began cutting back on higher education funding. At the same time, while the federal government was continuing to increase student financial assistance, it was not keeping pace with demand, and the mounting U.S. deficit made it clear that, at the very least, much smaller increases for academic research lay ahead. Finally, in the late 1980s, the collapse of Soviet communism foretold that there would be less money for defense-related R & D, a major source of guaranteed income, especially for large institutions. If they had heeded these signs, colleges and universities could have adopted austerity measures, taken on less debt, limited new construction, programs, and hiring, and aggressively built their endowments, but, ruled largely by shared governance, most chose instead to go on a spending binge.

Now the chickens have come home to roost. Administrators and faculty members alike have to face the fact that they cannot count on continually expanding sources of state and federal revenue. And they have to perform some of their basic missions better than in the past if they are to survive. But the shared governance system, like all forms of socialist management, simply is incapable of responding. It evolved, notes a recent Rand Corporation study, "in an environment of rapid, sustained growth. Budgets grew as fast as enrollments." Any changes in student or faculty demands "could be accommodated by increases in overall budgets; there was little need to think of reallocating resources from existing programs to new ones . . . allocation among institutions was largely ad hoc."[3] In other words, the shared goverance system can manage (or rather mismanage) very nicely in times of prosperity and even can deal with across-the-board budget cuts for short periods, but it cannot develop policies, procedures, and decision-making bodies to cope with the radical reform that is so desperately needed today.

For decades, faculty members, given unprecedented authority to determine their own budgets, have been spared the necessity of asking vital questions like: "How much will this new program cost?" or "How will we pay for it?" Administrators, freed of the responsibilities of being in charge, have joined the professoriate in the quest to raise more money in order to expand their own domains. The two groups have competed against one another for more money because more money has meant more power. And there has been another built-in incentive to spend more rather than less; any savings by individual departments have reverted to the central administration, and, in the case of public campuses, from the central administration to the state. Faculty members and administrators alike have gotten into the habit of spending all they can lay their hands on, and their cardinal rule, borrowed from the federal bureaucracy, has been: "Never come in under budget."

Despite all the evidence, shared governance seldom is blamed for any of these disastrous results. Ironically, most problems are attributed to too little power-sharing. The majority of today's faculty members claim, with perfect sincerity, that they and their colleagues have no real authority at all and that it is their president who is guilty not only of poor financial stewardship but of being an "autocrat" bent on destroying "academic freedom." This may seem like an exaggeration, but a recent national study of college presidencies notes that "faculty members almost universally discount the performance of their current presidents at a rate that must be 25–75 percent below that of other observers."[4] Faculties around the country at such schools as Elmira College, Lamar University, San Diego State University, Ferris State University, and, very nearly, the University of Notre Dame, have recently taken votes of "no confidence" and demanded that their presidents and/or other administrative leaders resign.[5] The arts and sciences faculty at Columbia University also stopped just short of a vote of "no confidence" in its president and provost in the early 1990s. The alternative strategy settled on had far more impact: Twenty-five department chairmen and leading faculty members in effect held a gun to the administration's head by threatening to quit if their budgets were cut.[6]

The real issue is power—who should control the campus? At spendthrift colleges and universities where "reform administrations" have tried to implement ordinary business practices, the result, says Arthur Levine, executive editor of *Change* magazine, "has been the unleashing of a political firestorm, with faculty at the center," and "an exodus of college presidents who tried to move in this direction."[7] To some extent, this is hardly surprising. Cutting budgets, cutting personnel, and cutting departments are moves that, however necessary, are bound to make college presidents unpopular. But "unpopular" is an understatement; if you asked most faculty members to draw a picture of their president, he likely would be wearing a hockey mask and holding a bloody chainsaw. And although it also is unsurprising that more presidents tend to bail out in times of crisis, it is deeply troubling that their *average* tenure has been whittled down to only three years at research universities and seven years at all other institutions. The presidents at Duke University, Columbia University, Yale University, Stanford University, the University of California, the University of Chicago, and the University of Texas were just a few of those who quit recently—three hundred to four hundred college presidents are resigning every year.[8]

Publicly, they claim that they are leaving to take advantage of "new career opportunities," but privately, they cite as the real reasons ceaseless battles with the faculty, enormous budget-cutting and fund-raising pressures, and the thorough politicization of campus life. Many of those who stay on confess, also off the record, that they face a constant and growing burden of dealing with stifling bureaucracy within their own institutions and/or university systems. Worst of all, they are opposed at every turn by their own faculty when it comes to making the most basic institutional and academic decisions. Says Stephen Joel Trachtenberg: "A funny thing happened to me on the way to the presidency of the University of Hartford." He goes on to describe the interview, which was:

> at enormous length about my opinions, feelings, intuitions, and preferences in matters of teaching, research, learning, and scholarship. This part of the interview, I must confess, I rather welcomed, since it implied that as president I would be expected to concern myself with the very activities that distinguish a university from other corporate or government endeavors. As it turned out, I was sadly mistaken, No sooner had I been inaugurated than I found out that any attempt on my part to actively participate in those professional activities was regarded with the same favor as a tap dancer at a funeral. The first role as university president, I was informed in no uncertain terms, is to bring the school to the attention of people with money in their pockets.[9]

If college presidents attempt to act as chief executives or call for major reforms, they are automatically branded as "authoritarian." In all the how-to advice and literature on becoming a college president, great stress is laid upon the "superior" model of the president as a "sympathetic listener," "faculty ally," "willing compromiser," and "goodwill ambassador." It is true that a successful college president must be all these things, but, first and foremost, he is supposed to be a *leader*, and this requires the clear and unequivocal authority to make basic day-to-day and long-term decisions about the institution he heads. Such authority is more important than ever before on today's politicized campuses; faculty members in one department may view those in other departments with hostility or envy, but they are adept at building coalitions in order to stymie the administration, which they regard as an "evil empire."

But most college presidents have traded their campus authority for external authority in areas like P.R. and fund raising. In "The Inside President," David Brooks Arnold says candidly that they have chosen to turn their backs on academic leadership rather than risk losing the fight for rightful control of their institutions.[10] The "new and improved," "kinder and gentler" modern prototypes have condemned traditional academic leadership and all hierarchical forms of control for "stifling dissent." Their primary role has not been to serve as chief executives of competitive businesses but as high-paid shills who have procured more and more state, federal, and private funding that the faculty (in at least equal partnership with the administration) has decided how to spend. Academic decisions also largely have been left up to the faculty; what has gone on in the classroom has not been the concern of college presidents. For their part, as sociologists David Riesman and Christopher Jencks noted over thirty years ago, faculty members have responded to the growing leadership vacuum quite predictably. They now consider themselves to be "independent professionals like doctors or lawyers, responsible primarily to themselves and their colleagues rather than their employers."[11]

But as we have learned through painful experience, no college or university can be run exclusively by consensus among "independent professionals" without running amok. College presidents need strong authority. This does not mean that they should pursue strength for strength's sake—clearly, the best kind of leadership depends on consensus, not coercion—but it *does* mean having firm expectations that everyone will cooperate and work within a framework of "corporate governance." Right now in American higher education there is a critical, immediate need not only to cut budgets substantially but to restructure the way virtually all educational enterprises operate. Imagine doing this through the shared governance system—it would be like allowing students to vote on the tuition they were charged or the grades they received ("rights" many student activists *are*, in fact, demanding). Just as there should be different rights and responsibilities in the student/faculty relationship, so, too, should there be different rights and responsibilities in the faculty/administrator relationship.

Restoring their own authority has to be college presidents' first task; they cannot tackle the budget, the curriculum, or any other issue until they have legitimate power to act. Only they can make the hard decisions that committees—any committees, whether made up of administrators or faculty members—by definition never can make. Only they can be held accountable for the success or failure of those decisions. I should add here that many thoughtful education critics have emphasized greater trustee involvement as a more important task. I agree with the inference that many trustees have been "derelict in their duty" and have not paid close enough attention to what is happening on the campuses they oversee. They *should* get more involved and exert an active influence. But their role is not to make policy decisions or to try to manage day-to-day academic and institutional affairs. They are meant to be the stewards, not the managers, of the institutions in their care.

Restoring presidential authority, then, is the real key to educational reform. It will not be easy—a decade earlier, it would have been impossible—but there will be a limited window of opportunity in the next several years as the seriousness of higher education's financial plight puts the backs of the professors—and administrators—up against the wall.

————— Marketplace Values —————

Modern higher education has been so heavily subsidized by government for so long that it no longer regards itself as accountable to those who are its real patrons or to the rules that apply to virtually all other businesses. Former Harvard University President Derek Bok admits, "All across the country they [Americans] hear about enterprises of every kind facing competitive challenges and having to pay much closer attention to the quality of everything they do. That is the revolution that is sweeping this country; the public naturally expects us to participate. And a lot of us are not."[12]

Educators have been more concerned with "revenue enhancement"—extracting money from government—than with striving to be competitive. They have allowed state and federal subsidies to create a false prosperity and have overfunded, overstaffed, and overbuilt their campuses to such an extent that they have eradicated "defects" that in reality were those campuses' greatest assets. Once, when colleges and universities were relatively poor, they spent prudently and grew only as they could afford it, which entailed careful planning. When they were small in size, there was a pervasive sense of community and constant interaction among administrators, faculty, and students—everyone "pulled together." When their campuses and facilities were modest, they concentrated more on what they could offer in terms of academic enrichment.

Today, while the spigot of direct government funding has not been completely shut off, its flow has been reduced significantly. Yet many educators are acting—and spending—as if nothing has changed. Old habits die hard, of course, and they still have not accepted the fact that government funding has subsidized the rot which is eating away at the very foundations of higher education. As someone who has experienced firsthand how tough it is to raise millions of dollars to keep even a small school going, I know how tempting it is to ignore such a conclusion. Government money is such easy money. There are literally hundreds of inducements to accept it, and it always appears—at first—to be "free money," without any strings attached. Heaven knows, there are plenty of politicians and bureaucrats who will claim that this is so.

Don't believe them. Nothing comes dearer than "free money." Hundreds of private colleges and universities have learned in recent years that even "indirect aid," that is, aid that goes to their students, makes them "federal recipients" and "wards of the state" as far as the government and the courts are concerned. Bureaucrats have used any excuse to invade their campuses and have made crusades out of such causes as "affirmative action," "fair labor standards," "health and safety," "consumer protection," and "academic freedom." Sometimes the invasion has even been welcomed because of the material benefits government provides; sometimes it has merely been tolerated because of the fear government inspires.

In addition to the way it wrongly compromises the independence of private institutions, government funding is also destructive because it wrongly shields colleges and universities from the normal, healthy forces of the marketplace. It eliminates competition, which is the only real incentive to practice good fiscal stewardship and remain responsive to issues of quality, affordability, and equal access. Critics will say, of course, that "privatizing" higher education means abolishing these things and that government subsidies are the lifeblood of higher education. But as Thomas Sowell points out, no one would be surprised if massive government subsidies to Sears had an adverse effect on Penney's or Montgomery Ward, or made Sears less concerned about pleasing its employees and customers and about offering quality goods and services at reasonable prices. The critics of privatization have not noticed, he continues, that in higher education throwing billions of dollars at academic research has taken more and more professors away from the classroom and made some of them as dictatorial and uncontrollable as feudal barons.[13] Nor have they noticed that the awe-inspiring "mega-universities" that government funds have helped erect are totally unsuited to the task of educating young undergraduates.

Thankfully, due to circumstances beyond their control, educators now must at the very least curb their addiction to government funding. The record-high revenues of the 1950s-1980s are over. In the 1990s, state and federal aid to colleges and universities is either declining or failing to keep up with the expansion of the system, and higher education has become just one budget priority competing among many. But educators are trying to replace lost federal and state revenues through massive campaigns directed at the private sector. The *Detroit News* calls it a "fundraising frenzy." Even schools with endowments in the billions of dollars have exhibited a panic mentality. Cornell University, Stanford University, Columbia University, Yale University, the University of Michigan, and the University of Pennsylvania have inaugurated new $1 billion-plus drives in recent years. Harvard University is planning one for *$2 billion.*[14] Even ardent supporters of private fund raising like Peter Buchanan, president of the Council for Advancement and Support of Education, are disgusted. He characterizes "megacampaigns" as "the dumbest thing I have ever seen," and the *Chronicle of Higher Education* reports that many laymen as well as experts are skeptical about why such well-endowed colleges and universities need so much money.[15]

Should the private sector give generously to higher education? Absolutely. But that does not mean that it should give blindly. Former Secretary of the Treasury William E. Simon wrote a brief *Wall Street Journal* article in the late 1980s that ought to serve as a manifesto for all would-be supporters. Called "Give to the College a Choice," it stated, "We in the business community have a right and a responsibility to steer our gifts to institutions committed to maintaining freedom."[16] He was not suggesting that businessmen dictate to higher education in the way that government does, but that they simply stop financing leftist attacks on the principles, values, and institutions that have allowed them to prosper. "Otherwise," he concluded, "we will have nobody to blame but ourselves for permitting the largesse of private enterprise to subsidize the slide into statism." In short, capitalists should stop giving away for free the rope to those in academe who are out to hang them.

Meanwhile, the best news of all may be that colleges and universities are (in many cases, literally) "going broke." More money didn't bail out the failing S & Ls in the 1980s; they simply misspent it in the same ways they had been misspending for years. Failing businesses only recover when they engage in a fundamental restructuring of the way they do business. Only now, as higher education is in the midst of its worst financial crisis since the Great Depression, are real rather than cosmetic reforms possible. In their annual "state of education" report in 1992, the editors of the *Chronicle of Higher Education* concluded that a review of priorities can be forestalled no longer; even "sacred cows" like low faculty workloads and high administrative/faculty salaries will have to be sacrificed since state and federal revenues cannot be counted on to pay for them.

But, like the state bureaucrats who sought to negate Proposition 13 in California in the 1980s, the majority of educators are cutting the "fire department" first: undergraduate teaching. The Rand Corporation reports: "There is no compelling evidence that the cuts higher education systems and institutions have made to date are focused on areas of waste and excess, or . . . have resulted in greater efficiency or responsiveness."[17] Education consultant Sean C. Rush comments: "During the past several years, the word 'productivity' has crept into the lexicon of higher education with all the subtlety of a Kansas tornado." But it is meaningless, he says, because colleges and universities are reluctant to make the hard decisions and acquire the discipline that goes along with it. At most institutions "productivity," Rush concludes, "like reading Leo Tolstoy's *War and Peace,* is something more often talked about than actually done."[18] Education researchers William Massey and Robert Zemsky have predicted that real budget cuts and quality gains will be made soon, but that they may be temporary. When the current crisis appears to have abated, all the old vices will return in force, and institutions still will not have rethought their fundamental financial or academic mission.[19] Two other education researchers, Gerald Gaither and Robby DeWitt, feel somewhat differently: "Colleges and universities have traditionally met such fiscal crises by 'muddling through' until better times return, and then eventually resuming their undisciplined spending patterns." But, they add, "many recent cases of severe financial strain have caught institutions badly prepared and unable to muddle through."[20] They will be permanently affected.

There is no overall rescue strategy that can be applied to a failing business when it is failing on the scale of American higher education. Right now, however, chances are good that quite a few campuses will try to make genuine and sound reforms—as a last resort, of course, but they will try to make them all the same. We can help them. Our job is to give generous philanthropic as well as moral support to the campuses that *do* try, and to foil any attempts to increase state or federal aid to higher education. The history of our nation proves that it doesn't take government money to be an American success story. This is an important lesson we must help educators learn all over again.

But there are risks that they won't learn the *right* lesson, and we have to be aware of the potential danger. Right now, taxpayers are on the hook for $250 billion or more in bad loans as a result of the S & L collapse, but that is peanuts compared to what it costs to run our colleges and universities; it wouldn't even pay for two years of operation at current spending levels. When the bottom fell out of the market, the government's first response was to clamp down on credit, which crippled thousands of small businesses. Hundreds of small private colleges are just as vulnerable in this case, and they are finding it harder than ever to raise funds, since they are competing not only against bigger private colleges and universities but, in the aftermath of state funding cuts, against public colleges and universities as well. The government's second response was to blame what happened to the S & Ls on deregulation. This also may happen with higher education; right now there are many regulation advocates calling loudly for the federal government to step in and take over higher education just as it took over the troubled thrift industry, which, according to sources such as *Forbes* and the *Wall Street Journal,* was the real cause of the S & L collapse. But even if it were to be more successful in this particular "takeover," government cannot guarantee that schools will become fiscally responsible or that students will learn, or that teachers will teach, or that productive scholarship and academic freedom will flourish. Regulating campuses only can lead to an even greater disaster than the failure of corrupt S & Ls, which, as many observers have noted, thrived on political influence.

ACADEMIC AND MORAL
——————VALUES——————

Colleges and universities have always held special status as places of integrity and idealism. Traditionally, those who teach have been revered in our society. But modern academics are so out of touch these days that they don't even realize how this has changed. At a recent seminar for a large crowd of business and community leaders from around the country, a well-known, liberal university scholar tried to validate his argument by declaring (in reverent tones) that it was based on data supplied by Harvard University. Upon hearing this, the audience booed, and the scholar was visibly taken aback. He did not realize that for millions of ordinary Americans "Harvard" has become a pejorative term, representing the worst, rather than the best, of academe.

Pollster Lou Harris reports that in the 1960s, an estimated 61 percent of all Americans placed a high degree of confidence in the "people running higher education." Today, only about 25 percent feel the same.[21] Martin Anderson adds:

Just listen to some of the voices knowledgeable about the world of academics. In 1988 Yale University's 19th president, A. Bartlett Giamatti, wrote that "for almost two decades the American people have been aware of and dismayed by the gap in the nation's colleges and universities, the gap between the grand, traditional and almost unexamined professions of high principle, lofty mission and splendid purpose—and institutional behavior that is often venal, self-serving, and shoddy." Venal, self-serving, and shoddy? In 1990 Bruce Wilshire, a professor at Rutgers University, published a book entitled, *The Moral Collapse of the University,* in which he wrote: "We must speak of the bankruptcy of the university as an educational institution. It is a humilating admission." Bankruptcy? In 1991 William Bennett, the former secretary of education, observed sadly that "in some ways universities are becoming increasingly irrelevant to the intellectual life of the nation." Irrelevant?

When educational leaders openly use such words as "venal," "shoddy," "bankrupt," and "irrelevant" to describe the state of higher education in America, we can be sure that something is seriously wrong.[22]

Once, when the academic community spoke, it was with the voice of authority. Educators occupied the moral high ground, as it were, and represented the pinnacles of achievement in learning, wisdom, and culture; they held the keys to a two-and-a-half-thousand-year-old intellectual treasury more precious than gold. Today, public esteem for education is still high, but educators have become laughingstocks. There is a popular saying: "There are some ideas that are so absurd that only an intellectual could believe them." Who, after all, can take seriously "cutting-edge" courses that range from exploring deconstructionism and Marxism to lesbianism and sadomasochism? Who can respect teachers who only spend three to six hours a week in the classroom and who consider research rather than teaching their true interest? Who can feel secure entrusting their eighteen-year-old son or daughter to a college or university that refuses to take a stand on issues of right and wrong and that abandons its moral obligations to students inside as well as outside the classroom?

Restoring traditional and time-tested academic and moral standards may be the hardest job of all, dwarfing any response to the mammoth financial crisis in modern higher education. Most educators will claim that it is impossible to turn back the clock and that no one would support such standards anymore, but it is up to us—as parents, donors, and taxpayers—to convince them that such standards are not only desirable, but necessary. Alexander W. Astin, a professor of education at UCLA, argues that it has become increasingly clear that the real problems of higher education are not about finances; they are about *values:*

> Values are fundamental to just about everything we do in undergraduate education: whom we admit and on what basis, what we teach them and how we teach it, what rules and requirements will govern our students' conduct, how to test and certify our students, whom to hire and the criteria for hiring, tenuring, and promoting them, the manner in which we treat each other as professional colleagues, the topics we choose for our own research and scholarship, and how we faculty use our discretionary time.[23]

For years, educators have been teaching our students the wrong values; they have traded discipline for a disdain for the work ethic, self-sacrifice for self-interest, broad intellectual inquiry for narrow pedantry, and the courage to make moral judgments for moral relativism and a hatred of all the "bourgeois trappings" of civilized society.

Here is where leadership values, again, are vitally important. College presidents not only must join but must lead the fight for a restoration of academic and moral values. In *A Memo to a College Trustee,* Beardsley Ruml explains that the president of a college or university is not just its highest-ranking officer—he is its "highest personal symbol."[24] He is the one who must develop and articulate a compelling vision that will unite the students, alumni, faculty, staff, donors, and trustees and lead them to set aside at least some of their parochial concerns and conflicts. In *How Academic Leadership Works,* Robert Birnbaum enlarges on this theme to argue that the college president's biggest impact should not be as a fund raiser or as an academician, but as a teacher of *morality*—he should set the tone for which values are cherished by students and faculty as well as which values underlie his institution's entire identity and mission.[25]

THE FALL OF THE
——————IVORY TOWER——————

A restoration of leadership values, of marketplace values, and of academic and moral values—any one of these constitutes a daunting challenge for American higher education, especially since what has troubled it in the modern era is what has troubled us as a nation: We have lost our sense of purpose, our consensus about the aims of human action. Our society, for years plagued by rootlessness and self-doubt, may be turning around, however—one can see evidence of the resurgence of values in even the most unlikely places, e.g., television, films, and the popular press. Certainly our flagging economy recovered at an amazing rate in the 1980s as just a few of the most egregious regulatory and tax burdens were lifted. As consumers and producers we again have come to know the fruits of competition. But, we are told by politicians, the media, and the educational establishment, competition is "bad" for our schools; educational reforms, educational management, and educational spending must emanate from Washington, D.C.

This book catalogues the ill effects of such statist thinking. It also suggests that too little competition and too much government have led to academic bankruptcy, moral bankruptcy, and, finally, to literal bankruptcy in our colleges and universities. The term "bankruptcy" derives from an Italian phrase, *banca rotta,* meaning "broken bench." It is an apt description of American higher education today; the entire system stands on the verge of collapse. Of course, the "ivory tower" will not come crashing down on some apocalyptic day of judgment. But its destruction is no less real simply because it happens gradually. In time, it will succumb to the forces of fiscal gravity, like a derelict building crumbling brick by brick.

"Big education" in public and private universities will continue to exist in some fashion, and the present Democratic administration and the federal bureaucracy will summon all their powers to shore up the damage through still more federal funding. But this tactic cannot reverse the internal rot which such funding caused in the first place. The process of decay is simply too far advanced. The real question is, therefore, what will we erect upon the ruins of the old system?

EPILOGUE

REBUILDING THE
IVORY TOWER

I am no seer, and there is no sense in pretending to be one, but I will be so bold as to make a few predictions about the future of American higher education. The most important is that radical change is unavoidable, because the educational system we have known for the last half-century is collapsing. Our colleges and universities are not passing through a troubled financial phase from which they will eventually recover in roughly the same, if somewhat diminished, shape as before; they are in the throes of a systemic crisis.

Most educators acknowledge this—partly, that is. American Association of Colleges President James Appleberry has remarked that "public higher education will be altered radically. . . ."[1] "We've been through budget squeezes before, but it's different this time," adds Lattie F. Coor, president of Arizona State University. This time, he says, it is "a fundamental shift in public policy as it relates to funding universities."[2] Richard Novak, president of the Association of Governing Boards of Universities and Colleges, confirms: "I think the downsizing will be permanent—even after a recovery."[3]

But the whole truth is that when they emerge from the

current crisis, all colleges and universities, public and private, truly will be different. Just as *perestroika,* which only was supposed to make socialism more cost-efficient and streamlined, ended up destroying socialism, downsizing and privatizing will change the nature as well as the scope of American higher education.

Another prediction is that we will continue to see a popular backlash against colleges and universities for years to come. Arthur Levine comments that academe "is facing more than a poor economy—it is undergoing a test of public trust." All its constituents "are asking hard questions about the cost, pricing, productivity, access, outcomes, and effectiveness of college. For the most part, we arrogantly ignore these questions—acting as if they were an insult to our integrity. Reduced financial support is one way in which the public is expressing its dissatisfaction—and our responses to date support their greatest fears."[4]

The financial crisis is also going to get worse before it gets better. State and federal revenues will not "save the day." Colleges and universities across the country are already going under or retrenching in dramatic ways. Foolishly, many are cutting essential services instead of bureaucracy and waste. All cuts, foolish or otherwise, will engender a great deal of protest in the media and will be fought by increasingly hostile interest groups representing students and faculty. But the atmosphere of crisis is just what is required to allow a number of college presidents to retake control of their campuses and become genuine leaders once again.

Though they will try to maintain their smorgasbord and boutique approaches to higher education, public "megauniversities" will no longer be able afford to do so, if only because they cannot spend money at the levels to which they became accustomed in the 1960s–1980s. The *Wall Street Journal* reports that most of the nation's state-sponsored schools are "under the ax," and that the budget cuts they have been forced to make are the result of more than just an economic downturn that has hit a few random institutions—two-thirds of all public colleges and universities have been affected.[5] The *Chronicle of Higher Education* vouchsafes that large institutions will have to adopt smaller programs, narrower missions, and insist on more productivity from their faculty and staff.[6] This will not happen overnight—they still have an awful lot of money to squander, and many will continue to lavish vast sums on "star professors," on research that does not contribute to the overall mission of the institution, and on "politically correct" departments and programs. But their worst excesses will be curbed, and very soon, state politicians will target specialty schools for elimination, asking, "Do we really need five schools of medicine, seven law schools, and nine schools of education in our state university system? Can we afford the tremendous drain on the public purse?"

Florida's Governor Lawton Chiles has already gone further than that: He has ordered public higher education officials to draw up a privatization plan for nearly all of the public colleges and universities within the state.[7] Although the kind of privatization he seems to have in mind is to make them public corporations instead of truly private enterprises, his action is enormously significant. Privatization of some form or another is also a very real possibility in states like California, where the public university system is barely surviving.

In addition, large private universities across the nation will dig deeply into their endowments and continue to slash programs, courses, faculty, and students to make up for huge losses in government revenues and previous overexpansion and overspending. While they will engage in a lot of rhetoric about a renewed commitment to quality teaching, undergraduate programs will remain mediocre at many of these institutions; others will successfully restore academic standards. (And, just as at large public universities, there will be dissension for years to come over budgets, salaries, tuitions, teaching loads, and reduced course offerings, making their campuses even more politicized and acrimonious; but downsizing will have a beneficial long-term effect on the way they operate and on their overall missions.)

The nation's 1,600-odd community and technical colleges will continue to gain enrollment and will fill an important, growing educational need for thousands of students. These institutions, which came into vogue in the early 1970s and which often do quite well on shoe-string budgets, will prosper as never before, as they are relatively cost-effective and are more attuned to regional markets and career training. Author and former Princeton professor Richard M. Huber points out that their students may pay ten times less tuition in order to be taught by full Ph.D.s instead of teaching assistants. And community college faculty, though low-paid, are often better-than-average classroom instructors who find it much more congenial to work with the older, highly motivated, nontraditional students that make up much of the student body. They tend to stick to teaching basic academic skills like reading and writing, which every successful student needs to acquire.

But many of these institutions are afflicted by the same problems as other colleges: low academic standards, rising operating costs, and dependence on government subsidies. Corruption involving federal grant and loan programs at trade schools will do further damage. They will go under, but new enterprises will take their place in what is the most dynamic market in higher education.

The real agents of genuine education reform will be the nation's smaller, private four-year liberal arts colleges. One factor in their favor is their sheer number: 1,158 compared to their 599 public counterparts. The bad news is that these schools are poorly endowed; therefore they are likely to be the greatest casualties in the current financial crisis. Those that have relied on state support as an important source of revenue will be in the most trouble, because inevitably the first support that states pull when economizing is from private colleges and universities, as we have seen recently in Florida, Maryland, New Jersey, New York, Pennsylvania, and South Carolina.[8]

It also is true that many of these schools have maintained a weak commitment to high academic standards, have watered down their curricula, and have undistinguished reputations. During the supposed "Golden Age" of higher education from

1960 to 1990, more than three hundred closed their doors.[9] Many more will close or merge now. But those that survive have both the opportunity and the means to pursue a new and prosperous future. There are huge numbers of students—and donors—looking for an alternative to "big education," to "political correctness," and to moral relativism in higher education. If these schools define themselves as a real alternative, and if they are willing to stake everything on a restoration of their commitment to quality undergraduate education, then there will be no limits to what they can achieve. Their first step, however, must be to restore their own institutional independence. That means paying their own way, for "he who pays the piper calls the tune," and up until now, as one former college president has observed, private higher education has been dancing to the government's melody.

To the extent that the American system of higher education makes room for private, independent colleges and universities, it will remain the best in the world. There is, simply, no other system like ours. By contrast, Great Britain has *one* private university; Germany has *one;* Australia has *none.* France and Japan together have a few hundred, but they are highly subsidized and/or regulated by the state. With all its faults, our system is the freest and most independent, and that is a strong foundation indeed on which to build the new "ivory tower."

ENDNOTES

CHAPTER 1
COLLEGES IN CRISIS

1. Marvin Lazerson and Ursula Wagner, "Rethinking How Colleges Operate," *Chronicle of Higher Education*, September 30, 1992, A44.
2. *Business Officer*, December 1991, 7.
3. James Harvey, "Footing the Bill: Financial Prospects for Higher Education," *Educational Record*, Fall 1992, 11.
4. Mel Elfin, "What Must Be Done: Cutting Costs While Improving Educational Quality Is the Main Aim of the New College Reform Movement," *America's Best Colleges, U.S. News & World Report*, 1992–93, 8.
5. Carolyn J. Mooney, "Death of a Campus," *Chronicle of Higher Education*, June 24, 1992, A13–14.
6. "Poisoned Ivy," *The Economist*, August 15, 1992, 18.
7. Many schools received higher than anticipated appropriations for their 1993–94 budgets, but virtually all observers agree that the sharp downward trend in funding will continue. *Chronicle of Higher Education Almanac*, August 25, 1993, 46.
8. In *Business Officer*, September 1992, 8.
9. Kent John Chabotar and James P. Honan, "Coping with Retrenchment: Strategies and Tactics," *Change*, November/December 1990, 28.
10. Ibid.
11. *Almanac of Higher Education, 1989–1990* (University of Chicago Press, 1989), 54, in Thomas Sowell, *Inside American Education: The Decline, the Deception, the Dogmas* (New York: Free Press, 1993), 14.
12. A few details of the Johns Hopkins case are discussed in *Arizona Alumnus*, University of Arizona, Fall 1992, 6.

13. "Poisoned Ivy," 18–20; Julie L. Nicklin, "Yale Opens a Campaign for
    $1.5 Billion, Largest Drive in U.S. Higher Education," *Chronicle of
    Higher Education*, May 13, 1992, A32; Elfin, "What Must Be Done," 8;
    Lazerson and Wagner, "Rethinking How Colleges Operate," A37–38;
    Chronicle of Higher Education, June 17, 1992, A30; Joye Mercer,
    "UCLA, under Pressure from State Budget Cuts, Stirs Anxiety and
    Anger with Plan to Close Four Schools, 'Old Ways' Won't Work, Says
    One Official," *Chronicle of Higher Education*, June 16, 1993, A28; *Chron-
    icle of Higher Education*, June 17, 1992, A26; Joye Mercer, "At Univer-
    sity of Maryland, Millions Are Freed in Program Cuts," *Chronicle of
    Higher Education*, July 29, 1992, A22; *Chronicle of Higher Education*, April
    21, 1993, A26; Carolyn J. Mooney, "Death of a Campus," *Chronicle of
    Higher Education*, June 24, 1992, A13–4; Joye Mercer, "Philadelphia
    Area Colleges Lose Millions in State Funds as Pennsylvania Cuts Direct
    Aid to Private Institutions," *Chronicle of Higher Education*, July 15, 1992,
    A26; "Spring Garden College Will Close in Fall," *Chronicle of Higher
    Education*, June 8, 1992, A5; *Chronicle of Higher Education*, July 29, 1992,
    A23; *Chronicle of Higher Education*, September 23, 1992, A31; Goldie
    Blumenstyk, "Loyola University of Chicago Will Close Its Dental
    School in June 1993," *Chronicle of Higher Education,* June 24, 1992, A26;
    "Faculty Members at Two Universities Vote No Confidence," *Chronicle
    of Higher Education*, September 16, 1992, A19; *Chronicle of Higher Educa-
    tion*, April 22, 1992, A40; *Chronicle of Higher Education*, May 20, 1992,
    A13; *Arizona State Outlook*, Arizona State University alumni newsletter,
    Fall 1992, 1; Mary Crystal Cage, "To Shield Academic Programs from
    Cuts, Many Colleges Pare Student Services," *Chronicle of Higher Educa-
    tion*, November 18, 1992, A26; Douglas Lederman, "A Painful Five-
    Year Struggle to Clean up Southern Methodist's Tarnished Image,"
    Chronicle of Higher Education, November 25, 1992, A25; Lucy Hodges,
    "U.S. Private Colleges Tighten Their Belts," *Times Higher Education
    Supplement,* September 14, 1990, 1; *Arizona Alumnus,* 6; *Chronicle
    of Higher Education*, April 22, 1992, A6–A7; Kim A. MacDonald, "Fed-
    eral Panel Recommends Closing Stanford Accelerators If Energy
    Department Physics Budget Fails to Match Inflation," *Chronicle of
    Higher Education,* April 22, 1992, A7; Kit Lively, "A Look at Two
    State Campuses Reveals Anguish of Adapting to Deep Budget Cuts,"
    Chronicle of Higher Education, June 9, 1993, A15, A19; "Oregon Col-
    leges Face Budget Cuts of 20 Percent After Legislature Kills Tax Plan,"
    Chronicle of Higher Education, June 8, 1992, A15; and Michele N-K
    Collison, "Private Colleges Unveil Tuition Discounts and Loans to

Woo Middle-Income Students," *Chronicle of Higher Education*, June 24, 1992, A27.

14. Joye Mercer, "Drop in State Support Leaves Ohio Colleges Wondering How Much Farther They Can Fall," *Chronicle of Higher Education*, September 9, 1992, A23–24.

15. Salma Abdelnour, "California Colleges Brace for Big Cuts in State Financing," *Chronicle of Higher Education*, September 9, 1992, A21, A25; and Kit Lively, "California Colleges Worry About How to Live with Deep Budget Cuts," *Chronicle of Higher Education*, September 9, 1992, A25.

16. Mercer, "UCLA, under Pressure from State Budget Cuts," A28; and Abdelnour, "California Colleges Brace for Big Cuts in State Financing," A21.

17. *Chronicle of Higher Education*, December 2, 1992, A4; *Chronicle of Higher Education*, November 25, 1992, A5; Jack McCurdy, "California State University Students Protest Budget Cuts," *Chronicle of Higher Education*, September 30, 1992, A26; "Students End Takeover of Bennington Office," *Chronicle of Higher Education*, May 3, 1992, A4; and Kit Lively, "LSU Students, Professors and Employees Protest Budget Cuts," *Chronicle of Higher Education*, November 25, 1992, A16.

18. Julie L. Nicklin, "Private Giving to Colleges Rose by 4 Percent in 1990–91," *Chronicle of Higher Education*, May 20, 1992, A25–26; and Elfin, "What Must Be Done," 10.

19. Jean Evangelauf, "Financial Support for College Students Climbs to a Record $30.8 Billion," *Chronicle of Higher Education*, September 16, 1992, A37; "Trends in Student Aid, 1982–1992," The College Board, September 1992, 3; and "Trends in Student Aid, 1983–1993," The College Board, September 1993, 3.

20. Harvey, "Footing the Bill," 12.

21. Kit Lively and Joye Mercer, "Higher Education and the States," *Chronicle of Higher Education*, January 6, 1993, A29.

22. *Chronicle of Higher Education*, April 15, 1992, A26; Goldie Blumenstyk, "College Officials and Policy Experts Ponder Implications of 'Privatizing' State Colleges," *Chronicle of Higher Education*, May 13, 1992, A25; *Arizona State Outlook*, 1; Ivy Weston, "UC Examines Options for Tackling Shortfall," *Daily Nexus*, January 19, 1993, 1; and Kit Lively, "Colleges Are Left Guessing as California Struggles to Adopt a Budget," *Chronicle of Higher Education*, July 15, 1992, A26.

23. Lively and Mercer, "Higher Education and the States," A33–38.

24. Lively, "Colleges Are Left Guessing as California Struggles to Adopt a Budget," A26.

25. Harvey, "Footing the Bill," 12.

26. "Trends in Student Aid: 1982–1992," 3.

27. Jim Zook, "Unexpectedly Tight Clinton Budget Dismays Higher Education Leaders," *Chronicle of Higher Education,* April 28, 1993, A21.

28. Ibid, A18.

29. In Charles Dervarics, "1994 Higher Education Budget Draws Some Negative Reviews from Education Associations," *Black Issues in Higher Education,* May 6, 1993, 8.

30. In Kit Lively, "Budget Outlook Prompts Some College Leaders to Speak Out for Higher State Taxes," *Chronicle of Higher Education,* October 7, 1992, A22.

31. "Institutions with High Default Rates," *Congressional Quarterly Almanac,* 1990, 626–627; and "Parents Increasingly Unable to Repay Student Loans," *Student Aid News,* October 16, 1992, 1.

32. Stafford Loan defaults increased 338 percent between 1983 and 1989. In "Abuses in Federal Student Aid Programs," Permanent Subcommittee on Investigations, U.S. Senate Committee on Governmental Affairs, May 17, 1991, 1.

33. Thomas J. DeLoughry, "U.S. May Drop 65 Colleges from Aid Programs in a Drive Against Institutions with High Default Rates on Loans," *Chronicle of Higher Education,* August 12, 1992, A23.

34. "Trade Association Questions Data," *Student Aid News,* August 21, 1992, 3.

35. *Chronicle of Higher Education,* January 13, 1993, A26.

36. William Norris, "U.S. Institutions Panic as Numberless Nightmare Looms," *Times Higher Education Supplement,* December 15, 1989, 10.

37. "Institutions with High Default Rates," 626–627; and "Education Bills Advanced in Committees," *Congressional Quarterly Almanac,* 1991, 365.

38. "Stafford Student Loans: Millions of Dollars Awarded to Ineligible Borrowers," U.S. General Accounting Office report to the chairman of the U.S. Senate Subcommittee on Governmental Affairs, December 12, 1990, 4.

39. "Guaranteed Loans Given to Prior Defaulters, Education Development Officials Say," *Business Officer,* July 1992, 8.

40. "Stafford Student Loans: Millions of Dollars Awarded to Ineligible Borrowers," 3; and appendix, 1.

41. "Stafford Student Loans: Millions of Dollars Awarded to Ineligible Borrowers," appendix, 28.

42. "Stafford Student Loans: Millions of Dollars Awarded to Ineligible Borrowers," 2; and *Department of Education Reports,* May 31, 1993, 8.

43. The GAO was basing its estimate on a loan interest rate of 8 percent and a special allowance rate of 3.25 percent and assumed students would stay in school for four years. "Stafford Student Loans: Millions of Dollars Awarded to Ineligible Borrowers," 5.

44. Ibid, 6.

45. Jill Zuckman, "A Student Shocker: Credit Checks," *Congressional Quarterly Almanac,* 1992, 407.

46. "Education Department Paying Banks Millions on Unused Student Loans, Inspector General Says," *Student Aid News,* November 15, 1991, 5.

47. "Florida Savings and Loan's Handling of $100 Million in GSLs Being Probed," *Student Aid News,* December 25, 1987, 8; and "Federal Government Seizes Largest Student Lender," *Student Aid News,* November 30, 1990, 4.

48. "Sallie Mae Affiliate Falsified Loan Collection Records," *Student Aid News,* January 24, 1992, 2; and "Kansas Banking Department Seizes Largest Stafford Loan Lender," *Student Aid News,* May 17, 1991, 6.

49. A compromise was worked out later. Robin Wilson, "Student Loan Industry Alarmed by U.S. Stance on Default Payments," *Chronicle of Higher Education,* March 8, 1989, A1, A22.

50. "Abuses in Federal Student Aid Programs," Permanent Subcommittee on Investigations, U.S. Senate Committee on Governmental Affairs, May 17, 1991, 21.

51. Parent Loans for Undergraduate Students and Supplemental Loans for Students defaults were not discussed in the GAO report. "Stafford Student Loans: Millions of Dollars Awarded to Ineligible Borrowers," 1.

52. Ibid., 9.

53. "Guaranteed Student Loans," U.S. Comptroller General, December 1992, 7.

54. Ibid.

55. Jim Zook, "Some Lawmakers Wary of Clinton Plan for Direct Loans to Students," *Chronicle of Higher Education,* May 12, 1993, A32.

56. "Senate Plan Would Reduce Top Pell Award," *Higher Education and National Affairs,* September 14, 1992, 1,4.

57. Thomas J. DeLoughry, "$1.4 Billion Shortage in Pell Grants Confounds Budget-Conscious Lawmakers and Administration," *Chronicle of Higher Education,* May 3, 1992, A21–22; and "Low Estimate of Pell Grant Needs Causes Funding Shortfall," *Business Officer,* July 1992, 8.

58. *Chronicle of Higher Education,* February 3, 1993, A27.

59. DeLoughry, "$1.4 Billion Shortage in Pell Grants Confounds Budget-Conscious Lawmakers and Administration," A21.

60. Ibid, A21–A22.
61. "Guaranteed Loans Given to Prior Defaulters, Education Department Officials Say," *Business Officer,* July 1992, 8.
62. All prisoners are eligible except those under death sentence or life imprisonment without parole. Jill Zuckman, "Higher Education Reauthorization," *Congressional Quarterly Almanac,* 1992, 3510; and "Prisoners Receiving Social Security and Other Federal Retirement, Disability and Education Benefits," General Accounting Office, July 22, 1982. In Susan Boren, "The Pell Grant Program: Background and Reauthorization Issues," Congressional Research Service, August 9, 1991, 20–21.
63. "Education Issues," U.S. Comptroller General, December 1992, 31–32.

CHAPTER 2
GOVERNMENT AND HIGHER EDUCATION

1. *Higher Education for American Democracy: A Report of the President's Commission on Higher Education,* 5 (U.S. Government Printing Office, 1947): 52.
2. In John Chodes, "Education for a Conquered Nation," *Chronicles,* March 1989, 21.
3. Prewar rates were similarly low. *Digest of Education Statistics,* U.S. Department of Education, 1991, Table 160, "Historical Summary of Faculty, Students, Degrees, and Finances in Institutions of Higher Education: 1869–70 to 1988–1989," 166.
4. George H. Douglas, *Education Without Impact: How Our Universities Fail the Young* (New York: Birch Lane Press, 1992), 3, 15.
5. Frederick Rudolph, *The American College and University: A History* (Alfred A. Knopf, 1962), in Rexford G. Moon, Jr., "Student Aid and the Federal Government," ed., Charles G. Dobbins, *Higher Education and the Federal Government: Papers Presented at the 45th Annual Meeting of the American Council on Education,* October 1962, 32.
6. *Higher Education for American Democracy,* 53.
7. Moon, "Student Aid and the Federal Government," 32.
8. *Digest of Education Statistics,* Table 160, 166.
9. Moon, "Student Aid and the Federal Government," 33.
10. Ibid.
11. In 1947, the official estimate for federal higher education spending was a little under $2 billion, but this did not include the hundreds of millions of

dollars spent on capital construction or on certain forms of research. *Higher Education for American Democracy*, 53–54.

12. Ibid., 3–4.

13. Public Law, 85–864, sec. 401.

14. Lawrence E. Gladieux and Thomas R. Wolanin, *Congress and the Colleges: The National Politics of Higher Education* (Lexington, MA: D.C. Heath & Company, 1976), 9.

15. John T. Wilson, *Academic Science, Higher Education, and the Federal Government, 1950–1983* (University of Chicago Press, 1983), 46.

16. Gladieux and Wolanin, 9.

17. David D. Henry, "A Program of Action for Higher Education," *Higher Education and the Federal Government: Papers Presented at the 45th Annual Meeting of the American Council on Education,* October 1962, 99.

18. Moon, "Student Aid and the Federal Government," 40–41.

19. Nathan M. Pusey, "The Carnegie Study of the Federal Government and Higher Education," *Higher Education and the Federal Government: Papers Presented at the 45th Annual Meeting of the American Council on Education,* October 1962, 18; and William G. Bowen, *The Federal Government and Princeton University* (Princeton University Press, 1962), 35.

20. Gladieux and Wolanin, 11.

21. Wilson, 49–50.

22. "Education Bill Advanced in Committees," *Congressional Quarterly Almanac,* 1991, 365.

23. Wilson, 61.

24. Ibid., 50.

25. "Minority Views of Senators Barry Goldwater and John G. Tower," Senate report on National Defense Education Amendments of 1961, 117, in Wilson, 51.

26. Wilson, 49.

27. Gladieux and Wolanin, 108, 230.

28. Ibid., 87, 108.

29. Ibid., 85, 108; and R. Frank Mensel, "The Chairman Puts Students First," *Junior College Journal,* December 1971, 13, 15.

30. Gladieux and Wolanin, 236.

31. Michael Mumper, "The Transformation of Federal Aid to College Students: Dynamics of Growth and Retrenchment," *Journal of Education Finance,* Winter 1991, 319–321.

32. Michael S. McPherson and Morton Owen Shapiro, "Does Student Aid Affect College Enrollment? New Evidence on a Persistent Controversy," *American Economic Review,* March 1991, 309.

33. Alison Bernstein, Ted Marchese and Frank Newman, "Government by Confrontation," *Change,* March/April 1985, 8.

34. Ibid.

35. Terry Hartle, "Federal Support for Higher Education in the 90s: Boom, Bust, or Something in Between?" *Change,* January/February 1990, 32.

36. National Direct Student Loans were not, as the name implies, direct loans. "Education Bills Advanced in Committees," *Congressional Quarterly Almanac,* 1991, 366.

37. Thomas J. DeLoughry, "House Panel's Draft Bill Would Increase Pell Grants, Drop Banks' Role in Loans," *Chronicle of Higher Education,* October 2, 1991, A1.

38. "Education Bills Advanced in Committees," *Congressional Quarterly Almanac,* 1991, 366.

39. Ibid., 372.

40. Jill Zuckman, "Who Are the Neediest?" *Congressional Quarterly Almanac,* 1992, 805.

41. Jill Zuckman, "House OK's College Aid Bill, Emphasis on Middle Class," *Congressional Quarterly Almanac,* 1992, 804.

42. Ibid.

43. Jill Zuckman, "Courting the Middle Class: Congress and Student Aid," *Congressional Quarterly Almanac,* 1992, 21.

44. *Chronicle of Higher Education,* March 3, 1993, A29.

45. "Education Bills Advanced in Committees," *Congressional Quarterly Almanac,* 1991, 368.

46. Ibid.

47. Jim Zook, "For Sallie Mae's Top Executives, 1992 Was a Very Good Year," *Chronicle of Higher Education,* June 9, 1993, A23.

48. Hough's estimate was $75 billion for a five-year start up, without counting tuition cost increases. Letter, March 5, 1993, 1.

49. Ibid., 369.

50. William F. Buckley Jr., "The Repristinization of Bill Clinton," *National Review,* June 21, 1993, 87.

51. Thomas J. DeLoughry, "House Votes to Approve Higher Education Act; Bush Threatens Veto," *Chronicle of Higher Education,* April 1, 1992, A1, A26.

52. Jill Zuckman, "Senators Boost College Aid in Reviewing 1965 Act," *Congressional Quarterly Almanac,* 1992, 406.

53. "On to College?" *Wall Street Journal,* September 8, 1992, A14.

54. Thomas J. DeLoughry, "College Officials Say Reauthorization Law

Benefits Some Students But that Aid Funds Will Be Scarce," *Chronicle of Higher Education,* July 29, 1992, A15.

55. Jill Zuckman, "Ford Drops Pell Entitlement from College Loan Bill," *Congressional Quarterly Almanac,* 1992, 731.
56. Jim Zook and Stephen Burd, "Senate Vote Virtually Ensures a $100 Cut in Maximum Pell Grant for 1993–94," *Chronicle of Higher Education,* September 23, 1992, A24.
57. Zuckman, "Ford Drops Pell Entitlement," 729.
58. Scott Jaschik, "223 College Presidents, Administrators, and Trustees Endorse Clinton," *Chronicle of Higher Education,* October 28, 1992, A33.
59. Jim Zook, "President Would Increase Education Department Spending by 25 Percent in Five Years, Cut $200 Million in Campus-Based Aid," *Chronicle of Higher Education,* April 14, 1993, A29.
60. *Department of Education Reports,* May 17, 1993, 4–5.
61. Gary Orfield, School of Education, Harvard University, in Jim Zook, "Department of Education Demonstrates Statehouse Orientations in Federal Policy," *Chronicle of Higher Education,* May 26, 1993, A21.
62. *Historical Statistics of the United States, Colonial Times to 1957,* U.S. Department of Commerce, Series H316–326, "Institutions of Higher Education — Faculty and Enrollment: 1870–1956," 210–211; and *Statistical Abstract of the United States,* 1975, Table 225, "Institutions of Higher Education — Faculty and Enrollment: 1940–1974," 136; and *Fact Book on Higher Education,* 1989–90, Table 45, "Enrollment by Level of Study, Selected Years, 1899–1900–1997," 70. All above in Martin Anderson, *Impostors in the Temple: American Intellectuals Are Destroying Our Universities and Cheating Our Students of Their Future* (New York: Simon and Schuster, 1992), 31; and *Chronicle of Higher Education Almanac,* August 25, 1993, 5.

CHAPTER 3
GOVERNMENT FUNDING TODAY

1. Lawrence E. Gladieux and Thomas R. Wolanin, *Congress and the Colleges: The National Politics of Higher Education* (Lexington, MA: D.C. Heath & Company, 1976), 12–13.
2. *Student Financial Aid: The Growth of Academic Credit's Other Meaning,* American Council on Education, 1992, in Esmeralda Barnes, "Increased Reliance on Loans Hurts Minority and Poor Students Most, Study Shows," *Black Issues in Higher Education,* December 31, 1992, 11.

3. Ibid., 10.

4. Jean Evangelauf, "Financial Support for College Students Climbs to a Record $30.8 Billion," *Chronicle of Higher Education,* September 16, 1992, A37; and "Trends in Student Aid: 1982–1992," The College Board, September 1992, 3.

5. James Cass and Max Birnbaum, *Comparative Guide to American Colleges* (New York: Harper & Row, 1989), 240, 292; and *The Marquette Investment,* Marquette Office of Admissions, in Thomas Sowell, *Inside American Education: The Decline, the Deception, the Dogmas* (New York: Free Press, 1993), 120; and Evangelauf, "Financial Support for College Students Climbs to a Record $30.8 Billion," A37.

6. Jim Zook, "National Service Urged as a Basis for Awarding of Student Aid," *Chronicle of Higher Education,* December 16, 1992, A21.

7. "Remarks by the President in National Service Address," White House press release, March 1, 1993.

8. David Wessell, "White House Gives Details of President's Five-Year Plan," *Wall Street Journal,* February 19, 1993, A4; Jeffrey H. Birnbaum and Cathy Trost, "Clinton's Program for National Service Could Start Small, Expand Gradually," *Wall Street Journal,* March 2, 1993, A20; Doug Bandow, "The National Service Boondoggle," *Wall Street Journal,* March 2, 1993, A18; and Joshua Gilder, "National Service and Fidel's Sugar Cane," *Wall Street Journal,* March 25, 1993, A14.

9. Bruce Chapman, "Pass National Service, Cripple Charity," *Wall Street Journal,* May 24, 1993, A10; Don Nickles, "National Servitude, Not National Service," *Wall Street Journal,* July 20, 1993, A14; and "The Newest Entitlement," *Wall Street Journal,* July 29, 1993, A14.

10. Bruce Chapman, president, Discovery Institute, phone interview, June 9, 1993.

11. Doug Bandow, "National Service: Utopias Revisited," *Policy Analysis,* March 15, 1993, 1.

12. Salma Abdelnour, "Programs for Community Service by College Students Get U.S. Aid," *Chronicle of Higher Education,* September 16, 1992, A28.

13. Gladieux and Wolanin, 42.

14. *Federal Programs for Higher Education: Needed Next Steps,* American Council on Education, 1969, in Gladieux and Wolanin, 44.

15. Gladieux and Wolanin, 45.

16. John T. Wilson, *Academic Science, Higher Education, and the Federal Government* (University of Chicago Press, 1983), 59.

17. In Wilson, 59.

18. "The Reauthorization of the Higher Education Act and Related Measures," Hearings before Subcommittee, 375–8; and Budget of the U.S. Government, Fiscal Year 1993, appendix 1, 445.

19. Vannevar Bush, *Science: The Endless Frontier* (National Science Foundation, 40th anniversary edition, 1990), 11.

20. Erich Bloch, preface to Vannevar Bush, *Science: The Endless Frontier,* xvi, xviii.

21. In real dollars, this was 20 percent less than in 1967, but it was still a huge sum by any estimation. Bloch, preface to *Science: The Endless Frontier,* xxi, xxii.

22. James Elek, "University of Michigan Bulks Up Research Funding,' *Michigan Review,* January 13, 1993, 3.

23. Jacques Barzun, "The Cults of 'Research' and 'Creativity,' " *Harper's,* October 1960, 69.

24. Roger Geiger, review of *Academic Science, Higher Education, and the Federal Government in Society,* July/August 1985, 91.

25. Wilson, 33.

26. *Chronicle of Higher Education,* April 15, 1992, A30.

27. Stephen Burd, "Rift Grows Between Scholars and U.S. Officials over Way Federal Funds Are Awarded," *Chronicle of Higher Education,* July 29, 1992, A18.

28. Ibid.

29. Office of Legislative and Public Affairs, phone interview, June 10, 1993; Geiger, review of *Academic Science, Higher Education, and the Federal Government,* 91.

30. Jack Goodman, "Congress Agrees to Rescind $8.1 Billion in Federal Spending It Approved for '92," *Chronicle of Higher Education,* May 27, 1992, A33; and Burd, "Rift Grows Between Scholars and U.S. Officials," A18.

31. Bloch, preface to *Science: The Endless Frontier,* xxv, xxviii.

32. Julius H. Comroe, Jr., ed., *Research and Medical Education* (Association of American Medical Colleges, 1962), 97.

33. Jim Zook and Stephen Burd, "Senate Vote Virtually Insures a $100 Cut in Maximum Pell Grant for 1993–94," *Chronicle of Higher Education,* September 23, 1992, A25; and Stephen Burd, "Researchers Say 1993 Budget Spells Disaster for Some NIH Institutes," *Chronicle of Higher Education,* February 12, 1992, A33.

34. O.B. Hardison, "NEH at Twenty: Has It Made a Difference?" *Change,* January/February 1986, 12.

35. Joseph A. Harris, "While You're Up, Get Me a Grant," *Reader's Digest,* June 1981, 169–172.

36. Stephen Burd, "Chairman of Humanities Has Politicized Grants Process, Critics Charge," *Chronicle of Higher Education,* April 22, 1992, A32–33.

37. The details on OERI and other "agencies within agencies" presented here are based on confidential interviews with former staff members.

38. Robin Wilson, "Trade Bill Provides $1.7 Billion for Education Programs, But Some of Them May Never Receive the Money," *Chronicle of Higher Education,* August 10, 1988, A19.

39. *Chronicle of Higher Education,* September 30, 1992, A23; and Colleen Cordes and Jack Goodman, "Congress Earmarked a Record $684 Million for Noncompetitive Projects on Campuses," *Chronicle of Higher Education,* April 15, 1992, A26.

40. Ibid, A1, A26.

41. Goodman, "Congress Agrees to Rescind $8.1 Billion in Federal Spending It Approved for '92," A33; Colleen Courdes and Katherine McCarron, "Academe Gets $763 Million in Year from Congressional Pork Barrel," *Chronicle of Higher Education,* June 16, 1993, A1, A21; and Colleen Courdes, "Curbing Earmarks: Study of Four Spending Bills Finds Academic Pork Down 50 Percent in One Year," *Chronicle of Higher Education,* November 3, 1993, A25.

42. Courdes and Goodman, "Congress Earmarked a Record $684 Million for Noncompetitive Projects on Campuses," A26.

43. Some of these earmarks may have been reduced as a result of Congress's $100 million budget reductions. Colleen Courdes and Jack Goodman, "College Projects that Received Congressional Earmarks," *Chronicle of Higher Education,* April 15, 1992, A31–36.

44. Ibid., A36.

45. Courdes and McCarron, "Academe Gets $763 Million in Year from Congressional Pork Barrel," A21.

46. The Clinton administration has proposed dropping these awards and using the funds for new programs like national service. Their fate is still uncertain.

47. Edward R. Hines, ed., "State Higher Education Appropriations, 1991–1992," State Higher Education Executive Officers, April, 1992, 1; and Fred Fischer, "State Financing of Higher Education: A New Look at an Old Problem," *Change,* January/February 1990, 44.

48. Minnesota dropped out of the top ten in 1992. These figures do not include local taxes and other sources—they reflect appropriations only. Hines, 2–4.

49. Scott Jaschik, "One Percent Decline in State Support for Colleges Thought to be First Two-Year Drop Ever," *Chronicle of Higher Education,* October 21, 1992, A21.

50. Hines, 2.

51. Jaschik, "One Percent Decline in State Support for Colleges Thought to be First Two-Year Drop Ever," A21.

52. Kit Lively, "Budget Outlook Prompts Some College Leaders to Speak Out for Higher Taxes," *Chronicle of Higher Education,* October 7, 1992, A22.

53. Ibid.

54. *Statistical Abstract of the United States,* U.S. Department of Commerce, 1990, Table 208, "School Expenditures by Type of Control and Level of Instruction, 1960–1989," 129, in Martin Anderson, *Impostors in the Temple: American Intellectuals Are Destroying Our Universities and Cheating Our Students of Their Future* (New York: Simon and Schuster, 1992), 28; and *Chronicle of Higher Education,* September 9, 1992, A4.

55. Anderson, 28.

56. *Fact Book on Higher Education, 1989–90,* American Council on Education, Table 96, "Current Fund Revenue of Public Institutions of Higher Education, Selected Fiscal Years, 1966–1986," 148–149, in Anderson, 28–29.

57. In Anderson, 29.

CHAPTER 4
THE POLITICS OF FUNDING

1. Commission on Financing Higher Education—1952, excerpted in *Institutional Aid: Federal Support to Colleges and Universities,* The Carnegie Commission on Higher Education, 1972, 101, in Lawrence E. Gladieux and Thomas R. Wolanin, *Congress and the Colleges: The National Politics of Higher Education* (Lexington, MA: D.C. Heath & Company, 1976), 456.

2. Fred Barnes and Rachel Flick Wildavsky, "Is Washington for Sale?" *Reader's Digest,* February 1992, 46.

3. *Chronicle of Higher Education,* February 3, 1993, A27.

4. In an unpublished Department of Education memo, Fall 1992.

5. Colin Norman, "How to Win Buildings and Influence Congress," *Science,* December 16, 1983, 1211–1213.

6. William Norris, "Lobbyists Win Back Colleges Lost Millions," *Times Higher Education Supplement*, November 24, 1992, 10.

7. Michael O'Keefe, "Self-Inflicted Laryngitis: How Long Can Higher Education Avoid Political Reality?" *Change*, March/April 1985, 11.

8. Bruce Foote, "Editor's Outlook," *MASFAA Newsletter*, Spring 1990.

9. Douglas Lederman, "Survey Reveals Salaries of Executives and Highest Paid Staff Members at 190 Colleges," *Chronicle of Higher Education*, May 5, 1993, A13.

10. Courtney Leatherman, "Salaries of Chief Executives in Higher Education Found to Have Grown by 6 Percent a Year Since 1988," *Chronicle of Higher Education*, July 3, 1991, A1.

11. Jean Merl, "UC Chief's Severance Package under Fire," *Los Angeles Times*, April 3, 1992, A3; and Jon Weiner, "Lavish Compensation Is Not Appropriate for Top Executives at Public Universities," *Chronicle of Higher Education*, November 25, 1992, B3–B4.

12. Lance Williams, "Outgoing UC Official Gets $204,000 Leave," *San Francisco Examiner*, May 22, 1993, A1, A9.

13. K. L. Billingsley, "State Education Funds Went for Cars, Bel-Air Mansion," *San Diego Union*, April 1, 1990, C3; and "Extra Cash?" *Insight*, December 21, 1992, 29.

14. Hayes E. Gahagen, former Maine state senator, phone interview, May 28, 1993.

15. *Chronicle of Higher Education*, April 1, 1992, A25.

16. David D. Henry, "A Program of Action for Higher Education," ed., Charles G. Dobbins, *Higher Education and the Federal Government, Papers Presented at the 45th Annual Meeting of the American Council on Education*, October 3–5, 1962, 99.

17. James J. Whalen, "Public Support and the Private Sector: A Partnership in Peril," *Educational Record*, Summer 1992, 36.

18. Morton Cooper, "The Grants Office," ed., Kathryn Mohrman, *Grants: View from the Campus*, Federal Resources Advisory Service, Association of American Colleges, 1979, 9.

19. Ibid., 90.

20. John Brademas, *The Politics of Education: Conflict and Consensus on Capitol Hill*, with Lynne P. Brown (University of Oklahoma Press, 1987), 22.

21. Gladieux and Wolanin, 112.

22. *Heritage Today*, Winter 1992, 6.

23. John Brademas, "Higher Education and the Nation's Future," *Education Digest*, February 1983, 10–12; John Brademas, "Achieving Diversity and

Unity Through Education: Reflections on Higher Education," *Change*, March 1983, 48, 50; and John Brademas, *The Politics of Education, 22.*

24. In William D. Ford, "Education and America's Future," *Education Digest*, March 1984, 6–8.

25. Gladieux and Wolanin, 110.

26. Ibid., 147.

27. Denise K. Magner, "Recruited by White House for Key Advice, Academics Find New Welcome in Washington," *Chronicle of Higher Education*, January 1, 1993, A28.

28. F. Phillips, "The Private College and Federal Aid," *Association of American Colleges Bulletin*, May 1949, 283, 287.

29. McGeorge Bundy, "Of Winds and Windmills: Free Universities and Public Policy," ed., Charles G. Dobbins, *Higher Education and the Federal Government, Papers Presented at the 45th Annual Meeting of the American Council on Education,* October 3–5, 1962, 93.

30. George Keller, *Academic Strategy* (Johns Hopkins University Press, 1983). In Alan Hamlin, "The President as Salesman," *Educational Record*, Winter 1990, 14.

31. Hamlin, "The President as Salesman," 11–14.

32. Based on a 50-state survey in *Michigan Higher Education: Meeting the Challenge of the Future*, Michigan Select Committee on Higher Education, March 26, 1986.

33. Joye Mercer, "Pennsylvania Private Colleges Lobby Fiercely Against Governor's Plan to Cut Aid," *Chronicle of Higher Education*, May 27, 1992, A22.

34. Reimbursements fluctuate slightly from year to year, based on state allocations and the number of eligible students, but generally are in the same dollar range. Michigan Senate Fiscal Agency, phone interview, March 5, 1993; and Michigan Office of Education, phone interview, June 16, 1993.

35. *Chronicle of Higher Education*, May 20, 1992, A24.

36. Jim Stewart, "Tuition Grants in Jeopardy," *Furman Reports*, Fall 1992, 4.

37. Whalen, 34–35.

38. Martin Anderson, *Impostors in the Temple: American Intellectuals Are Destroying Our Universities and Cheating Our Students of Their Future* (New York: Simon and Schuster, 1992), 29.

39. Mary P. McKeown and Kern Alexander, *Values in Conflict: Funding Priorities for Higher Education*, American Finance Association, 1986, 63; and "Michigan Higher Education: Meeting the Challenges of the

Future," Michigan Select Committee on Higher Education, March 25, 1986. In the Michigan survey, thirty-two states declared that they used formulas to determine funding, and eleven states declared that they did not. But the survey editors also note that many of the eleven simply have different definitions of what constitutes a formula and that they do depend on at least one variety.

40. From Lincoln A. Kallsen, College of Education, University of Minnesota.

CHAPTER 5
FEDERAL FUNDING AND FEDERAL CONTROL

1. Commission on Financing Higher Education report, Association of American Universities, November 19, 1952, in William F. Buckley Jr., "Hillsdale Rejects Federal Cash—and Control," *Detroit Free Press*, May 24, 1991, A9.

2. Nathan M. Pusey, "The Carnegie Study of the Federal Government and Higher Education," ed., Charles G. Dobbins, *Higher Education and the Federal Government: Papers Presented at the 45th Annual Meeting of the American Council on Education, October 3–5, 1962,* 19.

3. McGeorge Bundy, "Of Winds and Windmills: Free Universities and Public Policy," ed., Charles G. Dobbins, *Higher Education and the Federal Government: Papers Presented at the 45th Annual Meeting of the American Council on Education, October 3–5, 1962,* 90–91, 94.

4. David D. Henry, "A Program of Action for Higher Education," ed., Charles G. Dobbins, *Higher Education and the Federal Government: Papers Presented at the 45th Annual Meeting of the American Council on Education, October 3–5, 1962,* 107.

5. John T. Wilson, *Academic Science, Higher Education, and the Federal Government, 1950–1983* (University of Chicago Press, 1983), 44.

6. Homer D. Babbidge, "Scientists Affluent, Humanists Militant: Faction in Higher Education," *Graduate Journal Supplement* (University of Texas Press, 1962), 162, in Wilson, 44.

7. *Higher Education for American Democracy: A Report of the President's Commission on Higher Education,* 5 (U.S. Government Printing Office, 1947), 25, 57.

8. Wilson, 51.

9. Ibid, 53.

10. Lawrence E. Gladieux and Thomas R. Wolanin, *Congress and the Col-*

leges: The National Politics of Higher Education (D.C. Heath & Company, 1976), 117.

11. Ibid, 229.

12. In Charles B. Saunders, Jr., "Is Regulation Strangulation?" *The College Board Review,* Summer 1976, 2.

13. Details on the rise of affirmative action are from George Roche, *The Balancing Act: Quota Hiring in Higher Education,* 2nd ed. (Open Court, 1977).

14. In Roche, 4–5.

15. Ibid., 18–20.

16. Ibid., 20.

17. Lawrence A. Uzzell, "Want to Reform Public Education? First De-Fund the Department of Education," *Chronicles,* June 1990, 27.

18. In Lino A. Graglia, "Affirmative Discrimination," *National Review,* July 5, 1993, 26.

19. Michael S. Greve, "The Newest Move in Law Schools' Quota Game," *Wall Street Journal,* October 5, 1992, A12.

20. John H. Bunzel, "Choosing Freshman: Who Deserves an Edge?" *Wall Street Journal,* February 1, 1988, A24.

21. Ibid.

22. Scott Jaschik, "Education Department Says Affirmative Action Policies of Berkeley's Law School Violated Federal Anti-Bias Laws," *Chronicle of Higher Education,* October 7, 1992, A26.

23. Dinesh D' Souza, *Illiberal Education: The Politics of Race and Sex on Campus* (New York: Free Press, 1991), 4.

24. Ibid., 2–3.

25. Ibid., 5.

26. Joseph D. Grano, "Whites Need Not Apply at WSU," *Detroit News,* October 5, 1989, 19A.

27. Director of human resources, University of West Florida, memo, June 8, 1993.

28. George Cantor, "Failure of Schools Hampers University's Recruitment of Blacks," *Detroit News,* April 2, 1987, C17. The University of Michigan's double standards in admissions are not unique. Thomas Sowell has noted, for example, that Amherst College admits minorities with less than 400 on the verbal SAT while rejecting other students who scored above 750. Stanford University has denied admission to white and Asian applicants scoring above 700 on the verbal SAT while accepting large numbers of minority students scoring below 500. And at Duke University, minorities boasting totals 200 points less than other applicants also

have breezed through the admissions process. In Thomas Sowell, *Inside American Education: The Decline, the Deception, the Dogmas* (New York: Free Press, 1993), 123.

29. John Bunzel, "Affirmative Action: How It 'Works' at U-C Berkeley," *Public Interest*, Fall 1988, 22. In D' Souza, 39.

30. Shelby Steele, "The New Segregation," *Imprimis*, August 1992, 3; and Charles J. Sykes, *A Nation of Victims: The Decay of American Character* (New York: St. Martin's Press, 1992), 165.

31. George Will, "Constitutional Gymnastics," *Detroit News*, March 1984, n.p.

32. "Save Historically Black Schools," *Detroit News*, December 30, 1992, 8A.

33. "Color-Blinded," *The New Republic*, January 7 & 14, 1991, 7.

34. *Chronicle of Higher Education*, June 23, 1993, A5.

35. *National and International Religion Report,* June 14, 1993, 7.

36. Scott Jaschik, "Higher Court Deals Blow to Virginia Military Institute by Declining to Hear Its Appeal to Stay All-Male," *Chronicle of Higher Education*, June 2, 1993, A21.

37. "Auditors Say College Must Repay Millions," *Chronicle of Higher Education*, June 29, 1992, A5.

38. In William Bentley Ball, " 'Diversity': A Case Study," *University Bookman,* 1992, 4–13.

39. Joe Segall, "When Academic Quality Is Beside the Point," *Wall Street Journal,* October 29, 1990, A14.

40. Ibid.

41. Courtney Leatherman, "West Coast Accrediting Agency Hashes out a Policy on Racial Diversity for Campuses," *Chronicle of Higher Education*, November 18, 1992, A15.

42. Julie L. Nicklin, "Teacher Education Programs Debate the Need for Accrediting Agency's Stamp of Approval," *Chronicle of Higher Education*, May 6, 1992, A19, A22.

43. Uzzell, "Want to Reform Public Education," 27.

44. Llewellyn H. Rockwell, Jr., "The Conservative Sanction of Big Government," Ludwig von Mises Institute newsletter, n.d., 1.

45. Kelly R. Stern, "Regulations: Presidential Perceptions," *Educational Record*, Summer 1992, 20.

46. Ibid.

47. Ibid.

48. In *Student Aid News*, March 8, 1991, 8.

49. Stern, 16–21.
50. Thomas J. DeLoughry, "House Panel Wants to Overhaul Student Assistance," *Chronicle of Higher Education*, September 11, 1991, A33.
51. *Chronicle of Higher Education*, April 15, 1992, A30.
52. *Chronicle of Higher Education*, May 6, 1992, A27.
53. *Chronicle of Higher Education*, July 29, 1992, A2.
54. *Education Week,* March 23, 1988, 5.
55. Scott Jaschik, "House Panel Gives Preliminary Approval to Measure that Would Tax Some College Business Activities," *Chronicle of Higher Education*, June 1, 1988, A29.
56. Colleen Courdes, "Universities Angered by U.S. Proposal to Deny Them Patents on Some Research," *Chronicle of Higher Education,* September 22, 1993, A26.
57. Stephen Burd, "U.S. Proposes Regulations on Disclosure of Graduation Rates and Campus Crime Data," *Chronicle of Higher Education*, July 22, 1992, A24–25.
58. The University of Maryland narrowly escaped severe penalties for a 6 percent disparity between financial aid for male and female athletes by pledging to achieve full "gender equity" by 1998. *Chronicle of Higher Education*, November 25, 1992, A26.
59. *Chronicle of Higher Education*, June 2, 1993, A27.
60. *Chronicle of Higher Education*, May 26, 1992, B3.
61. "Task Force Calls for National Standards," *Higher Education and National Affairs*, September 14, 1992, 5.
62. "Twenty-Four States Found to Require Programs to Assess What College Students Learn," *Chronicle of Higher Education*, August 10, 1988, A19.
63. Emerelle McNair and Sandra E. Taylor, "Satisfactory Academic Progress Standards: Jeopardizing Efforts Toward Educational Equity," *Journal of Student Financial Aid*, Winter 1988, 10.
64. Graeme Baxter, associate director of the Consortium of Universities of the Washington Metropolitan Area, testifying before the Subcommittee on Postsecondary Education, Committee on Education and Labor, U.S. House of Representatives, May 9, 1979, 197.
65. In Ernest L. Boyer, keynote address at the National Association of Independent Colleges and Universities, February 3, 1993.
66. L. Gordon Crovitz, "Henry Hyde and the ACLU Propose a Fate Worse Than PCness," *Wall Street Journal*, May 1, 1991, A15.
67. Ibid.

CHAPTER 6
MISMANAGEMENT AND CORRUPTION

1. Most of these schools were named on NCAA sanction lists that appeared in the *Chronicle of Higher Education* on June 10, 1992, A30, and January 13, 1993, A35, and in a list on general sports investigations in the same source on April 1, 1992, A35.

2. Douglas Lederman, "Survey Suggests Many Division I Colleges Fail to Graduate Their Black Athletes," *Chronicle of Higher Education,* June 22, 1992, A31-A32; Raymie E. McKerrow and Norinne Hilchey Daly, "Student Athletes in Search of Balance," *Phi Kappa Journal,* Fall 1990, 43; and "Grading Graduates," *USA Today,* August 13, 1992, 8A.

3. James Tobin, "Sports: It's a Full Time Job for College Athletes," *Detroit News,* January 4, 1989, 4B; and "Studies of Intercollegiate Athletics," American Institutes of Research, 1988, 8.

4. Thomas Sowell, "The Moral Bankruptcy of Our Colleges," *Detroit News,* n.d., n.p.

5. Murray Sperber, *College Sports, Inc.: The Athletic Department vs. the University* (Henry Holt & Company, 1990), 2; Thomas Sowell, *Inside American Education: The Decline, the Deception, the Dogmas* (New York: Free Press, 1993), 232; Martin Anderson, "Price-Fixing, Finagling, and Football," *Washington Times,* August 25, 1992, F1; and Sowell, "The Moral Bankruptcy of Our Colleges," n.p.

6. In Sperber, 15.

7. Ibid., 15–16.

8. Ibid., 3, 16, 24, 86, 91.

9. Ibid., 5, 149.

10. Ibid., 5.

11. Ibid., 16, 149.

12. Ibid, 77, 149.

13. Ibid., 79.

14. *Chronicle of Higher Education,* April 21, 1993, A39.

15. In Sperber, 24.

16. Sperber, 25.

17. Ibid., 29.

18. Ibid., 23.

19. Ibid.

20. Ibid., 261.

21. Ibid., 82.

22. Ibid.

23. *Chronicle of Higher Education,* May 24, 1992, A29.

24. Sowell, *Inside American Education,* 48.

25. Sperber, 87.

26. Ibid., 87–88.

27. Ibid., 89.

28. Ibid.

29. *Chronicle of Higher Education,* May 10, 1992, A29.

30. Anderson, "Price-Fixing, Finagling and Football," F1.

31. Ibid.

32. Ibid.; and "Bowl Games Must Pay UBIT on Corporate Payments, IRS Rules," *Business Officer,* January 1992, 7.

33. *Chronicle of Higher Education,* January 13, 1993, A26.

34. *Almanac of Higher Education, 1989–1990* (University of Chicago Press, 1989), 54, in Sowell, *Inside American Education,* 14.

35. Robert Bell, *Impure Science: Fraud, Compromise, and Political Influence in Scientific Research* (New York: Wiley & Sons, 1992), 37–38.

36. Ibid., 39.

37. Kim A. McDonald, "Supercollider Scientists Left Dazed and Angry By Vote to Kill Project," *Chronicle of Higher Education,* July 1, 1992, A22; Bell, 72–73, 79; and *Chronicle of Higher Education,* November 3, 1993, A6-A7.

38. Bell, 37–79.

39. Ibid., 103–143; and Gregory Gordon, "Misconduct Costs University of Michigan $1 Million," *Detroit News,* May 13, 1993, 1.

40. Bell, xiv.

41. "Semiannual Report to Congress," Inspector General, National Science Foundation, October 1, 1992-March 31, 1993, 20–26.

42. *Chronicle of Higher Education,* April 1, 1992, A6.

43. Robert C. Cowen, "The Not-So-Hallowed Halls of Science," *Technology Review,* May/June 1983, 8.

44. Joseph P. Martino, *Science Funding: Politics and the Pork Barrel* (New Brunswick: Transaction Publishers, 1992), 371.

45. C. Michael Moriarty and Judy B. Purdy, "University Research: Planning for the 1990s," *Educational Record,* Summer 1992, 51.

46. Anderson, "Price-Fixing, Finagling, and Football," F1.

47. Brian Hecht, "Schools for Scandal," *The New Republic,* August 19 & 26, 1991, 15; "Federal Research: System for Reimbursing Universities' Indirect Costs Should Be Evaluated," General Accounting Office report to the Chairman, Subcommittee on Oversight and Investigations, House Committee on Energy and Commerce, August 1992, 2.

48. Dwight H. Purdy, "Silence, Shame Signs that 'U' Took a Wrong Turn," *Minneapolis Star Tribune,* August 21, 1993, 19A.

49. Hecht, "Schools for Scandal," 15.

50. "Financial Responsibilities at Universities," Hearings before the Subcommittee on Oversight and Investigations, House Committee on Energy and Commerce, March 13 and May 9, 1991, 4, 13.

51. Gordon C. Winston, "Hostility, Maximization, and the Public Trust," *Change,* July/August 1992, 20–27.

52. "Congress Hears More Charges of Improper Indirect Cost Billings," *Business Officer,* March 1992, 12.

53. Hecht, "Schools for Scandal," 14; "Federal Research: System for Reimbursing Universities' Indirect Costs Should Be Evaluated," 17; and "Financial Responsibilities at Universities," 3–4.

54. Gary Putka, "U.S. Is Reducing Research Funds to Universities," *Wall Street Journal,* May 6, 1991, B4; and "Federal Research: System for Reimbursing Universities' Indirect Costs Should Be Evaluated," 300.

55. "Federal Research: System for Reimbursing Universities' Indirect Costs Should Be Evaluated," 16.

56. Stanford was included in the twenty-two institutions surveyed. "Federal Research: System for Reimbursing Universities' Indirect Costs Should Be Evaluated," 16.

57. Anderson, "Price-Fixing, Finagling, and Football," F1; *Chronicle of Higher Education,* September 16, 1992, A32; Hecht, "Schools for Scandal," 14; Inspector General, Office of Audit Services, Public Health Service Audit Division, in "Hogwild! Universities Are Pigging Out," Young America's Foundation, 1; "Financial Responsibilities at Universities," 283–284, 307; and Chet Zarko, "University Research Policies Questioned," *Michigan Review,* October 7, 1992, 1.

58. Anderson, "Price-Fixing, Finagling, and Football," F1; and "Financial Responsibilities at Universities," 307, 400.

59. The exact amount was $10.6 million in academic year 1991–92. *Chronicle of Higher Education,* April 28, 1993, A18.

60. Jeff Muir, "Dingell Should Speak Out Against NEH Nominee," *Detroit News,* June 22, 1993, 11A; and "Hogwild! Universities Are Pigging Out," 1.

61. "HHS Report Proposes Three Options to Cut Indirect Cost Billings," *Business Officer,* January 1992, 6; "GAO Call for Limits on Reimbursements for Indirect Costs," American Council on Education, September 14, 1992, 1,4; Colleen Courdes, "Administration Announces Changes in Overhead Reimbursement," *Chronicle of Higher Education,* August 4,

1993, A21; Hecht, "Schools for Scandal," 15; and Gary Putka, "U.S. Is Reducing Research Funds to Universities," *Wall Street Journal,* May 6, 1991, B1.

62. *Chronicle of Higher Education,* May 27, 1992, A22.

63. Michele N-K Collison, "Reports of Spending Abuses Prompt Reviews of Student Government Policies," *Chronicle of Higher Education,* April 22, 1992, A37.

64. Ibid.

65. Sowell, *Inside American Education,* 119.

66. Ibid.

67. Gary Putka, "Do Colleges Collude on Financial Aid?" *Wall Street Journal,* May 2, 1989, B1.

68. Joye Mercer, "Five Community College Leaders Indicted in Ohio Contributions Scandal," *Chronicle of Higher Education,* June 24, 1992, A25; *Chronicle of Higher Education,* September 2, 1992, A51; Chronicle of Higher Education, June 3, 1992, A25; Sowell, *Inside American Education,* 117; Katherine S. Mangan, "Chief of Oklahoma State University Quits After Disclosure that University Money Went to Lottery Campaign," *Chronicle of Higher Education,* September 8, 1993, A32; Jon Weiner, "Lavish Compensation Is Not Appropriate for Top Executives at Public Universities," *Chronicle of Higher Education,* November 25, 1992, B3-B4; *Campus,* Winter 1993, 13; and Liz McMillen, "Stanford Bookstore Said to Have Lost $2 Million on Investment in Stocks," *Chronicle of Higher Education,* April 15, 1992, A40; *Chronicle of Higher Education,* December 2, 1992, A4; "President Admits Illegal Payments," *Times Higher Education Supplement,* June 7, 1991, 11; *Chronicle of Higher Education,* April 28, 1993, A31; Julie L. Nicklin, "Mississippi College Contends Its President Embezzled $3 Million," *Chronicle of Higher Education,* September 1, 1993, A43; *Chronicle of Higher Education,* October 28, 1992, A4; *Chronicle of Higher Education,* October 21, 1992, A4; *Chronicle of Higher Education,* July 15, 1992, A4; and *Hillsdale Daily News,* January 14, 1993, 5.

69. From former Department of Education financial officers, interview, January, 1993; and *Chronicle of Higher Education,* January 20, 1993, A4.

70. Julie L. Nicklin, "Fund Drives Flourish, But How Much Do They Really Raise?" *Chronicle of Higher Education,* October 21, 1992, A33.

71. Goldie Blumenstyk, "Accounting Board Proposes Changes in Way Colleges Present Bottom Line," *Chronicle of Higher Education,* November 25, 1992, A22.

72. Winston, 20.

73. Ibid.

74. Ibid.

75. Ibid.

76. Goldie Blumenstyk, "Colleges Race to Issue and Re-Fund Bonds to Take Advantage of Favorable Rates," *Chronicle of Higher Education,* October 28, 1992, A35.

77. Julie L. Nicklin, "Chief of Common Fund, Investment Group of Choice for Many Colleges, Steps Down," *Chronicle of Higher Education,* September 9, 1992, A29.

78. Winston, 20–27.

79. Martin Anderson, *Impostors in the Temple: American Intellectuals Are Destroying Our Universities and Cheating Our Students of Their Future* (New York: Simon and Schuster, 1992), 28.

80. As the economy recovered, so did Harvard. It made a 16.7 percent return the next year, but is still under criticism for its financial stewardship. Nicklin, "Chief of Common Fund, Investment Group of Choice for Many Colleges, Steps Down," A29; Liz McMillen, "College Endowments Gained Modest 7.2 Percent in 1990–91 as Recession Curbed Earnings for Second Year in a Row," *Chronicle of Higher Education,* February 12, 1992, A31; and *Chronicle of Higher Education,* December 1, 1993, A37.

81. The average rose to 13.1 percent in 1993, but was still below leading indexes. Julie L. Nicklin, "Small Colleges' Returns on Investments Match Those of Larger Institutions," *Chronicle of Higher Education,* January 26, 1993, A25; and McMillen, "College Endowments Gained Modest 7.2 Percent," A31; and *Chronicle of Higher Education,* December 1, 1993, A37.

82. *Chronicle of Higher Education,* September 9, 1992, A29.

83. S. Frederick Starr, "Private Colleges: Four Key Steps to Recovery," *Chronicle of Higher Education,* September 8, 1993, B1.

84. John Synodinos, "An Endowment Philosophy," *Currents,* November/December 1992, 24.

85. Ibid., 100.

86. Arthur Levine, "Why Colleges Are Continuing to Lose the Public Trust," *Change,* July/August 1992, 4.

Chapter 7
Soaring Tuitions, Soaring Costs

1. *Chronicle of Higher Education,* April 29, 1992, A5.

2. Jean Evangelauf, "Fees Rise Slowly This Year, But Surpass Inflation Rate

Again," *Chronicle of Higher Education,* October 3, 1990, A26; and Sean C. Rush, "Productivity or Quality? In Search of Higher Education's Yellow Brick Road," *Business Officer,* April 1992, 37.

3. The specific breakdown was 125–137 percent at public four-year institutions, 163–174 percent at private four-year institutions, and 114 percent at community colleges. John Brinkley, "College Tuition, Fees up 141 Percent in Decade, Study Says," *Rocky Mountain News,* September 15, 1992, 18; and "Study: Students Paying More, Getting Less," *Detroit News,* September 15, 1992, 2A.

4. Landmark College, which is not mentioned in this list, was charging $21,200 for students with disabilities like dyslexia. "College Costs Still Rising," *Jackson Citizen Patriot,* October 18, 1992, E2; Christopher Shea, "Idealism and Economic Pragmatism Mix in Debate over Value of Liberal Arts," *Chronicle of Higher Education,* February 24, 1993, A16; Jean Evangelauf, "Tuition at Public Colleges Is up 10 Percent This Year, College Board Study Finds," *Chronicle of Higher Education,* October 21, 1992, A43; and *Chronicle of Higher Education,* October 21, 1992, A39, A41–A42.

5. Daniel S. Cheever, Jr., "Tomorrow's Crisis: The Cost of College," *Harvard Magazine,* November/December 1992, 40.

6. "Sticker Shock at America's Colleges," *Compressed Air,* September 1992, 23.

7. Goldie Blumenstyk, "Private Colleges Scramble to Deal with Rising Costs of Financial Aid," *Chronicle of Higher Education,* April 21, 1993, A33.

8. "Poisoned Ivy," *The Economist,* August 15, 1992, 19.

9. In Joseph Pereira, "For Hard-Pressed Students Options Abound," *Wall Street Journal,* October 11, 1987, 25.

10. "Study: Students Paying More, Getting Less," 2A.

11. *Milwaukee Journal,* January 24, 1988, in Charles Sykes, *Professors and the Demise of Higher Education* (Regnery Gateway, St. Martin's Press, 1988), 36.

12. Robin Wilson, "Widespread Complaints: Undergraduates at Large Universities Found to Be Increasingly Dissatisfied," *Chronicle of Higher Education,* January 9, 1991, A1, in Thomas Sowell, *Inside American Education: The Decline, the Deception, the Dogmas* (New York: Free Press, 1993), 204.

13. *Wisconsin State Journal,* December 1, 1986, in Sykes, 37.

14. Mary Crystal Cage, "Fewer Students Get Bachelor's Degrees in Four Years, Study Finds," *Chronicle of Higher Education,* July 15, 1992, A31.

15. Ibid., A29.

16. Ibid.
17. Kit Lively, "California Colleges Worry About How to Live with Deep Budget Cuts," *Chronicle of Higher Education,* September 9, 1992, A25; and Jeff Ristine, "CSU Seeks Cash Boost by 2001," *San Diego Union-Tribune,* August 19, 1993, A3.
18. For some specific estimates, see Sowell, 118; *Chronicle of Higher Education,* April 29, 1992, B3; Evangelauf, "Tuition at Public Colleges Is up 10 Percent This Year," A36; and "Back to School Report," U.S. Department of Education, 1992, 6.
19. Joye Mercer, "Public College Officials Grope for Ways to Keep a Lid on Tuition," *Chronicle of Higher Education,* January 27, 1993, A32.
20. Evangelauf, "Tuition at Public Colleges Is up 10 Percent This Year," A36.
21. Thomas Sowell, "Aid for College Students Plentiful," *Gazette Telegraph,* February 10, 1985, G6.
22. Thomas P. Wallace, "Inequities of Low Tuition," *Chronicle of Higher Education,* April 1, 1992, A48.
23. Daniel Ritchie, "End State College Bargains for the Rich," *Wall Street Journal,* October 8, 1991, A22. *Chronicle of Higher Education,* June 10, 1992, B6-B7.
24. Ritchie, A22.
25. *Chronicle of Higher Education,* April 29, 1992, B3; and "Financial Stress, Proposal for Tougher Academic Standards Challenge New York's City University to Maintain Traditional Role," *Chronicle of Higher Education,* September 23, 1992, A25, A30.
26. *Chronicle of Higher Education,* April 29, 1992, B3.
27. Gary Putka, "Ivy League Discussions on Finances Extended to Tuition and Salaries," *Wall Street Journal,* May 8, 1992, 1.
28. Many schools also offer to forgive entire loan amounts if a student earns a certain G.P.A. Others agree to a fixed four-year tuition rate. Michele N-K Collison, "Private Colleges Unveil Tuition Discounts and Loans to Woo Middle-Income Students," *Chronicle of Higher Education,* June 24, 1992, A27.
29. Gary Putka, "Arithmetic on College Aid Varies Widely," *Wall Street Journal,* May 11, 1993, B1.
30. Jean Evangelauf, "Financial Support for Colleges Climbs to a Record $30.8 Billion," *Chronicle of Higher Education,* September 16, 1992, A37; Robin Wilson, "Forty-Six Percent of All Undergraduates Received Some Form of Financial Aid in Fall 1986, U.S. Study Shows," *Chronicle of Higher Education,* May 11, 1988, A26.

31. Michael S. McPherson and Morton Owen Shapiro, *Keeping College Affordable: Government and Educational Opportunity* (Washington, D.C.: Brookings Institution, 1991), 13, 18.

32. In "Alexander Astin Surveys the Class," *Lawlor Review*, Fall 1993, 11.

33. Allan W. Ostar, testimony before the House Subcommittee on Postsecondary Education, May 9, 1979, 244.

34. Some would argue, of course, that many colleges and universities raised prices reluctantly rather than eagerly; they were forced, as it were, to keep up with their competitors by taking advantage of all available government aid. But the net effect was the same.

35. Ibid., 246.

36. Ibid., 244.

37. James Buchanan and Nicos E. Devletoglou, *Academia in Anarchy: An Economic Diagnosis* (New York: Basic Books, 1970), 8.

38. Loren W. Loomis and Sean C. Rush, "A Double-Edged Sword: Assessing the Impact of Tuition Discounting," *Business Officer,* December 1991, 25–26.

39. Sowell, *Inside American Education*, 116.

40. "Controversy over Spending Practices Does Not End When President Quits," *Chronicle of Higher Education,* July 11, 1990, A20, in Sowell, *Inside American Education*, 115.

41. In Gary Putka, "Tracking Tuition: Why College Fees Are Rising So Sharply," *Wall Street Journal,* December 11, 1987, 25.

42. "Back to School Report," 6–7.

43. Martin Anderson, "What Me Teach? I'm a Professor," *Wall Street Journal,* September 8, 1992, A16.

44. *Chronicle of Higher Education,* April 29, 1992, B4.

45. "Study: Students Paying More, Getting Less," *Detroit News,* September 15, 1992, 2A; and Karen Grassmuck, "Big Increases in Academic Support Staff Prompt Growing Concern on Campus," *Chronicle of Higher Education,* March 28, 1990, A1, A23, in Sowell, *Inside American Education,* 115.

46. "Back to School Report," 6–7.

47. Carolyn J. Mooney, "Median Salary of Campus Administrators Kept Pace with Inflation," *Chronicle of Higher Education,* January 27, 1993, A21–23.

48. Rush, "Productivity or Quality," 38.

49. Courtney Leatherman, "Colleges Perplexed about Status of Health Insurance for Students in Wake of New Civil Rights Law," *Chronicle of Higher Education,* October 5, 1988, A25.

50. Paul Likoudis, "Cost of Federal Regulations Approaches $17,000 Per Family," *The Wanderer,* January 7, 1993, 1.
51. Charles B. Saunders, Jr., "Is Federal Regulation Strangulation?" *The College Board Review,* Summer 1976, 3.
52. Consultants for Educational Resources and Research, Inc., Washington D.C., phone interview, July 19, 1993.
53. *Chronicle of Higher Education,* April 28, 1993, A20.
54. *Chronicle of Higher Education,* September 30, 1992, A21.
55. Jim Zook, "With Education Act About to Take Effect, Colleges Lack Rules to Guide Compliance," *Chronicle of Higher Education,* June 23, 1993, A19.
56. Zook, "With Education Act About to Take Effect," A19.
57. Coalition for Student Loan Reform, letter, June 7, 1993, 2.
58. *Almanac of Higher Education* (University of Chicago Press, 1989), in Sowell, *Inside American Education,* 273; and "Holdings of Research Libraries in U.S. and Canada, 1991–92," *Chronicle of Higher Education,* March 10, 1992, A8.
59. All figures in 1988 dollars. Roger Benjamin et al., "The Redesign of Governance in Higher Education," Rand Corporation, February 1993, 19–20.
60. Michele N-K Collison, "Four Thousand Violent Crimes Committed on 580 Campuses: Use of Data Questioned," *Chronicle of Higher Education,* September 23, 1992, A32.
61. Peter Hughes, "Time to Tell the Whole Story: Uncovering the True Cost of University Athletics," *Business Officer,* May 1992, 46, 48.
62. "Athletics Revenues and Expenditures of NCAA Institutions," *Chronicle of Higher Education,* December 5, 1990, A36, in Sowell, *Inside American Education,* 235.
63. "Knight Commission Urges Financial Reform of College Athletics," *Business Officer,* May 1991, 10.
64. Murray Sperber, *College Sports, Inc.: The Athletic Department vs. the University* (New York: Henry Holt & Company, 1990), 130–131.
65. Sowell, *Inside American Education,* 103; Michele N-K Collison, "Private Colleges Unveil Tuition Discounts and Loans to Woo Middle Income Students," *Chronicle of Higher Education,* June 24, 1992, A27–28; and Richard Chait, "The Growing Hucksterism of College Admissions," *Chronicle of Higher Education,* May 20, 1992, B1.
66. Eric Schurenberg, "The Agony of College Admissions," *Money,* May 1989, 143; Richard Chait, "The Growing Hucksterism of College Admissions," B1-B2; and Kent John Chabotar and James P. Honan,

"Coping with Retrenchment: Strategies and Tactics," *Change,* November/December 1990, 34.

67. Mary Collins, "Higher Education Gets Lost in Fund Raising Frenzy," *Detroit News,* July 10, 1988, 17A.

68. Goldie Blumenstyk, "Private Colleges Scramble to Deal with Rising Costs of Financial Aid," *Chronicle of Higher Education,* April 21, 1993, A33; Rush, "Productivity or Quality," 38; and Diana Ortega, "University of California Officials: Rising Fees Not to Blame for Fewer Students," *Daily Nexus,* January 20, 1993, 12.

69. "Report Urges Government to Fund More Facilities, Programs," *Business Officer,* April 1992, 12; "The Decaying American Campus: A Ticking Time Bomb," Association of Physical Plant Administrators of Universities and Colleges and National Association of Business Officers, 1989, vii-viii; and Julie L. Nicklin, "Harvard University Reports $42 Million Deficit, Its First Since 1974," *Chronicle of Higher Education,* February 26, 1992, A33.

70. "Poisoned Ivy," *The Economist,* August 15, 1992, 19.

71. "Prospects for Long-Range Capital Planning in California Public Education: A Preliminary Review," California Postsecondary Education Commission, January 1992, 5.

72. Kim Clarke, "University of Michigan's Repairs Near Crisis Point," *Ann Arbor News,* April 19, 1992, A2.

73. Rush, "Productivity or Quality," 36; "Federal Share of Student Aid Load Dropping, Study Shows," *Business Officer,* October 1991, 12; Table 6 "Back to School Report."

74. Rush, "Productivity or Quality," 38.

CHAPTER 8
THE COLLEGE CURRICULUM AND POLITICAL CORRECTNESS

1. "Back to School Report," U.S. Department of Education, 1992, 1.

2. George H. Douglas, *Education Without Impact: How Our Universities Fail the Young* (New York: Birch Lane Press, 1992), 105–106.

3. In Charles J. Sykes, "How Colleges Are Failing Our Students," *Imprimis,* July 1990, 5.

4. Lynne V. Cheney, "Why We Need a Core Curriculum for College Students," *Imprimis,* May 1990, 3; Michigan State University graduate studies catalogue, 1989–1991, 86; Suzanne Alexander, "Ph.D. May Mean Doctor of Clambakes and Slumber Parties," *Wall Street Journal,* June 16, 1992, A1-A14; "Unsnarling the Black Hair Issue," *Wall Street*

Journal, August 21, 1992; Charles J. Sykes, *Profscam: Professors and the Demise of Higher Education* (Regnery Gateway, St. Martin's, 1988), 80, 102; *National On-Campus Report,* January 20, 1992, 5; Richard Norton Smith, *The Harvard Century: The Making of a University to a Nation;* and *Sports Illustrated,* in *The Brian Bex Report,* January 1992, 2146; Bryan Barnett, "Teaching and Research Are Inescapably Incompatible," *Chronicle of Higher Education,* June 3, 1992, A40; *Campus,* Spring 1993, 12; Charles J. Sykes, *A Nation of Victims: The Decay of the American Character* (Simon and Schuster, 1992), 191; and Brown University catalogue, 1991–1994, 316, 350, 427, and 451.

5. Cornell W. Clayton, "Politics and Liberal Education," *Chronicle of Higher Education,* April 8, 1992, B1.

6. Cheney, "Why We Need a Core Curriculum," 1.

7. Sykes, *Profscam,* 192.

8. Roger Benjamin et al., "The Redesign of Governance in Higher Education," Rand Corporation, February 1993, 9.

9. Kit Lively, "States Step up Efforts to End Remedial Courses at Four-Year Colleges," *Chronicle of Higher Education,* February 24, 1993, A28.

10. In "The College Curriculum: The Case for the Core," *Education Digest,* February 1990, 44–47.

11. "Index of Leading Cultural Indicators," Heritage Foundation, 1993; Thomas Sowell, *Inside American Education: The Decline, the Deception, the Dogmas* (New York: Free Press, 1993), 105; "The Admissions Game," *America's Best Colleges, U.S. News & World Report,* 1989, 44; Deidre Camody "Colleges' SAT Lists Can Be Creative Works," *New York Times,* November 23, 1987, B10; and B. Ann Wright, "The Rating Game," *The College Board Review,* Winter 1990–91, 16.

12. *USA Today,* October 11, 1988, 1.

13. *The Harvard Crimson*; and Lansing Lamont, *Campus Shock* (E.P. Dutton, 1981), 63, in Sykes, *Profscam,* 87.

14. Sowell, *Inside American Education,* 2.

15. Douglas, 113–114.

16. David Berkman, "Student Quality Fall Affects Journalism Schools," *Journalism Educator,* Winter 1985, in Sykes, *Profscam,* 85.

17. *Campus Life: In Search of Community,* Carnegie Foundation for the Advancement of Teaching (Princeton University Press, 1990), 10; and Susan Dodge, "Poorer Preparation for College Found in 25-Year Study of Freshmen," *Chronicle of Higher Education,* November 20, 1991, A39, in Sowell, 6.

18. Jacques Barzun, *Begin Here: The Forgotten Conditions of Teaching and Learning* (University of Chicago, 1991), 114.

19. Thomas Sowell, "Boomerang," *Forbes,* October 12, 1992, 62–63.

20. James Sledd, "A Basic Incompetence in the Defining of Basic Competencies," *English Journal,* November 1986, 26–28, in Sykes, *Profscam,* 93.

21. Christopher Shea, "What's Happened to Writing Skills? Professors Disagree on Whether Students' Work Has Worsened," *Chronicle of Higher Education,* February 3, 1993, A34.

22. Ibid.

23. Bill Johnson, "Speech Restrictions Act as Enemies of Diversity," *Detroit News,* May 17, 1991, A8; David Garraway, "The High Costs of Growing Bureaucracy," *Campus,* Winter 1993, 14; and Scott Jaschik, "High Court's Ruling on Bias Crimes May Permit 'Hate Speech' Penalties," *Chronicle of Higher Education,* June 23, 1993, A22.

24. Stanley Fish, "There's No Such Thing as Free Speech and It's a Good Thing Too," Hillsdale College lecture, February 1992, 3.

25. Alan M. Dershowitz, "Harvard Witch Hunt Burns Incorrect at Stake," *Los Angeles Times,* April 22, 1992, A11, in Lynne V. Cheney, "Telling the Truth: A Report on the State of the Humanities in Higher Education," National Endowment for the Humanities, September 1992, 10.

26. In Sykes, *A Nation of Victims,* 6, 166; *National On-Campus Report,* September 15, 1992, 4; *Michigan Review,* September 23, 1992, 2; "Michigan Mandate Progess Report," *Michigan Review,* September 30, 1992, 4; and "University of Connecticut Still Taking Flak over Laughter Rule," *Hartford Courant,* August 8, 1991, B8.

27. David DiSalvo, "On the Sensitivity Gravy Train," *Campus,* Spring 1993, 4, 15; *Chronicle of Higher Education,* April 1, 1992, A14; and *Heterodoxy,* December 1992, 3.

28. DiSalvo, 4; and Lisa Koven, "Help Wanted: 'Diversity Bureaucrats,' " *Campus,* Spring 1993, 2.

29. Benjamin Hart, *Poisoned Ivy* (New York: Stein and Day, 1984), 60–67.

30. Jeff Muir, "Universities Ignore Violence and Vandalism Against Conservative Student Publications," *Chronicle of Higher Education,* June 2, 1993, B2.

31. Sowell, *Inside American Education,* 211; and *Heterodoxy,* September 1993, 14.

32. Sowell, *Inside American Education,* 211; and Elizabeth Ellsworth, "Why Doesn't This Feel Empowering? Working Through Repressive Myths of Critical Pedagogy," *Harvard Educational Review,* August 1989, 319.

33. *Chronicle of Higher Education,* January 20, 1993, A16; Haverford College catalogue, 1990–91, 33.
34. *Chronicle of Higher Education,* September 2, 1992, A4.
35. "The Condom Parade," *National Review,* December 28, 1992, 12–13.
36. In Anne Matthews, "Deciphering Victorian Underwear and Other Seminars," *New York Times Magazine,* February 10, 1991, 58.
37. *Chronicle of Higher Education,* May 20, 1992, B4.
38. Charles Paine, "Relativism, Radical Pedagogy, and the Ideology of Paralysis," *College English,* April 1990, 563, in Cheney, "Telling the Truth," 13.
39. Cheney, "Telling the Truth," 31.
40. Ibid., 73.
41. In Sykes, *A Nation of Victims,* 169.
42. Benno C. Schmidt, Jr., "The University and Freedom," address, March 6, 1991, 1; and Derek Bok, "Worrying About the Future," *Harvard,* May/June 1991, 41.
43. Heather MacDonald, "Welcome Freshmen! Oppressor or Oppressed?" *Wall Street Journal,* September 29, 1992, A14.
44. "The Derisory Tower," *The New Republic,* February 18, 1991, 5, in Sowell, *Inside American Education,* 16.
45. In *Chronicle of Higher Education,* February 12, 1992, B5.
46. Bettina J. Huber, "Today's Literature Classroom: Findings from the MLA's 1990 Survey of Upper Division Courses," *ADE Bulletin,* Spring 1992, 48–53, in Cheney, "Telling the Truth," 23.
47. Peter S. Prescott, "Taking Offense," *Newsweek,* December 24, 1990, 48–51.
48. Douglas, 74.
49. Cheney, "Telling the Truth," 20.
50. Barzun, 191.
51. Sowell, *Inside American Education,* 163.
52. Shelby Steele, "The New Segregation," *Imprimis,* August 1992, 3.
53. Sykes, *A Nation of Victims,* 165.
54. William Raspberry, "Self Segregation Common on Campus," *Detroit News,* April 26, 1993, 11A; and Steele, 3.
55. Andrea Stone and John Larrabee, "Racism Taints Universities' Hallowed Halls," *USA Today,* November 9, 1992, 6A; Christopher Shea, "Protests Centering on Racial Issues Erupt on Many Campuses This Fall," *Chronicle of Higher Education,* November 25, 1992, A23; *Chronicle of Higher Education,* June 27, 1992, A5; *Chronicle of Higher Education,* June 17, 1992, A4; and "They Call It 'Diversity,' " *Wall Street Journal,* September 29, 1992, A14.

56. John Moody, letter to the editor, *Chronicle of Higher Education,* February 12, 1992, B5.

57. "They Call It 'Diversity,' " A14.

58. Sowell, *Inside American Education,* 161.

59. Raspberry, 11A.

CHAPTER 9
THE FACULTY AND THE COLLEGE COMMUNITY

1. Charles J. Sykes, *Profscam: Professors and the Demise of Higher Education* (Regnery Gateway, St. Martin's, 1988), 4; and Richard M. Huber, *How Professors Play the Cat Guarding the Cream: Why We're Paying More and Getting Less in Higher Education* (George Mason University Press, 1992), 11.

2. In *Chronicle of Higher Education,* September 23, 1992, A29; and Thomas Sowell, "It Doesn't Take a Scholar to Recognize a Rip-Off," *Detroit News,* September 30, 1992, n.p.

3. Sykes, 36.

4. Ibid.

5. Wisconsin Legislative Audit Bureau, April 8, 1986, in Sykes, 36.

6. Sykes, 40.

7. Martin Anderson, "What Me Teach? I'm a Professor," *Wall Street Journal,* September 8, 1992, A16.

8. Ibid.

9. Sykes, 41–43; David Hood, "Profscam at UNC," *Carolina Critic,* September 1989, 26, in Sowell, *Inside American Education: The Decline, the Deception, the Dogmas* (New York: Free Press, 1993), 204; and Martin Anderson, *Impostors in the Temple: American Intellectuals Are Destroying Our Universities and Cheating Our Students of Their Future* (New York: Simon & Schuster, 1992), 54–55.

10. Robin Wilson, "Widespread Complaints: Undergraduates at Large Universities Found to Be Increasingly Dissatisfied," *Chronicle of Higher Education,* January 9, 1991, A38, in Sowell, *Inside American Education,* 204.

11. Sykes, 41.

12. *National On-Campus Report,* September 15, 1992, 6.

13. Dennis Kelly, "Colleges Rely on Part-Time Faculty," *USA Today,* November 13, 1992, 1D.

14. Sowell, *Inside American Education,* 205.

15. Gordon C. Winston, "Hostility, Maximization, and the Public Trust," *Change,* July/August 1992, 20–27.

16. Jacques Barzun, *Begin Here: The Forgotten Conditions of Teaching and Learning* (University of Chicago, 1991), 70. As Charles J. Sykes has pointed out in numerous documented cases, winning a teaching award can be the kiss of death when it comes to gaining tenure.

17. Bryan Barnett, "Teaching and Research Are Inescapably Incompatible," *Chronicle of Higher Education,* June 3, 1992, A40.

18. David J. Powell, "LSA's Road to Insanity," *Michigan Review,* December 1990, 1, in Sowell, *Inside American Education,* 205.

19. In Michelle Renee Powers, "Pomp, Perks, and Politics: The Rise of the Super Prof," *Campus,* Winter 1993, 17.

20. Barzun, 8.

21. Douglas Lederman, "Survey Reveals Salaries of Executives and Highest Paid Staff Members at 190 Colleges," *Chronicle of Higher Education,* May 5, 1993, A17–A18.

22. "Pay and Benefits of Leaders at 190 Private Colleges and Universities: A Survey," *Chronicle of Higher Education,* May 5, 1993, A17–A18.

23. "Some Dynamic Aspects of Academic Careers: The Urgent Need to Match Aspirations with Compensation," *Academe,* March/April 1990, 5, in Sowell, *Inside American Education,* 116.

24. Anderson, *Impostors in the Temple,* 40; *Chronicle of Education Almanac,* August 25, 1993, 5.

25. Sykes, 39.

26. Anderson, *Impostors in the Temple,* 38.

27. Sykes, 101.

28. Chester E. Finn, Jr., "Higher Education on Trial: An Indictment," *Current,* October 1984, in Sykes, 101–102.

29. Robert Isoue, "How Colleges Can Cut Costs," *Wall Street Journal,* January 27, 1987, in Sykes, 102.

30. Anne Matthews, "Deciphering Victorian Underwear and Other Seminars," *New York Times Magazine,* February 10, 1991, 43.

31. Rachel Maines, "Evolution of the Potholder: From Technology to Popular Art," *Journal of Popular Culture,* Summer 1985, 3–33.

32. Sykes, 103.

33. Matthews, 43, 57; and Lynne V. Cheney, "Telling the Truth: A Report on the State of the Humanities in Higher Education," National Endowment for the Humanities, September 1992, 9.

34. Richard Mitchell, *The Graves of Academe* (New York: Simon and Schuster 1981), 69; and Sykes, 104–105.

35. *Chronicle of Higher Education,* August 12, 1992, A9.

36. Liz McMillen, "From Margin to Mainstream: Books in Gay and Lesbian Studies," *Chronicle of Higher Education,* June 22, 1992, A8.

37. Sykes, 103.

38. George H. Douglas, *Education Without Impact: How Our Universities Fail the Young* (New York: Birch Lane Press, 1992), 121.

39. Barzun, 11.

40. Jerry Buckley, "Paying for College," *U.S. News and World Report,* October 29, 1990, 90.

41. Martin Anderson, "The Galls of Ivy: Our Professors Do Everything But Teach," *Washington Post,* October 18, 1992, C3.

42. Douglas, 22.

43. Ibid., 125.

44. Sykes, 20.

45. Ibid., 24.

46. Gary Pavela, "Today's College Students Need Both Freedom and Structure," *Chronicle of Higher Education,* July 29, 1992, B1-B2.

47. Frank H.T. Rhodes, "The Student Decides," *America's Best Colleges, U.S. News and World Report,* 1987, 42, in Sowell, *Inside American Education,* 178.

48. Sandra F. MacGowan and Sarah McGinty, eds., *Fifty College Admissions Directors Speak to Parents* (New York: Harcourt Brace Jovanovich, 1988), 16, 43, in Sowell, *Inside American Education,* 178.

49. Cameron Humphries, "Funding 'Safe Sex': The Sexual Politics of Higher Education," *Campus,* Spring 1993, 3.

50. Ibid.

51. Sowell, *Inside American Education,* 180.

52. "Safe Sex Explorer's Action-Packed Starter Kit Handbook," 1986, in Thomas Sowell, *Choosing a College: A Guide for Parents and Students* (New York: Harper & Row, 1989), 99, 180.

53. Ibid., 99.

54. Ibid., 5, 101.

55. "Mandated Sensitivity," *Campus,* Winter 1991, 12, in Sowell, *Inside American Education,* 187.

56. *National On-Campus Report,* September 15, 1992, 3; "Moving Forward: Lesbians and Gays at Michigan State University," University-Wide Task Force on Lesbian and Gay Issues, Michigan State University, 1, 1992: n.p.; Carolyn J. Mooney, "Homosexuals in Academe: Fear of Backlash Clouds Reactions to Increased Tolerance," *Chronicle of Higher Education,"* September 23, 1992, A17–19; *Chronicle of Higher Education,*

December 16, 1992, A18; Michele N-K Collison, "Benefits for Gay Couples: More Colleges Are Providing Health Care for Partners of Homosexual Employees," *Chronicle of Higher Education,* November 3, 1993, A17; *Heterodoxy,* May 1992, 3; *National On-Campus Report,* January 20, 1992, 6; *Chronicle of Higher Education,* May 10, 1991, A27; Thomas Sowell, "Boomerang," *Forbes,* October 12, 1992, 62–63; *Stanford Daily,* March 7, 1990, 6; "Gays and Lesbians Talk About Campus Climate," *Chronicle of Higher Education,* September 23, 1992, A19; "Prostituting Feminism," *Detroit News,* November 19, 1992, 14A; Sykes, *A Nation of Victims: The Decay of the American Character* (St. Martin's, 1992), 225; "Campus Police Arrest Men for Sexual Acts," *Chronicle of Higher Education,* June 29, 1992, A4; and Sowell, *Inside American Education,* 184–185.

57. *Chronicle of Higher Education,* January 13, 1993, A29; Michele N-K Collison, "Four Thousand Violent Crimes Occurred on 580 Campuses in Past Three Years: Use of Data Questioned," *Chronicle of Higher Education,* September 23, 1992, A32.

58. "Crime Data From 2,400 Colleges and Universities," *Chronicle of Higher Education,* January 20, 1993, A34–43.

59. William Kibler, "Cheating," *Chronicle of Higher Education,* November 11, 1992, B1.

60. Don Feder, "Cultural Pollutants Erode Moral Ozone," *Boston Herald,* November 30, 1992, 23.

61. *National On-Campus Report,* January 20, 1992, 5.

62. Edward M. White, "Too Many Campuses Want to Sweep Student Plagiarism Under the Rug," *Chronicle of Higher Education,* February 24, 1993, A44.

63. Ibid.

64. Chris Gilleland, "Academic Dishonesty," *The Critic,* 14, in Sowell, *Inside American Education,* 2.

65. Kibler, B1.

66. George H. Douglas, letter to the editor, *Wall Street Journal,* September 28, 1992, A13.

67. Douglas, *Education Without Impact,* 165.

68. Claire L. Gaudiani, "The Cold War Is Over Between Generations," *Chronicle of Higher Education,* May 20, 1992, B3-B4.

CHAPTER 10
WHO CONTROLS THE CAMPUS—WHO CONTROLS THE FUTURE?

1. Martin Anderson, *Impostors in the Temple: American Intellectuals Are Destroying Our Universities and Cheating Our Students of Their Future* (New York: Simon & Schuster, 1992), 38–39.

2. Charles J. Sykes, *Profscam: Professors and the Demise of Higher Education* (Regnery Gateway, St. Martin's, 1988), 10–11.

3. "The Redesign of Governance in Higher Education," Institute on Education and Training, Rand Corporation, February, 1993, 22.

4. In Robert Birnbaum, "Will You Love Me in December as You Do in May?" *Journal of Higher Education,* January/February 1992, 1.

5. *Chronicle of Higher Education,* May 20, 1992, A13; and "Faculty Members at Two Universities Vote No Confidence," *Chronicle of Higher Education,* September 16, 1992, A19.

6. Robert L. Jacobsen, "Tensions Appear to Ease in Confrontation over Financial Management at Columbia University," *Chronicle of Higher Education,* May 6, 1992, A37–8.

7. Arthur Levine, "Why Colleges Are Continuing to Lose the Public Trust," *Change,* July/August 1992, 4.

8. Courtney Leatherman, "Spate of Resignations Prompts Concern About Health of the College Presidency," *Chronicle of Higher Education,* June 17, 1992, A13; and "The Redesign of Governance in Higher Education," 10.

9. In Richard M. Huber, *How Professors Play the Cat Guarding the Cream: Why We're Paying More and Getting Less in Higher Education* (Fairfax: George Mason University Press, 1992), 17–18.

10. David Brooks Arnold, "The Inside President," *AGB Reports,* January/February, 1988, 31.

11. In Sykes, 23.

12. In *Chronicle of Higher Education,* September 2, 1992, B2.

13. Thomas Sowell, *Inside American Education: The Decline, the Deception, the Dogmas* (New York: Free Press, 1993), 225.

14. Julie L. Nicklin, "Yale Opens a Campaign for $1.5 Billion, Largest Drive in U.S. Higher Education," *Chronicle of Higher Education,* May 13, 1992, A32; and Julie L. Nicklin, "University of Michigan's Capital Campaign Is Biggest Ever for a Public University," *Chronicle of Higher Education,* September 30, 1992, A27.

15. "Head of National Fund Raisers' Group Criticizes Big College Drives," *Chronicle of Higher Education,* July 22, 1992, A30.

16. William E. Simon, "Give to the College a Choice," *Wall Street Journal,* July 8, 1988, A15.
17. "The Redesign of Governance in Higher Education," 7.
18. Sean C. Rush, "Productivity or Quality? In Search of Higher Education's Yellow Brick Road," *Business Officer,* April 1992, 36.
19. William Massey and Robert Zemsky, "The Lattice and the Ratchet," *Policy Perspectives,* June 1990, in Rush, 39.
20. Gerald Gaither and Robby DeWitt, "Making Tough Choices: Retrenchment and Reallocations During Hard Times," *Business Officer,* July 1991, 31.
21. Louis Harris, "Planning to Get Real," American Association for Higher Education, March 1992, in James Harvey, "Footing the Bill: Financial Prospects for Higher Education," *Educational Record,* Fall 1992, 17.
22. Anderson, 24.
23. Alexander W. Astin, *What Matters in College: Four Critical Years Revisited* (San Francisco: Jossey-Bass, Inc., 1992), in *Chronicle of Higher Education,* November 11, 1992, B4.
24. Beardsley Ruml, *A Memo to a College Trustee* (McGraw Hill, 1959), 4.
25. Robert Birnbaum, *How Academic Leadership Works: Understanding Success and Failure in the College Presidency* (San Francisco: Jossey-Bass Publishers, 1992), xi–xii.

EPILOGUE
REBUILDING THE IVORY TOWER

1. "Nineteen States Cut Higher Education Budgets in Mid-Year, Survey Finds," *Business Officer,* March 1992, 11.
2. *Chronicle of Higher Education,* April 15, 1992, A26.
3. Sonia L. Nazario, "Funding Cuts Take a Toll at University," *Wall Street Journal,* October 5, 1992, B1.
4. Arthur Levine, "Why Colleges Are Continuing to Lose the Public Trust," *Change,* July/August 1992, 4.
5. Nazario, "Funding Cuts Take a Toll at University," B1.
6. *Chronicle of Higher Education Almanac,* August 25, 1993, 5; and Kit Lively, "A Look at Two State Campuses Reveals Anguish of Adapting to Deep Budget Cuts," *Chronicle of Higher Education,* June 9, 1993, A19.
7. Under this form of privatization, colleges and universities would act as public corporations with broad powers to manage their own affairs and the right to contract out many services to private sources. Kit Lively, "Florida's Governor Asks Higher Education Officials to Prepare a 'Priva-

tization' Plan for University System," *Chronicle of Higher Education,* September 22, 1993, A28.

8. Scott Jaschik, "One Percent Decline in State Support Thought to Be First Two-Year Drop Ever," *Chronicle of Higher Education,* October 21, 1993, A26.

9. James Harvey, "Footing the Bill: Financial Prospects for Higher Education," *Educational Record,* Fall 1992, 13.

INDEX